THE SUFFRAGETTE STORY AND THE PANKHURST FAMILY

THE SUFFRAGETTE STORY AND THE PANKHURST FAMILY

EMMELINE PANKHURST & HER THREE DAUGHTERS

SIOBHÁN COLGAN

First published in Great Britain in 2025 by
PEN AND SWORD HISTORY
An imprint of
Pen & Sword Books Ltd
Yorkshire – Philadelphia

ISBN 978 1 03611 601 9

A CIP catalogue record for this book is available from the British Library.

Typeset in Times New Roman 10.5/12.5 by
SJmagic DESIGN SERVICES, India.
Printed and bound in the UK by CPI Group (UK) Ltd.

The Publisher's authorised representative in the EU for product safety is Authorised Rep Compliance Ltd., Ground Floor, 71 Lower Baggot Street, Dublin D02 P593, Ireland.
www.arccompliance.com

For a complete list of Pen & Sword titles please contact
PEN & SWORD BOOKS LIMITED
George House, Units 12 & 13, Beevor Street, Off Pontefract Road,
Barnsley, South Yorkshire, S71 1HN, England
E-mail: enquiries@pen-and-sword.co.uk
Website: www.pen-and-sword.co.uk

or

PEN AND SWORD BOOKS
1950 Lawrence Rd, Havertown, PA 19083, USA
E-mail: uspen-and-sword@casematepublishers.com
Website: www.penandswordbooks.com

CONTENTS

Acknowledgements....vi
Introduction....vii
Chapter 1 An Early Awakening....1
Chapter 2 Foundations of Rebellion....9
Chapter 3 Drudge and Drill....22
Chapter 4 Like Mother, Like Daughters....31
Chapter 5 Family Frontlines....40
Chapter 6 Victories and Setbacks....54
Chapter 7 Building a Militant Movement....65
Chapter 8 Daughters of Defiance....73
Chapter 9 A Suffragette Split....83
Chapter 10 The Battle Cry....94
Chapter 11 Breaking Laws to Make Laws....105
Chapter 12 We Cannot Always Control Our Women....114
Chapter 13 America, a Truce and Two Terrible Deaths....123
Chapter 14 No Vote, No Census and a 'Torpedoed' Bill....136
Chapter 15 I Incite This Meeting to Rebellion....146
Chapter 16 Cat Among the Mice....164
Chapter 17 Family Fractures....175
Chapter 18 The Last Days of Militancy....185
Chapter 19 Patriotic Feminism....195
Chapter 20 Beyond Suffrage....207

Notes....216
Bibliography....228

ACKNOWLEDGEMENTS

I would like to express my heartfelt gratitude to those who have supported me throughout the journey of writing this book.

I am deeply grateful to everyone who made their archives and information available to me and accessible online. Their efforts preserve an extraordinary and vital part of our history, and making it freely available for all is a generous and important gesture.

Special thanks go to the organisations that provided images for this work, including the British Library, the Library of Congress, and the Women's Library at the London School of Economics.

I am also immensely thankful to the team at Pen and Sword. In particular, Sarah-Beth Watkins, for her unwavering patience and steadfast support over these past months, and Cecily Blench for helping me shape the manuscript into a clearer and more accurate book.

To my dear friend and fellow writer, Cecilia Bonner Donohoe, your guidance and inspiration have been invaluable. Our conversations about writing have sustained and encouraged me through this journey.

I owe my heartfelt gratitude to my parents, Sean and Pauline Colgan. Thank you for your unswerving support – always.

Finally, to my daughter, Enya-Sofia: my heart, my reason for everything, and the rebel I admire most.

INTRODUCTION

I have long been fascinated by the lives of Emmeline Pankhurst and her three daughters, and their significant role in forming a movement that forever changed the course of women's history in Britain.

When people hear the word 'suffragette' today, it often conjures up images of broken windows, burnt buildings, and hunger-striking women. However, the story of the suffragette movement did not begin with broken glass and arson attacks. It began with women challenging the status quo of the late Victorian society they were living in. How then did such women, often raised to be demure, proper and passive daughters, wives and mothers, transform into revolutionary activists who were willing to risk their very lives for the cause of women's suffrage? And what part did the intricate dynamics of the family at the heart of the struggle play in shaping all that happened?

These questions inspired me to write this book, and I hope I have sufficiently addressed them. My aim is not to judge the Pankhurst women, or any of the women who pushed the movement onwards, but to try and understand their world, and the choices and sacrifices they made.

Today, it's easy to dismiss Emmeline, Christabel, Sylvia, and Adela as extreme radicals, whose militancy was beyond what was necessary. Yet the truth is, we owe a debt of gratitude to Emmeline, her daughters, and the thousands of women who stood alongside them, enduring public ridicule, physical violence, imprisonment, and force-feeding, all in pursuit of a singular goal that we now benefit from, often without a second thought: votes for women.

CHAPTER 1

AN EARLY AWAKENING

Emmeline Goulden sat rapt. She had pleaded to be allowed to accompany her mother to one of the neighbourhood's rare suffrage meetings. Still, she had not expected the thrilling certainty she now felt as she sat listening to the eloquent woman at the front of the room. Moments earlier, the place had thrummed with the polite murmur of greetings, the soft rustling of skirts and the creak of wooden chairs as the gathered women gently shifted in their seats for comfort and a better view. Now, with Lydia Becker commanding the floor, it had stilled to a hushed silence.

Becker was not a striking woman in the conventional sense. Stout, with a broad face framed by wire-rimmed glasses and tightly pinned hair, she nonetheless had an imposing presence. As she spoke passionately about women's right to the same voting privileges as men, her voice was clear and authoritative, and her words, radical for the time, struck a profound chord in 14-year-old Emmeline. This moment would become a turning point in the young girl's life. In later years, the future suffragette leader would reflect on the occasion, referring to Becker as 'the Susan B. Anthony of the English movement'.[1]

The comparison was fitting. Lydia Becker possessed an unwavering sense of justice and, as a much sought-after speaker and powerful persuader, drew several influential people towards her. Beyond her activism, Becker was an accomplished amateur scientist. Though educated at home, her passion for botany led her to win a gold medal in 1862 for a scholarly paper on horticulture. Her expertise even fostered a long correspondence with Charles Darwin, and she contributed several plant species to his work, convincing him to send one of his papers (he sent three!) for presentation to the inaugural meeting of Becker's local women's scientific organisation, the Manchester Ladies' Literary Society. Her passion for plants, however, was equally matched by her dedication to women's enfranchisement and in January 1867 she helped establish the Manchester National Society for Women's Suffrage (MNSWS) one of the first organisations of its kind in England. Becker was appointed secretary and Dr Richard Pankhurst, the man who would later become the now-enthralled Emmeline's husband, was one of the earliest members of the Executive Committee.

In its first few years, the Manchester Society had focused on attempts to put women with the requisite property qualifications on the electoral register. Most of the women that they did manage to get on the register were subsequently removed by the Revising Barrister. This did not stop nine women, who had remained undetected on the registrar, from casting their votes anyway in the election of 1868, even though those votes were then considered invalid.

Three years after the official formation of the MNSWS, Becker co-founded the *Women's Suffrage Journal*, a publication that was delivered regularly to the Goulden household and greedily consumed by the impressionable Emmeline. It was partly as editor of this early publication, which presented the news of events that affected all areas of women's life, that she now stood in front of these gathered women and a teenage Emmeline, and urged them so eloquently to embrace the cause of suffrage.

Of course, she was speaking to a primarily converted audience, women who were already well-versed in ideas as daring as female enfranchisement. Manchester, the cradle of the Industrial Revolution, had long been a crucible of radicalism. The city's rapid industrialisation and seismic social changes had birthed several labour movements and reform campaigns, as workers through the years demanded better rights and representation. The concentration of industry and a burgeoning middle class also led to increased political awareness and activism. Ironically, Manchester's wealth owed much to slavery, and it was here, in the 1790s, that working-class communities led the charge against the transatlantic slave trade.

Manchester's radical pedigree was further cemented by one of the darkest chapters in its history, for this was the city in which the Peterloo Massacre occurred. A phrase coined to evoke the brutality of Napoleon's loss at Waterloo, the Peterloo Massacre unfolded in 1819 in the city's centrally located St Peter's Field during a peaceful protest against the working class's exclusion from political representation. Henry Hunt, the day's main speaker and a pioneering voice for workers' rights, had implored attendees to come 'armed with no other weapon but that of a self-approving conscience'.[2]

They did, which meant they were no match against the cavalry, paid for by aristocratic locals, that stormed the crowd that afternoon with sabres drawn. Chaos erupted. Men, women, and children desperately tried to flee, only to find themselves trampled under the hooves of charging horses. The scene was one of utter pandemonium; some were slashed by the constables' swords, others beaten with truncheons. When the dust settled, over 650 lay injured, and at least eighteen had died – among them, four women and a child.

What stood out, as historian Michael Bush notes in *The Casualties of Peterloo*, is that while women constituted perhaps an eighth of the crowd, they made up nearly a third of those injured. James Wroe, editor of the *Manchester Observer*, the city's first radical newspaper, would later highlight how the yeomanry appeared to explicitly target women during the stampede. It was Wroe who coined the term 'the Peterloo Massacre' and, along with many eyewitnesses on the day, firmly attested that the focus on women was no tragic accident but a deliberate act.

The reason for this was shocking but simple. In the months leading up to the protest, working-class women had played leading roles in organising the event. Women's reform clubs had sprung up across Manchester and its neighbouring towns, mobilising for universal male suffrage. However, the women's visible presence and defiance appeared to enrage the establishment, which saw their political engagement as a direct affront to male authority. As Bush explains, the attack on women was not merely a matter of circumstance.

> The considerations of protection, respite and mercy that men were normally expected to show to women… failed to come into operation… This was undoubtedly in reaction to the obtrusive behaviour of female reformers at recent political meetings… an unprecedented and successful invasion by women of a world traditionally accepted as a male prerogative.[3]

Rather than silencing them, however, the violence at Peterloo emboldened Manchester's women. Over the following decades, their courage grew and was passed from generation to generation, so that almost a century after the horrific events at St Peter's Field, a suffragette would mount a soap box in the centre of Manchester, demanding of the gathered crowd: 'We helped you carry your banners at Peterloo. Now it is your turn to help us carry ours.'[4]

Fourteen-year-old Emmeline was well aware of the occurrences at St Peter's Field. Her own grandfather, Robert's father, a fustian cutter, was there, pressed by his wife into attending, though she herself remained at home. He escaped the carnage by hiding in a cellar. Later, stories of grandad Goulden's experiences of that day would shock and thrill a very young Emmeline, forming an early seed from which her own rage against injustice would flourish. Like most Mancunians, Emmeline was probably aware that women had borne much of the suffering during the Peterloo Massacre. Whether this early knowledge influenced her later feminist convictions is uncertain.

Clearly, though, the Goulden family's connection to Manchester's radicalism went far beyond tales of Peterloo. While Emmeline's parents were not outspoken advocates for women's emancipation, they were deeply embedded in the city's reformist circles. Their middle-class home frequently hosted Manchester's radical elite, introducing the young Emmeline to many opinions and debates centred around social justice. Her father, Robert Goulden, had risen from humble beginnings as an errand boy in a Manchester mill to become the prosperous owner of a calico printing and bleaching works. With his success, he had moved his family from Moss Side, where Emmeline was born on 14 July 1858, to the grander home in Salford, modestly named Seedley Cottage, near his works. A committed liberal, Robert championed equality before the law, opposed imperialist wars, and was a fervent abolitionist. His anti-slavery activism earned him a place on the committee that welcomed American abolitionist Henry Ward Beecher to England in 1863.

Emmeline's mother, Sophia, had left her home on the Isle of Man at 18 to marry Robert and raise their eleven children in Manchester. She was known to be a strong-willed and forceful matriarch who had no problem presenting the Victorian ideals of 'the cult of the home' alongside her more radical beliefs in equality. Sophia managed the household with strict precision, growing her own vegetables, making jams and chutneys, and ensuring her sons' needs were prioritised above all else. Yet she still made time to read Harriet Beecher Stowe's *Uncle Tom's Cabin* to her daughters after they'd climbed into bed. Emmeline and Mary, the sister closest to her in age, were also often made accompany their mother to many of her charity fundraising events. In her biography *My Own Story*, Emmeline would later recall that as a child of five she already knew the meaning of the words 'slavery' and 'emancipation'.[5] That the headstrong and heroic-minded Emmeline took her temperament from her mother is undeniable. But she was also undoubtedly influenced by her father and both her parents' equal commitment to social reform.

Emmeline left her first suffrage meeting that night as a 'conscious and confirmed suffragette'. Reflecting on this pivotal moment, she later wrote wryly, '[With my] temperament and my surroundings, I could scarcely have been otherwise.'[6] Yet before fully immersing herself in the cause that would one day define her life, Emmeline firstly wanted an education equal to her brothers'.

However, despite their progressive politics, the Gouldens held the conservative Victorian views of the day regarding the education of their daughters. Both Robert and Sophia believed their daughters' primary roles were to become capable wives and mothers, and their schooling should reflect that goal. Emmeline had been nicknamed 'the dictionary' by her brothers for her precocious intellect, and though Robert encouraged Emmeline and her younger sister Mary to read the daily newspaper, he didn't believe that such learnedness would benefit them in the same way it would their brothers. Once, when Emmeline was supposed to be sleeping, she heard her father lament, 'What a pity she wasn't born a lad.' To Emmeline it was no great pity at all – she was happy to be a woman. But she realised the entrenched truth behind the comment, later explaining: 'It was made quite clear that men considered themselves superior to women, and that women apparently acquiesced in that belief.'[7]

Nonetheless, it's likely that as the second child and eldest daughter, the clever young Emmeline, with her bright eyes, high cheekbones and raven-black hair, was a favourite. As a result, her parents would have been keen for her to access what educational opportunities were available to her. They would not have been blind to the benefits that a 'finishing school' abroad would have in enhancing her marriage prospects as a cultured and accomplished young woman, either. So it was that in 1873, 15-year-old Emmeline travelled with her father to France, where he left her at the École Normale. A good school in the pleasant Parisian suburb of Neuilly, the École Normale had the reputation for ensuring girls learnt more than how to sew a ribbon onto a dress sleeve. For Emmeline, it was the beginning of a broader education and a new adventure.

❁❁❁

In 1873, the French capital was still reeling from the country's defeat in the Franco-Prussian War. To the young, spirited, and impressionable Emmeline, the city burned bright with this recent patriotic history. Bullet holes were still visible across Parisian landmarks, while buildings reduced to rubble offered a silent reproach to its citizens of the demoralising 1871 Paris siege.

At the École Normale, which in the previous conflict had been used as an infirmary for the war-wounded, Emmeline was guided by the school's director, Mlle. Marchef-Girard. A noted educator who would later be appointed government inspector of schools in France, Mlle. Marchef-Girard believed her girls should receive a robust education similar to that given to boys. The curriculum, which Emmeline praised in her later writings, included accountancy, chemistry and other sciences alongside embroidery and sewing.

The young Mancunian's friend and roommate during this period was Noémie Rochefort. Similar in thought and temperament to Emmeline, she was the daughter of Henri Rochefort, a well-known French Republican and communist, and journalist with the political daily newspaper, *Le Cri du peuple*. Rochefort had taken part in the disastrous self-styled socialist government that ruled France for two months in 1871 and which was known as the Paris Commune. Upon its failure, he and others had escaped into exile, and Noémie, proud of her father but fearful for his future, shared her worries with her new friend along with stories of her father's escapades. Emmeline listened earnestly to these tales of revolutionaries and men willing to take extreme action to create a new political playing field. As she did, the belief that one needed to suffer for the greater cause began to take shape.

Of course, at this stage, it was a romantic vision, further enhanced by its particular French flavour. For, in truth, Emmeline had long been in love with the ideals of France. She had discovered Thomas Carlyle's *History of the French Revolution* when she was around 9 years old and, greatly admiring it, had re-read the book several times. She loved the fact that her birthday landed on the anniversary of the storming of the Bastille Prison in 1789 (though several historians dispute this, claiming she was actually born on 15 July). Later, she would highlight the connection between her birth and this day celebrating the courage of France's citizens who fought for their right to democracy and freedom from tyranny, stating in a 1908 speech: 'I have always thought that the fact that I was born on that day had some kind of influence over my life.'

It's not difficult to see why Emmeline felt such a kinship with the French Revolution. The late eighteenth century in France had been a time of transformative thinking. Fuelled by the Enlightenment, ideas of liberty, class equality and human rights gained traction while revolutionary ideals swept across the whole of Europe. In the drawing rooms of Parisian high society, evening discussions known as 'salons' were organised by the wives of politically connected and ambitious men. These salons became hotbeds of civic debate and dissent, and the stylish salonnières who organised them found they could exert political influence through their ability to draw together influential friends and family members. Eventually, these women's support for equality for men turned into a demand for equality for all.

As the road towards revolution fanned outwards, the voices of the French working class joined those of the intellectuals in calling for a new 'free' France, wherein they had access to civic rights, include access to basic food supplies. The political role of women expanded from the salons to the streets. France's working-class women were central to key events from the storming of the Bastille in 1789 to the aptly named Women's March on Versailles that same year, an event that marked the end of the monarchy in Versailles. They also led bread riots in the spring months of 1792 and 1793, protesting the soaring cost of food. These demonstrations, entwined with the demonstrations of revolutionaries, would eventually help lead to the execution by the guillotine of Louis XVI and Marie Antoinette. For the young and idealistic Emmeline, these acts of courage and solidarity must have seemed nothing short of heroic. Reflecting on her childhood in her autobiography, she wrote, 'While my childhood was protected by love and a comfortable home … I began instinctively to feel that there was something lacking, even in my own home, some false conception of family relations, some incomplete ideal.'[8]

Despite women's active participation in these early revolutionary events, the French Revolution failed to secure political rights for them. The leading male revolutionaries never gave any real thought to the possibility that rights for women would be a component of 'individual liberty and equality'. Nevertheless, women remained actively engaged in the struggle, pushing boundaries and participating in the societal upheavals that defined this world-changing rebellion.

In England, many were seized by the revolutionary zeitgeist of this political moment. Artists celebrated it, with the poet William Wordsworth encapsulating the Romantic sentiment around the storming of the Bastille with the words, 'Bliss was it in that dawn to be alive.'[9] Political thinkers on both sides of the Channel explored how these ideals could reshape society, fuelling debates on human rights and individual freedoms. Among these thinkers was Mary

Wollstonecraft, whose 1792 work *A Vindication of the Rights of Woman* became one of the earliest feminist treatises. Wollstonecraft, who was the mother of *Frankenstein* author Mary Shelley, argued that women, possessing the same capacity for reason as men, were entitled to the same rights and responsibilities. She called for educational opportunities for women, asserting that society, family, and marriage would all benefit from such reforms. Two years earlier, Catherine Macaulay had articulated similar ideas in her *Letters on Education* (1790), advocating for equal education for women and men. While Macaulay acknowledged that women had the commonly accepted vices of vanity, duplicity, and ignorance, she argued these traits were the result of inadequate education rather than inherent flaws.

These were heady days of revolutionary dreaming, when thinkers across Western Europe envisioned a new age of parity along both social and gender lines. The writings of Wollstonecraft, Macaulay, and other French and British women provided an intellectual foundation for future suffrage movements, including the one Emmeline would later lead. In her 1933 essay *Reed of Steel*, a biographical account of Emmeline's life, British author Rebecca West would go so far as to claim: 'She [Emmeline Pankhurst] was the last popular leader to act on inspiration derived from the principles of the French Revolution; she put her body and soul at the service of Liberty, Equality and Fraternity, and earned a triumph for them.'[10]

Such revolutionary ideas and histories swirled in the young Emmeline's mind as she explored Paris during her time at the École Normale. On days when there were no classes, she roamed the cobbled streets and river boardwalks, savouring her newfound freedom and romanticising the fervour with which Parisians had defended their city from the advancing Prussians. The romance of Paris would stay with her throughout all her life, and be a factor in the patriotic stance she later took during the First World War. Her exposure to French sentiments against the Prussians also seeded in her a lifelong anti-German attitude. But she embraced all aspects of the continental culture, picking up the language quickly and enjoying the elegant French style of dress. In subsequent years, she loved to take younger suffragettes clothes shopping during their visits to Paris. Such was her passion for the city that her daughter Christabel later wrote in *Unshackled: How We Won the Vote*:

> This whole excursion into the intellectual life of Paris was one of the great experiences of Mother's youth. Her beauty, her Englishness and simplicity, made her very attractive; her quickness of sympathy and her fluent, pretty French enabled her to fit into this Paris world, and she more than half longed to stay there always.[11]

But this was not to be. After four years of education, Emmeline returned home to Manchester, her formal schooling complete. However, her time in Paris had set a precedent; her younger sister Mary was also sent to the École Normale. Visiting her sister during this time gave Emmeline the chance to return to the once war-battered streets of her beloved city. These visits also opened the door to an even deeper taste of Parisian life, thanks to her friend Noémie, who introduced her to the vibrant political and cultural circles in which she moved.

When Noémie married a Swiss artist, not long after her time at the school, the two young women hatched a bold plan to find Emmeline a French husband. This, they envisioned, would allow them to build a fun, full life together in Paris. Emmeline was game, and so a suitor was promptly found. However, when the young man in question declared that he'd gladly marry the pretty English rose but only if her father paid a dowry, the plan unravelled. Furious at the very idea of 'selling' his daughter, especially to a foreigner, Robert Goulden quickly put an end to the match. She was brought back to England, her romance abruptly and unceremoniously concluded.

While deeply annoyed with her father, Emmeline didn't seem too concerned about the loss of her would-be lover. As Christabel observed:

> At the time she must have thought her way narrowed. But her temperament would not let her mope in Manchester and, after all, her heart had not been engaged. Only one ever won and held it – my father. It was simply a wider life she had wanted and always would want.[12]

This, of course, was true. For Emmeline, Paris had offered a glimpse of that wider life – a life of freedom, possibility, and intellectual excitement. More than that, these early years in France had helped to further politicise her and built upon her secret belief that, after all, she was destined to do 'some great thing'.[13]

CHAPTER 2

FOUNDATIONS OF REBELLION

Emmeline returned from France as a strikingly beautiful young woman, with a slender figure, dark, shiny hair and olive skin. Yet with plans of finding a husband and settling into a Parisian life now firmly quashed by her father, she set aside ideas of matrimony, resolving to create a broader, more meaningful life in Manchester.

However, as a young nineteenth-century woman living in her father's house, her first duty was to her parents, and she and her sister Mary, who had also returned from France, were tasked with tending to their eight younger siblings. Sophia Goulden was particularly anxious that her sons enjoyed the comforts of home for as long as was feasible while they prepared for a later life of worthwhile occupation. Her consistent urgings to Emmeline and Mary to maintain a clean and tidy house and attend to their brothers' needs prompted the disgruntled sisters on one occasion to comment archly that if their mother was in favour of women's rights she didn't show it at home!

Mostly, Emmeline missed the intellectually stimulating and varied days of Paris. When it was possible, she would hurry with her mother to Jackson's Row, a central city street rising gently towards what was once St Peter's Field, and on which the office of the Manchester Society for Women's Suffrage was based. Beyond the headquarters' door, the fight for justice became more palpable to 19-year-old Emmeline. Members penned letters, planned petitions, and engaged in passionate discussions around electorate reform that favoured women. Emmeline carried out basic administrative duties when she could. Mostly, she listened and learned, tentatively joining in the often heavy political conversations, while silently shaping her own opinions and convictions in the process.

One of the members with whom she felt an immediate kinship was Dr Richard Pankhurst. Small in stature, with reddish hair and a similarly coloured bristling beard, the 43-year-old Pankhurst was not, by any standards, a handsome man. But his fervent commitment to fighting injustice greatly appealed to Emmeline.

A barrister by profession, Richard Pankhurst had been called to the Bar at Lincoln's Inn four years after he had graduated Doctor of Laws with Gold Medal from the University of London. He had joined the northern assizes circuit, which had brought him back to his boyhood city of Manchester. Here he lived in the family home in Old Trafford with his ageing parents.

Richard continued his practice, yet his true passion was not law but politics. He was a member of the Liberal Party, which, at the time, was the primary opposition party to the Conservatives, and a founder member of the Manchester Liberal Association. Extremist in his thinking, he supported several generally unpopular political causes of the day including universal free secular education, Irish Home Rule and an Independent India.

However, the still relatively young Liberal Party was happy to indulge independent-minded intellectuals like John Stuart Mill, James Bryce, Henry Fawcett and Peter Taylor, men who easily blended elements of liberalism with strands of other political philosophies. As such, Richard's support for less favoured causes was not entirely out of step with others in the party. In any case, he was liked in Manchester where his more socialist tendencies led to him being affectionally referred to as the 'Red Doctor' in the city's radical circles.

Sharp-minded and sympathetic to the women's cause, Richard was also a founding member of the Manchester Society for Women's Suffrage along with the pioneering activist for women's rights, Elizabeth Wolstenholme Elmy. In 1869, he drafted the Municipal Franchise Act. Not only did this act extended the vote to women ratepayers in local elections but it also enabled women to serve as Poor Law Guardians (and therefore be involved in local government), a role his future wife would later take on.

In 1870, the Red Doctor authored what would later become the Married Women's Property Act of 1882. This ground-breaking Act granted married women absolute control over their property and earnings for the first time in British history.

Richard enjoyed a particular friendship with Lydia Becker, who described him as 'a very clever little man with some extraordinary sentiments about life in general and women in particular'. There is some suggestion that Becker may have harboured romantic feelings for Richard Pankhurst, though no evidence exists to suggest they were ever realised or reciprocated. Whatever Becker's feelings towards the passionate politico, to Emmeline, he was a kindred spirit. Though he was twenty-four years her senior, their friendship grew quickly and within weeks they were in love.

Sophia Goulden disapproved of the speed of the relationship, and more openly of Emmeline's behaviour, which she claimed was not in keeping with 'a proper maidenly reserve' expected of a middle-class woman of the time. But Emmeline didn't care. She was in love and, remarkably, it was with a man whose passion for political justice mirrored her own. In one of the many love letters the couple exchanged, Richard wrote:

> In all my happiness with you, I feel most deeply the responsibilities that are gathering around us … Every struggling cause shall be ours. Help me in this future, unceasingly. Herein is the strength – with bliss added – of two lives made one by that love which seeks more the other than self.[1]

The romance between Emmeline and Dr Pankhurst accelerated further when, shortly after his father had passed away, Richard's mother was also taken ill and died. The Red Doctor sank deeply into a state of sadness, alarming Emmeline. She was aware that as the eldest son of a small family, he felt his parents' passing acutely, more so considering he was now left alone – and lonely – in the family home.

The couple had already talked of marriage, but now Emmeline pushed the possibility forward. In their earlier conversations concerning their future together, Emmeline had suggested that they enter into a free union. There were several reasons to do this. Richard had helped form the Manchester Married Women's Property Committee, which actively lobbied for a change to English Common Law. The law at this time posited that a woman, upon marriage, surrendered all property to her husband and ceased to be a legal entity in her own right. Dr Pankhurst was still a member of the committee and sidestepping marriage would, as Emmeline saw it, be a public act of support of his staunch beliefs. Additionally, it would prevent her from having to forfeit her own legal rights.

However, while a free union offered obvious practical benefits to women, the stigma which was so often attached to such an arrangement could easily destroy that same woman's reputation – though it generally left the man's reputation intact.

Emmeline's future husband was more acutely aware of this than most. Elizabeth Wolstenholme Elmy, his good friend and colleagues in the Manchester Married Women's Property Committee, had become pregnant while in a free union. She and her partner, Benjamin John Elmy, had married three months before the birth of their child, but the issue continued to cause waves of consternation within suffrage circles. Finally, Millicent Garrett Fawcett, a woman who was already emerging as a leader in female suffrage ranks, insisted that Elmy step down from her role on the committee on the precept 'that what happened before you were married has been and is a great injury to the cause of women'.

Richard Pankhurst did not want Emmeline to be similarly vilified nor excluded from all future political life. He persuaded her that marriage was a better route and the couple tied the knot in a small ceremony at St Luke's Church, Pendleton, on 18 December 1879.

Emmeline settled down to married life in her new home at 1 Drayton Terrace, Old Trafford, in Manchester. Almost immediately, she fell pregnant with their first child, and a daughter, Christabel Harriette, was born on 22 September 1880.

Dark-haired and broad-faced, Christabel had been named for the eponymous romantic heroine in Samuel Coleridge's 1797 gothic poem:

> The lovely lady, Christabel,
> Whom her father loves so well.

With its themes of female power and love, the poem had become a symbol of female emancipation and was a fitting appellation for the Pankhursts to bestow upon their firstborn.

A second daughter, Estelle Sylvia, was born on 5 May 1882, while the Pankhursts' first son, Henry Francis Robert, later to be known simply as 'Frank', was born in 1884.

Sylvia (she dropped the 'Estelle' when a young adult) was a placid baby, while Frank, with his dark hair, long lashes and quick, bubbly laughter, quickly became the favoured child of the family.

The role of motherhood and its attending domestic life occurred swiftly for Emmeline. But she had little desire to embrace the archetype of dedicated Victorian wife, and refused to see it as her sole lot in life. She was not good at managing home affairs nor had any interest in being so. Christabel was the only one of her children that Emmeline nursed herself, handing her other infants over to the care of a young nurse that the Pankhursts employed.

'I was never so absorbed with home life and children, however,' Emmeline later wrote in *My Own Story*, 'that I lost interest in community affairs. Dr Pankhurst did not desire that I turn myself into a household machine. It was his firm belief that society as well as the family stands in need of women's services.'[2]

When Christabel was still an infant, Emmeline served on the executive committee of the Women's Suffrage Society, and also on the committee for the Married Women's Property Act. A hard worker and a passionate believer, she remained, nonetheless, the youngest and least informed of the women involved. But she had bold ambitions, and right now they were directed towards helping her husband become the morally upright Member of Parliament Emmeline believed he was destined to be and which, she felt, her city – and England – sorely needed.

❖ ❖ ❖

Manchester, in the early nineteenth century, was an overcrowded, polluted city, swollen with industrial ambition. The relentless expansion of its cotton industry had spun fortunes for many businessmen and factory owners, while grinding down the poorer working class. The town's rapid growth mirrored the broader transformations of a newly industrialised Britain, where the agricultural rhythms of life gave way to the mechanical regularity of factory work. Here, long working hours, poor conditions, and a rigid, punitive work culture became the new norm.

No member of a working-class family was exempt from earning a wage (such as they were). The 1851 British census starkly illustrated this reality: over 33,228 boys and 37,058 girls, all under the age of 15, were employed in the cotton mills, making it the third most common occupation for children at the time. The conditions they endured were appalling; children as young as 5 worked gruelling twelve- to sixteen-hour days, six days a week, in factories that were stifling, dim, and crowded, earning a mere 4 shillings (less than 25p today) a week for their toil.[3]

The inequality and exploitation was obvious to anyone who cared to look, and, as a consequence, Manchester had become a centre for radical thought, a place simmering with the desire for change. The author of the *Communist Manifesto*, Karl Marx, had been living in London since 1849. But through Friedrich Engels, whose family owned a Manchester cotton mill, he had ties to the bustling, smoke-belching city and was a frequent visitor. In the summer of 1845 he and Engels developed the habit of sitting and reading together at Manchester's Chetham library, always choosing the same desk, which, today, remains exactly where the two men enjoyed their studies under the colourful light of a stained glass window.[4]

Engels had laid bare the brutal realities of Manchester's industrial landscape in his 1845 work, *The Condition of the Working Class in England*. In it, he painted a grim portrait of neighbourhoods where filth and decay were so pervasive that residents had to wind their way through piles of human waste and refuse on a daily basis, and the stench of tanneries, bonemills and gasworks filled the air.

By the 1870s, little had improved. The city was still an overcrowded hub of towering mills, teeming streets, and filthy lower-class neighbourhoods. Various health and safety acts had started to be formed, and while the use of child workers was going into decline, the full prohibition of employing children under 14 would not come until 1933. However, the century of rapid industrialisation that had transformed Manchester – and indeed much of Europe – did more than just reshape the urban landscape. It had also given people new ways to think about society, the role of all people, and the urgent changes that now needed to come.

Following the birth of Sylvia, the Pankhursts decided to relocate to Emmeline's larger family home in Salford. Money was already tight, and Richard Pankhurst had plans to resign from the Liberal Party of which he was a member and run as an Independent in the next election.

The last few years with the Liberals had been fraught. A staunch pacifist, Richard disagreed with many of his political colleagues' wishes to join forces with Turkey against Russia and Serbia in their war over the autonomy of Bosnia and Herzegovina. Regular disputes over this and other issues had made it clear to Richard that his radical views were becoming less accepted by his Liberal colleagues and, in truth, would have difficulty thriving in any political party.

Emmeline's parents were supportive of their daughter's husband and held high hopes for his success in both his law practice and as a politician. Her father acted as Dr Pankhurst's agent and, though as a self-made man with his own printing works, he did not hold many of the same socialist-leaning views that his son-in-law did, he still supported him in his decision to stand as an Independent in the next election.

That time came sooner rather than later. Less than two months after Dr Pankhurst had shared his resignation with the Liberal Party, a by-election was called in Manchester. As the Liberals did not contest the seat, the fight was between Pankhurst and the Tory candidate. The Liberals, furious with Pankhurst for snubbing them, encouraged their members not to vote for him, however. This, along with Pankhurst's controversial views on universal suffrage, the disestablishment of the Church of England and the abolition of the House of Lords, not to mention his support for Irish Home Rule, led him to suffer a massive defeat of 6,216 votes against his Tory challenger's 18,188.

Emmeline had done much to support her husband in the lead-up to the count. She had helped him with his election address and contacted people she felt would aid his campaign. One of those had been Lydia Becker. To her immense shock, Becker had refused. Likely, this was to do with the fact that ten years earlier Pankhurst had vehemently argued against his old friend's support for a women's suffrage bill that only included single women. The bill which, at the time, had the sponsorship of the Tory MP William Forsythe would give 800,000 women the vote and was, as Becker saw it, an inroad into eventual full voting rights for women. Richard and the other women working hard to pass the Married Women's Property Act, steadfastly refused, however, and Becker was said never to have forgiven him for allowing this chance to pass them by.

It's also possible, of course, that when the attractive, deeply-in-love Emmeline appeared in front of Becker pleading for the latter to support the former's husband, old wounds relating to the affection Becker may have once harboured for Dr Pankhurst split open again. Whatever the reason, Emmeline left Becker in tears and though she continued to admire the woman who had convinced her of the suffrage cause all those years ago, their friendship would never be the same thereafter.

Pankhurst's loss at the polls negatively affected the couple's home life too. While Robert Goulden had initially supported his son-in-law, the fallout of Pankhurst's election failure had included many prominent liberals boycotting his business. The resulting economic difficulties caused problems between

Emmeline's husband and her father. Moreover, both men continued to clash around their political differences, and heated conversations and the men's raised voices were daily heard throughout the house.

Eventually, with Emmeline now expecting a fourth child, the couple decided to leave Seedley Cottage. They moved back to Manchester proper, renting a small house in Chorlton upon Medlock. Emmeline's sister, Mary, moved with them, ostensibly to help Emmeline who, struck down with regular migraines and dyspepsia, was not having an easy pregnancy. However, Mary was just as keen to get out from the strained atmosphere of the family cottage, where arguments over money and criticisms hurled towards Emmeline and her husband had become something of a constant.

The Pankhursts' own financial situation was fragile, however, so Emmeline approached her father for help. When he refused, she was furious and never spoke to him again. Robert Goulden died seven years later at his wife's family home in the Isle of Man. He had moved there with Sophia and Emmeline's older brother, Walter. While Emmeline had lost the chance to make amends with her father, and despite the ongoing tensions between her and her mother, she and Sophia Goulden slowly began rebuilding their relationship over the next few decades.

On 19 June 1885, later than expected, Adela Constantia Mary was born at the Pankhurst's new home at 66 Carter Street. Though the Pankhursts bestowed their fourth child with a beautiful name (popular at the time as a variant of the beloved Queen Adelaide, wife to the earlier William IV, who had been admired for her deep commitment to civic work), the baby girl's birth was not celebrated in the same way as that of her earlier siblings. Money remained a worry in the household, and Richard's recent election failure along with the bitterness Emmeline now felt towards her parents had fully redirected the couple's energy towards the Red Doctor's political aspirations.

Adela, as it transpired, was a sickly infant. She regularly suffered bouts of bronchitis, and her small, spindly legs were placed in splints from early infancy to help strengthen her hips. When she was just a few months old, Emmeline took on another young nurse, Susannah Jones, to take care of her youngest child, freeing her up to travel to London so that she could help her husband in yet another bid to claim a seat in Parliament as the candidate for the Liberal and Radical Association. In her later years, Adela would blame this early neglect on the reasons for her illnesses and the lack of a bond that she and her mother had.[5]

Emmeline's months in London came to nought. If the Red Doctor had been a figure to admire in Manchester, in London he suffered immense ridicule. His Tory opponent in the November by-election for the industrial Rotherhithe division of Southwark labelled him 'a slum politician' and savagely queried his credentials as 'a gentleman'.

Richard, as a staunch Home Ruler, believed he at least had the Irish working class vote but this turned out to be false; Charles Stuart Parnell, the leader of the Irish Home Rule struggle and a member of the British Parliament, directed his followers not to vote for Pankhurst. Parnell had nothing against Richard, but he was a tactical politician whose fight for Home Rule included sabotaging the majority government, which, at this time was Liberal. Emmeline, initially shocked at Parnell's 'betrayal' of her beloved, was forced into admiring Parnell's ruthlessness and would employ similar tactics later on as leader of the Suffragette movement.

The Rotherhithe election was another huge failure for Pankhurst. Additionally, the good doctor had sued his opponent for defamation but lost his case. Money continued to drain from the family purse, and so it was decided that if Richard were to have any chance at a political career, the Pankhursts had to move to London.

Young, beautiful and energetic, the 28-year-old Emmeline was excited to be caught within the colourful chaos and commotions of life in a vibrant city once again. She decided to open a 'fancy goods' shop that, she dreamed, would provide the financial foundations upon which the Pankhurst family and her husband's career would thrive.

The couple settled on 165 Hampstead Road, a rather rough working-class area which, they were assured by their estate agent, was 'up-and-coming'. The property consisted of a ground-floor store with cramped living quarters above, nestled amidst a jumble of shops, groceries, taverns, and homes. With the premises requiring refurbishment, the children were temporarily housed in nearby lodgings with Susannah, allowing Emmeline and Richard to focus on preparing their new home and business. Outside, the street thrummed with life – market stalls and street vendors clamoured amidst the dirt and grime of London city, hawking their wares to the teeming throngs of predominantly working-class folk. If the prospect of competition from the street's varied merchants troubled Emmeline, she gave no sign. Flushed with the possibility of finding success as a businesswoman in London, she dived enthusiastically into organising her shop's layout, ordering stock, and settling on a name for her new enterprise. The name she chose was Emerson and Co., likely a nod to Ralph Waldo Emerson's famed adage: 'Nothing great was ever achieved without enthusiasm.'

With the property ready, and the children moved in upstairs, Emmeline was finally ready to throw open the doors to what she envisioned would be a stream of ready customers. Unfortunately, she was to be quickly disappointed. Emmeline's carefully selected elegant houseware was too fancy for the local clientele who could find cheaper and just as useful items on the stalls that continued to crowd the pavements outside Emerson and Co.'s shop windows.

The late 1880s was also 'a time of tremendous unrest, of labour agitations, of strikes and lockouts'.[6] The year that Emmeline opened her shop, London itself was struggling with unemployment riots and the ongoing tension between police and Irish protestors finally spilled over into the violence of Bloody Sunday on 13 November 1887. None of this helped to encourage more affluent shoppers to trek along to the side of the city where Emerson and Co. was situated.

The money that Emmeline had hoped the shop would provide didn't transpire and Richard, to support his family, began commuting to Manchester where he could still earn money through his northern circuit law practice. With little to do on the shop floor, Emmeline often left her sister Mary in charge and travelled with her husband back to the political environment she knew and loved so well.

The children were left in the care of gentle Susannah, whom they all loved. Yet it didn't stop the inevitable sibling rivalries and resentments from arising. Christabel was considered the cleverest of them all and was regularly commended for her 'incredible memory'. However, she was a placid, somewhat lazy child who seldom engaged in the nursery room squabbles. Instead, when she was old enough to read, she preferred to ignore her siblings and immerse herself in the passions of others through her chosen books – works by the Brontës, George Eliot, Dickens, Dumas, Hans Andersen, and Hardy.

Adela and Sylvia, however, found themselves in constant conflict, a situation exacerbated by the endless hours they were compelled to spend in each other's company. Like many younger children, Adela often felt overshadowed by her elder sisters, and was a somewhat solitary child. She wrote later, 'My father treated his elder daughters as if they were grown up when they were only little children. He gave them an exaggerated idea of their own importance and made them intensely self-conscious.'

Of her sister Sylvia, she claimed: '[Sylvia] dominated the family because she had a supreme self-love and a tenacity of purpose greater than belongs to most people… with her long face and in the sharp, shrill voice, she was a fearful "tell-tale".'[7]

One afternoon, with Richard and Emmeline in Manchester, Susannah decided to take the children to the park. It was early September, and already the leaves had started to turn golden and red, crisp under the little group's feet. Christabel and Sylvia ran through the fallen foliage in glee, while Susannah pushed the pram with 3-year-old Adela inside, her legs still in splints. Beside her, 4-year-old Frank, usually the first to struggle out of his nursemaid's grip at any possibility to be playful, shuffled alongside her, coughing and wheezing.

By the time they returned home, his symptoms had worsened and Susannah immediately alerted his mother in Manchester. Emmeline rushed back only to find her young boy in a critical condition. Doctors were called in but wrongly diagnosed him as having croup, discovering too late that it was, in fact, diphtheria. A deadly bacterial infection, diphtheria was spread through the air or by contact with contaminated objects. That it had no cure in the 1880s made it one of the most feared childhood diseases.

Emmeline remained with her young son throughout the night but nothing could be done for him. He died in the early morning of 11 September, with his mother's anguished screams waking up a startled household. In her wretchedness, Emmeline cried out that she wished Sylvia or Adela had been taken instead, and could not be soothed in her grief. She later insisted that two portraits of her dark-eyed son be put away out of sight, and at any stage to hear little Frank's name uttered brought on a fresh attack of tortured weeping.

When Richard heard the news of his son's death he was devastated. And though the profound sorrow it left him with never subsided, according to Christabel, it did seem to ignite in him a deeper flame of tenderness towards his remaining offspring.[8]

Richard was in his 50s now, and much of his married life had been centred on his political ambitions and finding ways to provide for his family. While these priorities didn't shift, he began to carve out a little more space in his life for his girls.

Emmeline's scars equally never healed. When it was discovered that defective drainage at the back of the building was likely the cause of little Frank's diphtheria, she was distraught at the idea that her and Richard's decision to live in such a poor neighbourhood had resulted in her dear boy's death.

However, rather than crumble, Emmeline channelled her grief into her work. She resolved more than ever to win her husband a seat in the House of Commons where he could be a voice for those who had no choice but to live in such impoverished conditions. She, on the other hand, had such a choice, and almost immediately after Frank's death she moved her family out of Hampstead Road.

The Pankhursts rented a handsome house on the corner of Russell Square in Bloomsbury. The building was typical of the era. It was tall with rooms for a maid, the nursery and Susannah squeezed along the top, a kitchen and cook's room in the basement, and a living space comprised of a study and drawing room for Emmeline and Richard in the middle of the house. Across the street, the flower-strewn lawns of Russell Square, corralled by iron railings, offered a safe space for the children to play when Susannah brought them for their afternoon constitutionals.

The area was decidedly middle class, comfortable and somewhat staid. It had yet to achieve its status as a fashionable refuge for London's literati. Instead, stuffy men of law and academia strode along the leafy streets, while nursemaids in long, drab bell-like skirts steered scampering children in through the park's gates.

Emmeline had closed the shop on Hampstead Road. But after the family's move to Russell Square, she reopened it in Berners Street, just north of Oxford Street, and then later, in the more upmarket neighbourhood of Regent Street. She used the excess stock from the shop as eclectic decoration for the family home. Voguish Persian plates, Chinese teapots, Japanese bead blinds and rugs in brilliant Eastern colours adorned the rooms and hallways. In the drawing room, which Emmeline had painted a bright, daffodil yellow, her favourite colour, a frieze of yellow irises ran around the wall while fashionable William Morris drapes cascaded down the windows.

Emmeline was determined to become a part of London's radical elite, and held regular salons similar to those she had heard about in the glory days of the French Revolution. Pregnant again, she was, in appearance, still very much a woman of her day. She preferred her veil when she was outdoors, and her long velvet dresses to the short skirts worn by socialist and woman's rights activist, Annie Bessant, or the trousers preferred by nonconformist Helen Taylor, stepdaughter to the great reformist John Stuart Mill, who had been a close friend of Richard's.

Both Bessant and Taylor were regulars to the Pankhursts' salons, along with other great reformers and radicals of the day. Emmeline and Richard were already members of the newly formed Fabian Society, and other pacifist and left-of-centre groups, and many of these members were regular guests. These included labour leaders Ben Tillet and Tom Mann, the Italian anarchist Errico Malatesta, the Russian refugee Prince Pyotr Kropotkin, artist, socialist, and textile designer William Morris, and the American slavery abolitionist and suffragist William Lloyd Garrison and Elizabeth Cady Stanton when they were in the city.

Emmeline was also thrilled to welcome to her home the elderly Count Henri de Rochefort, her early hero and father of her old school friend, Noémie. Finally apprehended by the Versailles government, Rochefort had been condemned to life imprisonment but had narrowly escaped to America before travelling on to London, where he now lived. Rochefort's presence in the English capital meant that Emmeline was also visited by Noémie, now a mother with three children of her own, and the two women spent several afternoons reminiscing fondly about their years of teenage freedom in Paris.

Emmeline saw her salons as a success. Conversations flowed with dreams, debate and eager plans to construct a better world built on equality and justice. In amongst the swell of chatter and gay laughter, the Pankhursts' dutiful daughters, their bodies pinched in tight frocks of white silk or wool, served neatly cut sandwiches and strawberries and cream. The girls loved these gatherings, and would often sit agog, listening to the rise and fall of the many voices. These were stolen moments of belonging, rarely felt in a household where the complete devotion of their parents to each other and their various political commitments left little room for their children's needs.

To many, however, there may have been a certain social clumsiness to Emmeline's salon. Years later, the writer Rebecca West, though an unapologetic admirer of the suffragette leader, would write of them: '[What] a naïve and ludicrous parody it must have seemed to those who really knew the world, of the real social functions of power, where great ladies shining with diamonds received at the head of wide staircases under magnificent chandeliers.'[9]

Emmeline gave birth to another son on 7 July 1889 and named him Henry Francis in honour of his deceased brother. Indeed, when discovering her fifth child was a boy, she proclaimed joyfully, 'It is Frank come again.'[10]

If the arrival of Harry, as he was called, suggested to some that Emmeline might slow down her work and the fierce ambitions she had for her husband, they were mistaken. During the previous December, a bitter split had occurred in the Central Committee of the National Society of Women's Suffrage, the umbrella organisation of all suffrage societies across Britain. Several members believed the National Society could better flourish if it affiliated itself with other non-suffrage women's organisations. This change in rules was hotly opposed by certain members, including Lydia Becker and the secretary of the National Society of Women's Suffrage, Millicent Garrett Fawcett.

Emmeline, whose membership was still with the Manchester Society, paid a 5-shilling subscription to the National Society so that she could attend the meeting to vote on this matter. After three hours of angry argument, the majority voted in favour of changing the rules, at which point Becker and Fawcett walked out. They would go on to retain the 'old' organisation with its original name, while the remaining majority would welcome in fresh members under the banner of a new organisation now called the Central National Society for Women's Suffrage.

However, with its base on Parliament Street, it was more often than not simply referred to as the Parliament Street Society. Sylvia Pankhurst later claimed her mother was going to vote against changing the rules. What made her change her mind and move with the majority is unknown. Perhaps she saw in the large numbers greater benefits for her husband's political career. Or maybe she was still bitter over Lydia Becker's earlier 'betrayal' of her husband, and for that reason took the position to stand against her. Whatever the reason, Emmeline joined the 'radical left-wing' as Becker dubbed them.

Yet trouble continued to brew within the newly expanded Central National Society for Women's Suffrage. The group did not speak as one on many of the major issues involving women's rights, in particular the issue around the married women's claim. When, at the group's first annual meeting, Richard Pankhurst unsuccessfully implored those in attendance to withdraw support for bills which explicitly excluded married women, he and Emmeline knew they would have their work cut out for them in a way that they had not been expecting.

It was for this reason that three weeks after Harry had been born, the couple helped establish the Women's Franchise League (WFL). Early members of the organisation included well-known agitators such as Josephine Butler, leader of the Ladies National Association for the Repeal of the Contagious Diseases Acts and Harriot Stanton Blatch, daughter of US suffragist Elizabeth Cady Stanton.

Emmeline was still recovering from the birth of Harry, along with a sudden life-threatening haemorrhaging that had occurred only days after her labour, and had sent a panic-stricken Susannah out onto a bustling Russell Square, calling on any passing doctor to help with a cry of, 'My mistress is dying!' Her plea had been answered and a local passing doctor had hurried up the stairs to the master bedroom and saved Emmeline's life.

A terrified Christabel, Sylvia and 4-year-old Adela had been rushed to the basement in the meantime, where they were left to huddle on their own for hours, sure their mother was going to die. Richard, who had travelled to Manchester for a few days of work, was telegraphed and returned home in great distress. But the crisis had passed. Emmeline remained in bed for a few further days and then rose to return to her work. Death may have threatened, but the cause was more important.

CHAPTER 3

DRUDGE AND DRILL

The nursery room feels cold. With the fire unlit, the only warmth is a weak splash of sunlight filtering through the rattling windows. Still, the older children are accustomed to it, and busy themselves with setting up props before their seated parents. At last, they're ready. Ten-year-old Christabel steps forward to announce their latest sketch, her chestnut curls revealing a pretty face and the confident smile of a mother's favourite. Behind her, 8-year-old Sylvia, a constant shadow to her older sister, dares a quick glance towards her father. Here is her hero, seldom seen in the nursery but now fixing the full force of his attention on his children. Next to him their mother, perching upright like a bird anxious to take flight, smiles stiffly, her mood as yet unknown. Only 5-year-old Adela and toddler Harry feel the hard edge of the room's chill and stand shivering. Both born with weak constitutions and prone to illness, they find little comfort in their father's presence. His large flat face, fiery beard, and cold, quizzical eyes are more terrifying than delightful to the younger children.

The children's theatrical offering, carefully crafted and narrated by the elder Christabel, tells a tale of a poor widow struggling to support a large family who in a twist of fate is rescued by a wealthy benefactor who then takes the families troubles on as his own. The sketch is a success, and greeted with hearty applause and effusive praise from their parents. The narrative, undoubtedly tailored to their father's ideology, reflects his constant lectures on socialism and capitalist greed – topics that along with suffrage and the evils of religion, have long coloured their lives. For youngsters, Adela and Harry, these are subjects that prick them with fear and confusion; they dread the possibility of being quizzed by their father on matters they scarcely understand. Yet for the elder daughters, his commands are a familiar refrain: 'Life is nothing without enthusiasm. Work for others! My four children are the pillars of my house, but if you ever go back to religion, you will not have been worth the upbringing.' These words, harsh and absolute, echo in their minds, a testament to the weight of their father's expectations and the fervour of his beliefs.

In truth, growing up a Pankhurst child was not an easy experience. Emmeline's nature demanded drama and constant action, otherwise she was prone to sulks and black moods. Richard, on the other hand, was so absorbed in his political work that he rarely had time to spend with his children. When he did, he interacted clumsily, with little patience or paternal warmth towards them. The couple's deep dedication to each other and their causes increased the distance between themselves and their children, and only by the girls' and Harry's attempts to be seen to support their parents' path did the familial ties between all remain intact.

That said, Emmeline was a constant in their lives in other ways. Despite her and Richard's commitment to radical politics and a vision of a modern future, at home, the Pankhursts upheld the conservative values of their time, mirroring the household of Emmeline's own childhood.

The children had a standard Victorian breakfast every day – porridge on weekdays and Saturdays, with bread and butter on Sunday and an occasional egg between the four of them. Lunch was a cold cut of meat with boiled potatoes and cabbage. The children ate with their nursemaid, but on Sunday, Emmeline and Richard made a special effort to sit down to a family meal with fruit and a piece of cake for dessert, if the children were lucky.

A spoonful of cod liver oil was also a daily requirement and refusal to endure it or eat any of the food given to them would typically result in a thrashing from their mother. This was the norm in Victorian Britain; harsh discipline was believed to be a good tutor. Once, when Sylvia refused her daily dose of cod liver oil, her mother tied her to the bedpost for the day until the rebellious child finally relented. Unlike the other children, who would quickly submit when Emmeline raised her hand, Sylvia stubbornly held out as long as she could. As an adult, she would overhear her mother tell a friend that she had to stop smacking Sylvia when her daughter was still very young because 'when she had employed the means of bringing me to contrition, I had made her feel that she might kill me before I would give way'.

Adela, on the other hand, loved and feared her mother in equal measure. To Emmeline, young Adela was either 'a pet or a problem'.[1] When Emmeline was feeling happy and loving, she would stroke her young daughter's hair, praising whatever artistic endeavour Adela was attempting, be it a drawing or an article for the family's monthly newsletters, *The Home News* and *Universal Mirror*, which the children wrote and illustrated. But at other times, it was Adela who felt the brunt of her mother's explosive tempers. In these moments, Emmeline would turn on her, calling her a 'stupid, silly lump' among other cutting comments.

The strongest bond that Emmeline forged among her children was with the confident, self-composed Christabel. The rapport and mutual respect that the pair had for each other would last throughout their lives and was never mirrored in Emmeline's relationships with her other two daughters or even Harry.

It may have been that Christabel, as the oldest child, possessed the keenest insight into her parents' complex frailties, making her more empathetic towards them than fearful of their ways. In Richard, she saw not solely an overbearing patriarch, but a grieving father, and a man whose ambitions were consistently and cruelly thwarted. While in her mother, Christabel was aware of a woman chafing against the heavy shackles of Victorian propriety, frustrated by the constraints that sought to confine her. Her mother's energy, she knew, came from a desperate need to make a difference, and to be part of a world where that counted.

The young Christabel, for her part, was not interested in making their family politics her life. Like all the Pankhurst girls, she had been encouraged in the pursuit of arts and had emerged as a talented dancer. It was Emmeline's deepest desire that Christabel fashion a career for herself as a ballerina and her darkest fear that, instead, her favoured daughter – or any of her female offspring – ended up a governess.

Sylvia had shown promise as an artist, and her talent was further shaped by her aunt, Mary, who acted as the girls' tutor at home, teaching them to read and draw. Adela had a strong imagination and loved stories (something she had perhaps gotten from her mother who, as the later suffragette leader, would spend free evenings reading gothic and romance novels rather than heavy tomes on English law!). This along with visits to the British Museum and London's many art galleries sufficed as the girls' education during their youngest years. While Emmeline was determined her children should be educated, she loathed the idea of the British school system, believing it crushed a child's creativity and individuality. Richard agreed, but suggested their children attend a Marxist education collective, though Emmeline did not want this either.

However, the children would enter the school system in later childhood. Financial hardship had continued to dog the family. When the lease on Russell Square expired in early 1893, Emmeline and Richard decided to close the shop, loosen their ties with the Women's Franchise League and move to the North of England. It was here that the girls went to school for the first time.

Richard had fallen ill and had to take the cure at Smedley Hydro. The rest of the Pankhursts took furnished rooms near the beach at Southport, where he later joined them. It was a blissful time for the children. There was no nursery or separate dinner times from their parents. The whole family lived together, ate together and spent long hours outdoors enjoying the bracing sea breeze. Emmeline and Richard would stroll by the water's edge while the children frolicked along the sandy shore collecting seashells and building sandcastles.[2]

When Aunt Mary left to marry John Clarke, much to the dismay of Emmeline who enjoyed a close bond with her sister, the girls were enrolled in the local school and stayed there for a single term. Adela in particular flourished in her new classroom environment. School for her was very much a sanctuary, a place away from her siblings whom she fought often with. 'We lived too much together within ourselves to be healthy minded,' Sylvia later noted, 'and brooded over troubles that children in more healthy surroundings would have forgotten in five minutes.' Adela would later claim it was in this first school that she uncovered her true personality. Perhaps, more accurately, it was here that she discovered the thrall of religion.[3]

As a result of her family's asserted atheism, Adela was relegated to the back of the room during scripture class. Feigning attention to her other studies, she nonetheless drank in the biblical tales – The Creation, Cain and Abel, David and Goliath – with a fervour that kindled her already vivid imagination. These stories, filled with wonder and moral gravitas, became a private sanctuary of belief, a secret faith that was hers alone.

With Richard on the mend, the family uprooted again and in the summer of 1893 moved into a modest farmhouse in the small resort town of Disley in Cheshire. The arrival of the railway in the 1850s had provided Disley with a fast, reliable link to Manchester, and many businessmen, like Richard, lived with their families in this rural idyll while travelling to town by railroad.

Emmeline's moods had lightened too. As the children romped through the countryside, picking blackberries and riding ponies, she often joined them in their fun. It was a rare time of rest and release for her. Yet as the first leaves of autumn began to fall, the Pankhursts' circumstances shifted once more. Susannah, the children's beloved caretaker, followed in Mary's footsteps and left to marry. As a result, Emmeline and Richard decided a move back to Manchester proper was a must.

Back in Emmeline and Richard's hometown, the family settled into a spacious two-storey house on Buckingham Crescent, now known as Daisy Bank Road. The neighbourhood, perched on the edge of the crowded industrial city, offered a surprising pastoral charm with its tree-lined gardens and a field stretching out before the Pankhurst's home. With no one left to care for the children at home except their mother, the girls were enrolled in the prestigious Manchester Girls' High School, an institution that prided itself on providing girls with an education equal to that of boys.

Emmeline immersed herself in her work once more. Her old friend and sometime adversary, Lydia Becker, had died in 1890 and the reins of the Manchester National Society for Women's Suffrage passed to Esther Roper, a dynamic leader from Lancashire. Under Roper's strong guidance, the group shifted its priorities. Historically focused on middle-class women and once opposed to including married women in suffrage measures, the MNSWS began actively involving married and working-class women in its efforts. Emmeline was happy to join the society's executive committee, adding it to her growing list of commitments.

The city of Manchester was still very much the smog-ridden Dickensian 'Coketown', with appalling poverty evident on every corner. The winter that the Pankhursts returned was particularly brutal, and as temperatures dropped, death rates climbed in the teeming inner-city slums. Unemployment was spiralling but with no unemployment benefit, those who lost their jobs struggled to pay the steep rents. Families were forced out of their homes and pushed onto the icy streets, where the elderly and infants in particular had the slimmest chance of survival.

Desperate to feed the multitudes, Dr Pankhurst, who was already involved in the local mining strike, organised a relief committee that, on good days, fed up to 2,000 impoverished people. Emmeline helped out. She walked the bustling markets, often with the children in tow, entreating stallholders for whatever they could spare for the relief effort. The elder Pankhurst girls, Sylvia and Christabel, were pulled in to help at soup kitchens, ladling out a thin broth to the men, women and children who queued up, their faces etched with the desperation of those on the brink. These were drastic times, and on the rare occasions the Red Doctor was at home with the children he would declaim to them his favourite mottos, 'Drudge and drill! Drudge and drill!' and 'Work for others!'

The Pankhursts' politics had been veering even more towards socialism over the last few years. Frustrated by the Liberal Party's growing indifference to women's suffrage and its failure to address the crushing poverty so visible in Manchester, they made a bold decision. In 1894, Richard and Emmeline finally severed ties with the party and joined the newly formed Independent Labour Party (ILP).

The ILP had been formed with the unique focus of representing the interests of the ordinary working people in parliament. Moreover, it included women members who were to have the same rights and say in the organisation as men, and it encouraged several affiliated committees, councils and groups dedicated to serving the interests of both. The decision to join cost Richard dearly in terms of Liberal clients and friends who had stayed with him even after he had resigned from the party years earlier. However, it also earned him a place on the ILP National Council. Additionally, that winter, Emmeline broke new ground by being elected as the ILP member of the Chorlton Board of Poor Law Guardians, one of the first women in Britain to assume such a position.

The Boards of Guardians were made up of community members that administered the Poor Law and dispersed money coming from the Poor Taxes in ways that they felt made the most difference. They controlled the local workhouse, hospital, poor schools and several other institutes that administered to the impoverished. Emmeline quickly discovered that the Chorlton Board of Poor Law Guardians had been badly governed, with greater attention being given to saving the rates than dispersing them. She immediately set about instigating changes. Some were modest yet meaningful, such as replacing the hard, backless benches in the workhouse dining rooms with comfortable chairs, allowing the elderly to dine with dignity. Other initiatives were more ambitious, like attempting to establish a cottage system for orphaned children, complete with proper sleeping and eating facilities, a gymnasium, and even a swimming pool.

Emmeline was also horrified at the workhouse's treatment of poor unmarried mothers, many of whom were no more than girls. These women faced a grim choice: they could either surrender their child and remain in the workhouse, where they would be fed and clothed but subjected to gruelling labour, or they could leave with their newborn, 'without hope, without a home, without money, without anywhere to go', as Emmeline wrote in her biography, *My Own Story*.[4] It was a dire situation, and one that she and later female guardians demanded be reformed under the Poor Law. However, their pleas fell on deaf ears. Meaningful change, Emmeline quickly realised, was unlikely to come from the predominantly male Board of Guardians who were largely indifferent to the plight of these women and children. Additionally, in the hallowed halls of government, class, not gender, held the greater political sway; despite the passage of the third Reform Act in 1884, which had extended voting rights, 40 per cent of British men still had no right to vote. As such, the needs of the female underclass were greatly overlooked.

But to Emmeline, the forgotten lives of these women greatly disturbed her. 'I thought I had been a suffragist before I became a Poor Law Guardian,' she would later write, 'but now I began to think about the vote in women's hands not only as a right but as a desperate necessity. These poor unprotected mothers and their babies I am sure were potent factors in my education as a militant.'[5]

At home, Emmeline once again opened her doors to the radical elite, transforming her household into a salon where new ideas and revolutionary opinions could be freely shared and debated. Keir Hardie, the leader of the ILP, was a frequent guest and became a close friend of the family. Unionist Tom Mann, Robert Blatchford, the publisher of the socialist newspaper *The Clarion*, and Eleanor Marx, the daughter of communist leader Karl Marx, were also regular visitors. The Pankhurst girls were once again brought in to deliver plates of sandwiches and pour drinks, and sit quietly while soaking up the ideas of socialism, Fabianism and Marxism, that roiled around them.

But these were happier times. The older girls were much more aware of the important social causes that their parents were involved in, and were excited that so many of the leading men and women of those causes often ended up sitting on their parents sofas, sipping strong tea and passionately sharing their ideas.

For quiet, serious Sylvia, it was the presence of Keir Hardie that she most looked forward to. A politician who 'walked the talk', having grown up in dire poverty and toiled in the mines as a child, in him Sylvia saw not just a political figure but a beacon of hope and a testament to the power of conviction.

James Keir Hardie had been born in Lanarkshire, Scotland, to a then unmarried farm girl who later married a ship's carpenter and early trade unionist. The couple had eight more children and to help the family, Hardie had begun working as a baker's delivery boy when he was 7 before becoming a miner at the tender age of 10. The harshness of these early years was tempered by the influence of his stepfather's trade unionism and his mother's insistence that he learn to read and write. Hardie was active in forming workers' unions first in Lanark and, following being fired in Lanark for his strike activity, in Ayr. Rising in the ranks of the miners' union, he also wrote articles in the pro-labour press to help make ends meet, later establishing his own publications, *The Miner* and *Labour Leader*.

While Hardie harboured personal ambitions and a desire to escape the grim conditions of the mines, his true aspiration centred on the possibilities of collective action. In 1888, he helped found the Scottish Labour Party, becoming the party's secretary. Despite a setback in his first parliamentary bid, he succeeded in 1892. The following year, he played a pivotal role in organising the Independent Labour Party (ILP). His arrival into national politics was marked by both defeat and resurgence; he lost his seat in 1895 but returned triumphantly in 1900, where he continued to serve for another six years.

It was during these first political forays that Hardie met and formed a friendship with the Pankhursts. As early supporters of the burgeoning ILP, Richard and Emmeline's commitment quickly fostered a deep friendship with Keir Hardie. Despite having a wife in Scotland, Hardie spent considerable time in Manchester as well as London where he kept rooms, and while in the northern city often visited the Pankhursts' home. For Sylvia, these visits were a source of secret delight. In her 1911 account on the history of the women's militant suffrage movement, she recalled her anticipation, rushing home from school, hoping to find him there:

> Seeing the library door open, I hastened upstairs to the angle where one could see who was sitting in the big armchair by the fire. There he was: his majestic head surrounded by ample curls going grey and shining with glints of silver and golden brown: his great forehead deeply lined: his eyes, two deep wells of kindness… Kneeling on the stairs to watch him, I felt that I could have rushed into his arms… Like a sturdy oak with its huge trunk seamed and gnarled, he seemed to carry with him the spirit of nature in the great open spaces.

At the time, Sylvia might not have recognised her feelings as love, enveloped as she was in the awkwardness of early adolescence. Yet this marked the genesis of a profound friendship and later, a love affair that would shape and guide her adult life. This connection, with all its complexities, brought to Sylvia not just personal affection but also an enduring influence, steering her towards the ideals and struggles that would define her own unique journey.

In hindsight, it made sense that Sylvia, or any of the children, would find their first loves in the home they lived in; their social lives were largely confined to this space and they were discouraged from forming friendships beyond these bounds. Instead, their time was spent helping at soup kitchens, going on family cycles with the working-class Clarion Cycle Club, or attending 'Cinderella' coffee parties for slum children. At these latter events, the stark contrast between their own lives and the ragged, barefoot children scrambling for meagre portions must have left a deep impression on the three girls, though the impact seems to have been felt differently by each. The youngest, Adela, was horrified by what she saw. Sylvia sympathised, while the teenage Christabel seemed largely indifferent. It's possible that Christabel resented being forced into such close contact with poverty, and perhaps felt frustrated by the class consciousness thrust upon her. This could explain why, later on, she fought to have the Women's Social and Political Union recognised as class-blind, and eventually even dropped the pretence of representing the working class at all. For Christabel, the real battle was always over gender, not class. However, despite, or even because of their differing responses, it was this period in Manchester that, as Adela later reflected in her own writings on the Suffragette Movement, helped shape 'three of the most complete agitators that have troubled the social peace of Britain'.

In July 1895, 60-year-old Dr Pankhurst, still struggling with poor health, was invited by the ILP to make another bid for Parliament, standing as a candidate for West Gorton in southeastern Lancashire. Emmeline and the children, filled with hope, joined him in canvassing the working-class neighbourhoods. Even Harry, as immersed in the political expectations of his home as his sisters, helped out, taking days off school to campaign alongside his mother and scrawl slogans for his father on roadside pavements. However, Richard suffered another crushing defeat. Sylvia, who claimed, 'I saw my father a lofty embodiment of the human mind, faring forth amid uncharted waters,'[6] wept bitterly when the results were announced, only to be sternly rebuked by her mother for her unseemly show of emotion.

This would be Richard's final political endeavour. Over the following years, plagued by chronic stomach pain that often left him immobile, the Red Doctor's health deteriorated further. In the summer of 1898, Emmeline decided to take 17-year-old Christabel to Geneva for a finishing year with her old friend Noémie Rochefort DuFaux, intending to bring back Noémie's daughter in exchange. However, during her absence, Richard's condition worsened dramatically. Poor 16-year-old Sylvia was faced with the terror of trying to nurse her father alone and summoned the doctor. Yet there was little he could do; Richard's stomach ulcers had perforated. Richard had sent a telegram to his wife with the words: 'I am not well. Please come home, my love.' But now

Sylvia rushed another to her mother. A desperate Emmeline was already racing back to Britain, but it was too late. On 5 July 1898, at the age of 63, her beloved husband and political soulmate passed away. At the time, Emmeline was still on a train hurtling across England. She received the news just as the train was pulling into Manchester, and collapsed with a cry of anguish.

By the time she arrived home, her sister Mary and brother Herbert were already there, doing their best to comfort the heartbroken children. Sylvia, in particular, was inconsolable, consumed by guilt and the mistaken belief that she could have done more to save her father. He had been her idol and she never truly got over the loss.

For her husband's tombstone, the grief-stricken Emmeline chose a line from Walt Whitman: 'Faithful and True, and my loving Comrade.' The secular funeral that happened on the following Sunday, 9 July, began with Dr Pankhurst's coffin carried on an open carriage covered in red flowers. It was flanked by large numbers of representatives of the ILP and a group from the Clarion Cycle Club wearing white rosettes. Hundreds of people then gathered at the graveside to hear the eulogies – friends, colleagues and members of every political group that the Red Doctor had ever been involved in. It was a fitting passing for a man who had touched so many lives.

CHAPTER

4

LIKE MOTHER, LIKE DAUGHTERS

In the Pankhurst household, Richard's death had rent a great void in their lives. A heavy sadness descended on the family. Emmeline turned away even more from the children, unable to come to terms with her loss. Sylvia regularly shared a bed with her mother, though only as a bedmate to weep through their grief together until the early hours of the morning. 'It was the collapse of our happy life,' Christabel, who had then returned from Geneva, wrote years later.[1] In truth, this collapse had as much to do with the crippling debts that Richard had left behind him as it had to do with the grief they felt. He had made no will and left no funds for the family's survival. The house on Buckingham Crescent was given up, and all its furnishings sold. The Pankhursts moved to a smaller residence in the then-crowded Nelson Street. The new home, one of a row of two-storey brick terraced cottages with a small garden at the back, was much closer to the smog-choked, industrial centre of the city, and depressed the children even further.

Though 62 Nelson Street had three entertaining rooms, five bedrooms, a bath and WC, and an office, the living space was still cramped. According to the 1901 census, those residing in the house at that time included Emmeline and her four children, together with her two brothers, Walter and Herbert Goulden, the latter's son, and the family's two servants, the cook, Ellen Coyle, and Mary Leaver, the housemaid.

With no means to support her family, Emmeline knew she had to pick herself up and find work. She had refused an offer of financial help from family friend, Robert Blatchford, though she encouraged him to use the money to set up a fund in her husband's name.

Despite the lessons of her previous business failures in London, Emmeline re-launched Emerson's on Manchester's King Street. Christabel was frequently dragged in to stack shelves and serve behind the counter, though she spent most of her time flicking through recent novels. As expected, the shop soon became a financial burden. Emmeline also stepped down from her role on the Board of Guardians but was quickly offered a paid position as registrar of Births and Deaths for the Rushholme district. In this new position she was once again confronted with the appalling conditions and lack of care afforded to impoverished women and children. It was not uncommon for girls as young as 13 to enter her office to register the birth of their illegitimate child, often accompanied by a male relative – sometimes even the girl's own father – who was responsible for the young mother's pregnancy.[2] This grim reality only deepened Emmeline's resolve to advocate for laws that would provide equal protection and representation for women, mirroring the rights enjoyed by men.

With the shop, the job, and her determination to continue working for needy causes, she required more support than ever and her sister Mary stepped up to help her when she could. To manage expenses, Adela was withdrawn from the costly Manchester High School for Girls and sent to a cheaper, though more austere boarding school on Ducie Road. Harry, too, was sent away to a cheaper boarding school. A melancholy and forlorn boy, Harry struggled with severe short-sightedness. However, Emmeline refused to get him spectacles, deeming them unsightly. Consequently, he found reading difficult, was often bullied, and ran away from school on several occasions.

As the family gradually returned to their daily routines, Emmeline granted Sylvia the use of a room as an art studio. Sylvia's artistic talent had caught the attention of Charles Rowley, a prominent dealer in Pre-Raphaelite art who had visited the Pankhurst home to appraise Richard's collection for sale. He urged Emmeline to nurture her daughter's gift. In 1901, Sylvia's dedication paid off when she won a scholarship to the Manchester School of Art, much to Emmeline's delight. Later that year, Sylvia was awarded a National Silver Medal for mosaic design, earning her another scholarship – a travelling studentship that allowed her to study art at a location of her choice in Europe. She chose Italy. An excited Emmeline decided to accompany her as far as Geneva to visit her childhood friend, Noemie, whom she had left in great distress three years earlier upon learning of her husband's worsening health. As it turned out, the three women all ended up travelling to Venice together, where the older women indulged in shopping and sightseeing while the young Sylvia immersed herself in the surrounding art and dedicated herself to painting.

When Emmeline finally had to return to England, Sylvia sobbed at their parting, so happy had she been during their easy time together. However, she soon recovered and joined the Academia di Belle Arti, throwing herself into the artistic life of Venice. She made friends and like any young girl of her age gossiped shyly about love and other frivolous female concerns. When she wasn't attending art classes or roaming the galleries, she would sit and paint or spend time with her close friend, the young Polish countess, Sophie

Bertelli Algarotti. However, when the time came that Sylvia too had to return to Manchester, she felt ready to do so. In her private papers, she reflected:

> My decision to return to Manchester was made without hesitation. I was clearly aware I was leaving a life of security where I was happy and beloved and which attracted me above all because therein I might study and improve the art which was very precious to me… but I permitted myself no doubts and no regrets.

Meanwhile, the 'clever Christabel' had begun taking courses in logic under Professor Samuel Alexander at Owens College and a year after Sylvia had found her path to art college, she made her great escape from Emerson's counter. To get herself out of working in the family shop, Christabel had gotten involved with the Manchester Women's Trade Union Council, and in 1901 was appointed to the executive committee of the North of England Society for Women's Suffrage. It was through these affiliations that she met Esther Roper, already known to her mother, and Eva Gore-Booth. The women were life partners and prominent figures in the North of England Society for Women's Suffrage and the Women's Trade Union Council, respectively. They had ventured north to rally female mill workers around suffrage, believing that working-class women suffered as much from having a lack of voice as any woman in Britain. In fact, more so. With their appallingly low wages and no political route to changing that, the vote was 'a weapon of self-defence'.[3] Hearing a passionate speech given by Christabel at this time and recognising her latent leadership potential, they spurred her on to become even more involved in the women's movement.

The women's encouragement ignited a bold impulse in Christabel. Though she had been raised in a politically charged household, her role, as she understood it, was to adhere to her parents' teachings. She held the same views as Sylvia, who wrote in *The Suffragette Movement* (1931):

> To what a treadmill he [Richard Pankhurst] condemned us helpless, hopeless children and his poor wife with her gaiety, her beauty. 'Working for others', was interpreted to mean, of course, adopting his political and religious views and sacrificing everything to them … the children counted for nothing at all beside the cause…

For all her community service, Christabel had never thought to step out from under her parents' shadow and commit fully to a purpose. Now, with Roper and Gore-Booth's encouragement, she joined the North of England's Society for Women's Suffrage, where both women were executive committee members, and resolved to turn her energies towards advocating for women's suffrage. She later wrote in *Unshackled: The Story of How We Won the Vote*:

> I had been reared in the suffrage cause and the principle of equality had been lived out in our home. In fact, it was the sharp contrast between practical suffragism in the home circle and the inequality I saw meted out to women in general in the outer world that made me see in the suffrage cause one, not of merely academic interest, but of … practical importance. Here, then was an aim in life for me – the liberation of politically fettered womanhood.[4]

As a part of this, Christabel also decided to study for her matriculation. Emmeline supported her daughter's newfound dedication to both activism and academics, and advised her to follow in her father Richard Pankhurst's footsteps and study law. The suggestion resonated with Christabel. As she reflected: 'It seemed that a knowledge of law might be useful in work for woman suffrage, and useful it was indeed to prove.'

Christabel applied to Lincoln's Inn, her father's alma mater, though was denied entry on the basis of her gender. Undeterred, she appealed the decision and was invited to address a gathering of lawyers at the Union Society in London, yet her bid for admission remained unsuccessful. Determined to continue, she enrolled in law studies at Manchester University. She would go on to excel in her studies, achieving joint first-class honours in the LL.B. exam in 1906, even while balancing her numerous commitments to the suffrage cause that had since developed.

While Sylvia was blossoming as an artist and Christabel was studying and finding her voice as an advocate for women's liberation, Adela remained directionless, caught in the undertow of her sisters' burgeoning ambitions. She had finally been withdrawn from Ducie Road after repeated lice infestations and returned to Manchester High School. There, the new headmistress, impressed by her writing and intellect, suggested she aim for an Oxford History scholarship. Both Emmeline and Sylvia furiously shot down the idea, deeming it a betrayal of Adela's late father, who had harboured a deep disdain for Oxford and all it stood for. For Adela, watching the support her sisters received while she felt belittled and overlooked, her days at school were marked by a profound sense of isolation and resentment. She was particularly offended by Sylvia, whom she felt had acted out of spite in dashing Adela's dreams of an Oxford education. Isolating herself even further from her siblings, she spent her remaining school years engulfed in self-pity and a simmering animosity.

There were attempts to engage her mother by supporting Emmeline's causes. For instance, in 1899 the Boer War had broken out and Emmeline, a pacifist as her husband had been, was furious with the Fabian Society's refusal to condemn Britain's participation. She and sixteen other members resigned. Adela bravely attempted to voice her own pacifist views in her school, only to have a book thrown at her head. Harry too took a public pacifist stand in his school, was beaten up and left unconscious on the street. These events, along with the horrific tales Adela heard of the treatment of the Dutch Boer women and children in the concentration camps, served to fuel the young Adela's hatred of British jingoistic capitalism. She saw the Dutch in South Africa as the underdogs, and during the later First World War, would, in her muddled, empathetic thinking, also extend this sympathy to the German antagonists. At 17 years of age, Adela also developed an interest in socialism, brought on primarily by a visit to Chorlton's workhouse with a young Russian socialist friend, Marie Koss. Until then, the idea of class struggle had felt abstract – something her father had lectured about at length but never truly come alive. That changed the moment she stepped into the grim, overcrowded institution. A row of tiny coffins was laid outside, while inside the gloomy building the suffering cries of diseased and dying babies left alone in iron cots met the two horrified girls. When the nurse noted the direction of their shocked gaze, she claimed the cause of the suffering was down to 'social evil'.[5]

At home, Adela mentioned the nurse's comment to Emmeline, who promptly handed her Friedrich Engels's *The Origin of the Family, Private Property and the State*. Adela devoured the text eagerly, and this newfound curiosity about the ideology that had formed the very basis of her father's powerful beliefs brought her closer than ever before to her mother.

The family were proud of Christabel's work and it had renewed their interest in the area of women's quest for the vote. However, Emmeline had been feeling decidedly sidelined by Christabel, who spent increasing time with her mentors, Esther Roper and Eva Gore-Booth, and so she began taking Adela to ILP women's suffrage meetings in working-class, industrial areas. At one such gathering, where Emmeline was scheduled to speak but was delayed, Adela was asked to step in. With trepidation, she ascended the stage but soon found her voice, passionately advocating for the intertwined causes of socialism and women's suffrage as the remedy for the plight of poor women. It was her first time addressing a public crowd, and she revelled in it.

After that, she took on more of her mother's speaking engagements, enthusiastically committing herself to her mother's causes. Her memory of those small children's coffins along with the many pauper children she had met through the work of her parents also encouraged her to step beyond the safety of Emerson's counter, where she had been forced to work once Christabel began her studies, and apply for a job as a pupil-teacher in a working-class school. Though she received a paltry wage for her lack of formal training, she embraced the position eagerly. Perhaps she believed that in her work in the school and with her mother, she had finally found her place in the family.

❁ ❁ ❁

The campaign for female suffrage had always been among the most persisting crusades in the Pankhurst household. As the century moved towards its close, it was a cause that had gradually found steadier feet in the public sphere. Throughout Queen Victoria's sixty-year reign, the ideals of women's rigid domestic role had gone virtually unchallenged. But as the century drew to a close, and the now more-or-less reclusive 80-year-old Queen had less of an influence on the public mind, the weight of these constraints began to chafe. The long-held expectations of docility and domesticity started to feel increasingly suffocating. Women, once confined by these rigid societal norms, were starting to assert their desire for freedom, seeking to redefine their roles and claim their place beyond their private parlour rooms. Yet the lack of legal rights around marriage, widowhood, and divorce left them with few options.

Though by the end of the 1800s, the Married Women's Property Acts allowed women to own property, they could hold on to little else, including their children in cases of divorce or separation. Widows, too, could find themselves destitute if their late husband's will left property to others, with no legal recourse.

In addition, most professions such as law, medicine, and higher education were closed to women, whether married or single. Even when women could find work, conditions were poor, with low wages and limited opportunities for advancement. For single women, job loss meant no state welfare safety net, leaving many facing poverty. In a society that neither encouraged nor valued independence in women, there were also few legal protections against abuse, harassment, or violence, leaving them vulnerable and unsupported.

It was into this repressive social climate of the mid-1890s that the 'New Woman' emerged. This was a term introduced by the feminist writer Sarah Grand in her 1894 article, 'The New Aspect of the Woman Question', which gained further prominence when used by English novelist Ouida (Maria Louisa Ramé) and American author Henry James. The fight for female social and political freedoms had been happening since Mary Wollstonecraft had penned *A Vindication of the Rights of Women*, but this new label encapsulated the growing number of educated, independent and unmarried Victorian women advocating for greater meaning in their lives and, as a reflection of that, a more significant role in the governance of their countries. These 'New Women' were easily identifiable by their short-cropped hair, their bicycles, and their daring 'bloomers' – a divided skirt that afforded them greater freedom, particularly when cycling. Though several of their detractors dismissed these sartorial choices as mere provocations, they were, in fact, potent symbols of a deeper determination for autonomy and purpose.

For many New Women, this was their time to finally push the idea of female suffrage centre stage. Throughout this era, suffragist groups had sprung up in Edinburgh, Dublin, and other areas of southern and northern England as well as London, and Manchester. In 1897, the National Union of Women's Suffrage Societies (NUWSS) was founded, with the graceful Millicent Fawcett as its chair. Born into a privileged, liberal-minded family in Suffolk in 1847, Millicent was married to the blind Liberal MP Henry Fawcett. Her sister,

Elizabeth Garrett Anderson, was Britain's first woman doctor, while another sibling, Agnes, co-founded one of Britain's and the world's first all-female interior design firms, A & R Garrett House Decorators, with their cousin Rhoda. Millicent had been an active participant in the women's suffragist movement since her youth. She wrote, 'I cannot say I *became* a suffragist. I always was one, from the time I was old enough to think at all about the principles of Representative Government.'[6]

Millicent and Henry Fawcett, like Emmeline and Richard, were a couple of singular purposes and vision. They were ardent proponents of proportional representation and the rights of trade unions, and staunch defenders of individual liberties and the principles of free trade. Their commitment to advancing the cause of women was unwavering and Millicent wrote several essays and articles on women's education and suffrage. In Cambridge, the couple championed Henry Sidgwick's initiative to offer lectures for women – a scheme inaugurated in their drawing room in 1869, while in 1875, Millicent herself co-founded Newnham Hall (later College), the only college in Cambridge and elsewhere run by women, for women. As a founder, she also took an active role on its council. Later, in 1887, she further supported fellow feminist Emily Davies's contentious campaign to open Cambridge degrees to women, a bold move that stirred both excitement and resistance.

Millicent joined the London Suffrage Committee in 1868, making her début as a speaker for the cause at the first public suffrage meeting held in London a year later. With her clear, sweet-toned voice, she was a popular speaker among the many upper-middle-class 'New Women'. Following the split within the Central Committee for Women's Suffrage and the proliferation of various suffragist groups across Britain, Fawcett was invited to become President of the Special Appeal Committee, established in 1893 to encourage unity among suffrage societies working towards a common goal. Henry Fawcett had died in November 1884, leaving Millicent a widow at only 34 years old. Though she had retreated from public life in the years that immediately followed, she now accepted this role of president. At that time, seventeen individual groups, including the Central Committee for Women's Suffrage, the London Society for Women's Suffrage, the Edinburgh Society for Women's Suffrage, and others, campaigned for women's right to vote.

On 14 October 1897, these groups united to form the National Union of Women's Suffrage Societies (NUWSS), marking a pivotal moment in the early women's rights movement in Britain. Millicent Fawcett, a natural leader, would guide the NUWSS for the next two decades.

The NUWSS was dominated by middle- and upper-class women, many of whom were connected to Liberal politicians or moved in similar social circles. Consequently, a significant portion of the membership adhered to the Victorian ideal of womanhood, highlighting women's roles as refined, respectable, and protective of their private domestic interests.

To attract working-class women to the NUWSS, the organisation emphasised that female enfranchisement did not undermine the role of homemaker but rather safeguarded it. Millicent and her colleagues believed that women's unique perspectives justified their need for the vote. In the *Nineteenth Century Magazine*, in June 1889, she wrote:

> We do not want women to be bad imitations of men. We neither deny nor minimise the differences between men and women. The claim of women to representation depends to a large extent on those differences. Women bring something to the service of the state different from that which can be brought by men.

The NUWSS was dedicated to moral reform, actively campaigning against violence towards women, and the trafficking of women and girls, as well as women's suffrage. They believed in gently pushing for reform through petitions and letters sent to their public representatives.

Meanwhile, Emmeline maintained her connections with members of the waning Women's Franchise League (it would end for good in 1903). Additionally, as a member of the Independent Labour Party (ILP), she believed that the party offered a promising platform for advancing the 'Woman Question'. Keir Hardie, the Pankhursts' family friend and the ILP's sole Member of Parliament, was staunchly sympathetic to the cause of women's suffrage. He and Emmeline had spent many evenings in the house on Buckingham Crescent discussing equality for women and the need for the women's vote. Though several of Hardie's ILP colleagues believed the fight was actually for 'adult suffrage', whereby property and financial qualifications would not restrict any man or woman, Emmeline feared that arguing for both men and women to be given full franchise was placing too much emphasis on men's rights and overlooking those of women. For many, adult suffrage was, she knew, a byword for 'Manhood Suffrage', and she shared her fears with Hardie, who accepted those fears as valid.

In 1903, Emmeline's friend and Labour ally, Robert Blatchford, heeded her advice and raised funds for the ILP to construct a hall on St James Road, in the working-class district of High Town, Manchester, as a memorial to Richard Pankhurst. Emmeline enlisted Sylvia to decorate it, and the young artistic Pankhurst spent weeks transforming the space, painting roses, doves, and vibrant peacock feathers – symbols of love, peace, and beauty – across the entrance and walls. By late summer, the hall was ready for its grand opening.

However, only weeks after the inauguration, Emmeline and her daughters discovered that the local ILP branch using Pankhurst Hall would not permit women to join. Outraged, they saw this as a profound betrayal. To make matters worse, it soon became clear that several ILP members were uneasy about advocating for parliamentary votes for women, arguing that the focus should remain on securing suffrage for all men first, with women's rights to be addressed only after. For Emmeline, the path forward was becoming unmistakably clear. The movement needed the old wisdom of previous suffragists, but it also demanded a youthful energy and bravery from the 'New Women' who were refusing to accept a lesser role in society. Earlier that year, the American women's rights activist Susan B. Anthony had paid a visit to Manchester and those involved in the women's struggle had met with her. After she had left, Christabel, who had been deeply impressed by the eminent reformer, had lamented that it was 'Unendurable to think of another generation of women wasting their lives begging for the vote. We must not lose any more time. We must act.'[7]

This declaration provided the impetus Emmeline needed. On 10 October 1903, she invited a small group of ILP women to her home at 62 Nelson Street. Christabel sat alongside her mother as a second facilitator of the meeting. Adela was also there. At 18 years old, she was the youngest in attendance, sitting quietly among the seasoned activists who eagerly circled the wooden kitchen table. Outside, the clamour of smog-filled, congested Manchester persisted, indifferent to the momentous decision unfolding within. 'Women, we must do the work ourselves,' Emmeline told those gathered, and so they began. There, in that modest room, the women founded an organisation that would forever change the British political landscape and the lives of countless others.

CHAPTER

5

FAMILY FRONTLINES

The Women's Social and Political Union (WSPU) was established as a pressure group with a clear mission to secure the right to vote for women. Although its founders, primarily socialists and working women from the Independent Labour Party (ILP), had resolved not to tie themselves to any single political party, they saw their movement as complementary to the broader ILP. They did not rely on the party but rather aimed to leverage their existing connections within it. Christabel, however, was sceptical of any potential alliance with the ILP. Influenced by her mentors, Eva Gore-Booth and Esther Roper, she had grown more radical in her thinking, believing that Labour men cared relatively little for franchise reform, and vehemently rejected the notion that the Labour party could be relied upon to champion women's rights. 'Why are women expected to have such confidence in the men of the Labour party?' she had written in the *ILP News*'s public forum. 'Working-men are as unjust to women as are those of other classes.'

Emmeline did not disagree with Christabel. Alongside the recent experience with the ILP group in Pankhurst Hall, many of the political movers and shakers who came to stay at Nelson Street openly dismissed the notion of prioritising women's enfranchisement, insisting that the true divide was not between men and women, but between classes. Similarly, most of the other founding members of the WSPU were unwavering in their understanding that true social change for women hinged on a singular focus: securing the vote for women. Around Emmeline's kitchen table on that fateful first evening, they drafted a manifesto that left no room for doubt. 'Social reform can never be satisfactory,' they declared, 'as long as one-half of the nation is not represented.' But they understood too that achieving this goal required more than just resolve; it demanded strategic alliances. Winning over members of the ILP and employing the established methods of current suffragist societies – such as lobbying MPs and pushing for Private Members' Bills – were necessary steps toward realising their vision.

That's not to say that the older members of the early WSPU were content to simply follow the well-worn paths of their feminist peers. They had come together to carve out a new, uncharted route toward female enfranchisement. Even in the organisation's very structure, the differences were significant, if subtle. Most suffrage groups welcomed both women and men who supported the cause. In stark contrast, the WSPU made a bold decision to limit its membership exclusively to women. Men were welcomed to support, but only women could join. Moreover, while the broader suffragist movement emphasised peaceful campaigning, the WSPU was committed to direct action. They would be 'satisfied with nothing but action on our question,' Emmeline later noted. '"Deeds, not words", was to be our permanent motto.'

This motto was not just a declaration but a guiding principle that reflected their willingness to do whatever was necessary to draw attention to their cause. Although this approach would eventually become synonymous with civil disobedience, Emmeline and her fellow members knew from the outset that while traditional methods of instigating parliamentary change were necessary, something more was needed to catapult their movement into the public spotlight.

Emmeline's conviction deepened on 3 February 1904, during the opening day of Parliament. She joined a delegation of mainly NUWSS suffragists in London, a yearly ritual of meeting with 'friendly' MPs to present their case and seek assurances of support for women's suffrage. To Emmeline, these encounters were but a charade, a farce of superficial sympathies and empty assurances.

In her autobiography, she recounts the ritual:

> The ladies made their speeches and the members made theirs. The ladies thanked the friendly members for their sympathy and the members renewed their assurances that they believed in women's suffrage and would vote for it when they had an opportunity to do so. Then the deputation, a trifle sad, but entirely tranquil, took its departure and the members resumed the real business of life, which was support of their parties' policies.

During this particular spring morning meeting, as the women prepared to take their leave, Emmeline cornered the Liberal MP Sir Charles McLaren (spelled as M'Laren in various sources including Emmeline's own book), pressing him to disclose whether any Parliamentarian was poised to introduce a suffrage bill. If not, then she demanded to know what concrete actions were McLaren and his 'friendly' colleagues planning to take to show their professed support.

Her questions greatly flustered the politician and stunned the other women, who were aghast at her breach of decorum. McLaren mumbled his earlier-given assurances and clumsily made his escape, and when all the women were out on the street again, Emmeline faced sharp rebukes for potentially alienating McLaren and other ostensibly supportive MPs. Unperturbed, she remained resolute; words alone would not suffice, she sought deeds.

In those early days, the WSPU was poorly funded. Membership was small and each member contributed what they could with Emmeline supplying the remaining money needed. The group met weekly, often in the Pankhurst home or in rented rooms. Mrs Rachel Scott was appointed as the first honorary secretary and neither Emmeline or Christabel had taken an executive position; they believed that to do so would make the organisation appear like a 'family party'. The younger Pankhurst girls didn't hold office in the WSPU either. Sylvia had not even been at the inaugural meeting and Adela, though enthusiastic, lacked the influence and charm that Christabel and Emmeline naturally commanded. Yet, despite their careful avoidance of overt leadership, it was clear that the WSPU was very much a 'Pankhurst' endeavour. Emmeline and Christabel, with their undeniable passion and charisma, were already steering the group's direction.

The members were constantly at work, often gathered around the Pankhursts' kitchen table writing letters to various organisations and seeking invitations to speak. At the time, the WSPU had only five speakers: Emmeline, her three daughters, and Teresa Billington, a spirited and free-thinking agnostic. Emmeline had first encountered Teresa through her work as a teacher with the Education Committee and quickly recognised her potential, encouraging her to join the Independent Labour Party (ILP). With no fear of speaking up at Labour and trade union meetings in Manchester, it was obvious Teresa was a gifted orator. Emmeline introduced her to Keir Hardie, who invited her to work as the first woman organiser for the ILP, speaking on women's suffrage. When the WSPU was formed, it was only natural that she would become one of its leading figures.

Teresa and the other speakers travelled around Manchester, addressing any organisations that accepted their requests to talk to their members. Eventually, two more speakers joined their ranks. These were Nellie Martel, a tireless advocate who had helped secure the vote for women in New South Wales and had become the first woman to stand as an independent candidate for the Australian Senate in 1903, and Flora Drummond, whose bold, headline-grabbing stunts would soon make her one of the movement's most formidable figures. Together, they embarked on an exhausting campaign across northern England, speaking at ILP meetings, Trade Union gatherings, on soapboxes on street corners, in crowded village greens, and during the rush and ruckus of market days. Their message was clear: women should have the vote on equal terms with men.

However, speaking engagements alone were not enough. While they could connect with ordinary people open to hearing their message, enacting change in the corridors of power was not so easily won from a soapbox. Before they could make real progress, a change in strategy was necessary. Emmeline had already set things in motion by confronting Sir Charles McLaren, demanding concrete actions rather than vague promises. Christabel, however, was determined to push further. Frustrated by the tired, repetitive tactics that had plagued the suffrage movement since her grandmother's time, she sought a new approach – one that would lift the 'women's question' out of the dim waiting rooms of the House of Commons and into the full glare of national debate. The challenge was formidable; envisioning what had never been done before was no easy task. But in the early spring of 1904, Christabel caught a glimpse of what could be.

At that time, the incumbent Conservative Party, under the leadership of Arthur James Balfour, clung desperately to its dwindling power while the Liberals confidently reached for it. The costly Boer War had ended in 1902, burdening the Conservative government with £210 million in expenses (around £25 billion today) and over 120,000 British and Imperial casualties, including 22,000 deaths. This financial strain, coupled with rising issues around taxation and protectionist tariffs, appeared to foreshadow the government's decline.

Furiously campaigning across the country, the Liberals had organised a public meeting at the Manchester Trade Hall. The gathering was essentially an hour-and-a-half-long address by a young and ambitious politician named Winston Churchill. At that point, Churchill, a Tory MP, was on the verge of leaving his party, driven by his opposition to their proposed tariff reforms. With his mop of red hair and moody eyes, the young Churchill, not yet 30, had already achieved some fame for his daring escape from a Boer prison during the South African War. Upon returning to England, he had left the army to pursue a political career, narrowly winning a seat as the Conservative candidate for Oldham in the 1900 general election. However, his outspoken stance against protectionism made it unlikely that he would retain his seat as a Tory. He planned to switch to the Liberals, positioning himself as a Liberal champion of free trade. The seat in North West Manchester appeared ready to swing from Conservative to Liberal, and Churchill had been invited by the Liberals to contest it.

His speech at the Free Trade Hall on 19 February 1904 drew a large crowd, but somehow Christabel managed to secure a place on the platform. Churchill spoke at length, passionately defending his unwavering commitment to free trade. Just as he was proposing the formal adoption of a resolution affirming this principle, Christabel stood up to ask if he could include women's suffrage in his proposal.

The ruffled Churchill turned to the other dignitaries, whose own shocked expressions revealed to him they'd be of little help. Christabel, her heart pounding, her feet unsteady, approached the Chairman with her written proposal for the addition, which he had no choice but to read out. However, after doing so, he pointed out that the organisers wanted the resolution to be adopted unanimously, and adding a contentious issue like women's suffrage would make that impossible. Christabel retreated, but the encounter had illuminated something crucial for her. In their startled and evasive responses, she had glimpsed an as yet unused path for the women of the WSPU to take.

'This was the first militant step – the hardest to me, because it was the first,' she wrote in *Unshackled.*

> To move from my place on the platform to the speaker's table in the teeth of the astonishment and opposition of will of that immense throng, those civic and county leaders and those Members of Parliament, was the most difficult thing I have ever done … [but] something had been gained. Women's claim to vote had been imposed upon the attention of political leaders and the public, at one of the decisive political meetings of the century.

While Christabel was trying to figure out how this new approach, this disruption of the norm, could work, Emmeline was applying her grit to the old methods. That April, she attended the annual conference of the Independent Labour Party, determined to gain their support to present a suffrage bill before Parliament during their next session.

She knew she would have a battle on her hands. The minority that was openly opposed to directing energy towards a separate bill for votes for women had strengthened. She gave a rousing speech, claiming, 'No man was excluded because he was a man, but every woman was precluded because she was a woman.' After much deliberation, and to the surprise of many, the resolution was accepted: Labour's MPs would be instructed to put forth a women's suffrage measure alongside that of adult suffrage when the new session of Parliament convened the following February. The bill they would champion was none other than the original draft that Richard Pankhurst had penned years earlier. At the same meeting, Emmeline was re-elected to the National Administrative Council (NAC) of the ILP, a development that excited members of the WSPU, who knew her position could help in securing further ILP backing for the proposed franchise bill.

Yet the path ahead was far from straightforward. The British government permitted private bills to be discussed only once a week, and with numerous MPs eager to present their own proposals, they would draw lots on the first day of Parliament to determine whose bills would be discussed. This reality placed significant pressure on Emmeline and the WSPU to rally as much support as possible from Labour MPs, thereby increasing their odds of seeing their bill brought to the floor.

And so they got to work, fervently composing letters to each and every Labour MP they had connections with. It was not just the kitchen table in Nelson Street that was nightly surrounded by earnest women writing these urgent appeals. The WSPU reach was growing, and women across the North of England and elsewhere frantically lobbied their MPs. Even Richard's old friend, the now elderly Elizabeth Wolstenholme Elmy, had joined the WSPU, and happily dispatched several letters daily from her home in Congleton.

During all this time, Sylvia, who had not been present at the inaugural meeting, had fallen into easy step with what was needed to be done. However, in autumn 1904, after sitting for the London Royal College of Art (RCA) entrance exam, she was awarded a two-year attendance scholarship of £5 a month. This necessitated a move to the capital, a prospect she found both thrilling and daunting; though she had lived away from her family during her time in Italy, Venice was not the vast, impersonal expanse that London was.

Sylvia rented lodgings off the Fulham Road, costing 10 shillings a week, and supplemented her income by selling her designs for cotton prints. Despite the meagre earnings, she sent most of it back home to her family in Manchester, where finances remained tight. Yet Emmeline, now the household's financial decision-maker, did not prioritise this extra income. Though appreciative of her daughter's efforts, she soon redirected Sylvia's focus, arguing that her time would be better spent gathering signatures for the Women's Franchise Bill rather than working in her free time to earn a few extra shillings. For Sylvia, this meant setting aside her evening design work to traverse London's boroughs, attending meetings, and canvassing support from local trade unions and ILP branches.

It was lonely work, not made lighter by her first few weeks at the RCA. Sylvia found herself adrift in an environment where her fellow students seemed to effortlessly forge friendships, their conversations flowing with laughter and shared thoughts on art and artists. Naturally reserved and accustomed to the older, politically engaged circles that frequented her home in Manchester, she kept mostly to herself. However, among her professors, she quickly gained a reputation as a troublemaker. Sylvia had discovered that the college only rarely awarded scholarships to women. Ignited by a sense of injustice, she enlisted the help of Keir Hardie, who, as an MP, had a base in London, asking him to table a parliamentary question. He duly did this, discovering a disheartening ratio in the process: the RCA only awarded one female scholarship for every thirteen given to men.

Yet even with her social clumsiness around her classmates and the unpopular reputation she had developed with the college board, Sylvia did finally manage to make friends with two other students. Austin Osman Spare was an avant-garde painter influenced by symbolism, Art Nouveau, and the occult, whose unconventional paintings often shocked the other students. At just 18, Austin was also a writer and his book *Earth, Inferno, Destiny, Humanity and the Chaos of Creation* had been published by the Cooperative Printing Society. With his pale skin and hair, eccentric manner of dress, and provocative art, he was a rebel the other female students were a little scared of, but Sylvia found him interesting and they formed a quick friendship. The pretty and good-natured

Amy K. Browning was another who shared Sylvia's indignation over the college's gender biases and would later win a Silver Medal at the Paris Salon des Artistes. Though not politically active, Amy's sense of justice resonated with Sylvia, and she became a warm confidante, someone with whom Sylvia could share her dreams and fears. Though neither Austin nor Amy were heavily involved in the suffrage movement or politics of any kind, they supported and listened to Sylvia, and would remain her lifelong friends and allies.

Another significant bond Sylvia deepened during her RCA years was with Keir Hardie. As a salve to her loneliness, Sylvia had joined the Fulham branch of the ILP, finding herself among the serious-minded, older company she was much more used to. She was regularly invited to the flat of Margaret and Ramsay MacDonald (a future Labour Prime Minister) who threw 'At Homes', much like her mother's London salons of bygone days. Here she encountered an array of engaging, interesting people. These included Dora Montefiore, an Anglo-Australian suffragist and founding member of the Womanhood Suffrage League of New South Wales, and, of course, Hardie. Their friendship quickly rekindled to the extent Sylvia began visiting Hardie at his own lodgings at 14 Nevill's Court.

Sometimes, 15-year-old Harry accompanied her. Still shy and sickly but now, at least, fitted with spectacles, he was attending boarding school in London. On the weekends that he didn't return home to help the WSPU, the two would meet, sometimes stopping in a café to share a currant bun and chat before taking the tram to Hardie's home. These visits fostered a deep sibling bond between Sylvia and Harry, one that had been elusive in their home while growing up, the demands of their parents' causes often overshadowing the importance of family intimacy.

The soirées with ILP members were enjoyable, yet Sylvia found true comfort in Hardie's cluttered home. It wasn't merely the warm glow of the candlelight under which he worked or his ritual of boiling tea over the hearth, an act she loved to watch, that soothed Sylvia; she had a deep admiration for his intellect and Christian socialist ambitions. In all likelihood, his compassionate discourse on the plight of the poor and underprivileged stirred memories of the father she missed profoundly and his enduring belief that the noblest pursuit in life was to 'work for others'.

To the 47-year-old Keir Hardie, the regular appearance of 21-year-old Sylvia in his life must have been a breath of fresh air. Despite his immense popularity with the ordinary person on the street, Hardie was a lonely man. His whole life was dominated by his work and the worries and fears of failure that he wove through it. His image was very much that of a 'kindly grandfather', but in parliamentary circles Hardie was known to be quarrelsome and prone to arguments with fellow socialists – hardly the foundations of lasting friendships! He was often referred to as 'queer Hardie' thanks to his penchant for donning clothes that caused the more staid and conservative in the House of Commons to, at the very least, frown when they saw him – a deerstalker, tweed cap or trilby on his head; a red cravat around his neck and a kimono; sometimes wandering the corridors of power in sandals, bare-legged and unbothered by the disapproving glances of his colleagues.

Sylvia filled the well of loneliness within him, just as he likely did for her. She also presented him with the semblance of a social life, something that had long been a casualty of his strict work ethic and his puritanical disdain for common pleasures like the theatre and drinking. They went for long walks, strolling through London's leafy parks, and sat in city cafés drinking black coffee, a beverage Hardie had never tasted until he met Sylvia. In his earlier years he had married. But the relationship was not a happy one for either of them, and Hardie's wife, Lillie, remained in Scotland in their Ayrshire home with their children while he rarely made the time to visit.

It was inevitable then that he and Sylvia would grow close. Hardie, a staunch supporter of the suffragist cause, found a kindred spirit in Sylvia, whose own political beliefs were increasingly shaped by his socialist ideals and the influence of the ILP. Their shared political vision, coupled with an emotional comfort both had long been bereft of, forged a profound connection between them. It was a friendship that naturally blossomed into love, a love that they would nurture discreetly, yet steadfastly, until 1912.

In Manchester, the first year of the WSPU's activities passed swiftly. The women had travelled to the mill and factory towns of Lancashire, Cheshire and Yorkshire, slowly gaining support. In between, Adela continued her teaching and Christabel her studies. Emmeline's sister, Mary Clarke, had left her husband, who had turned out to be cruel and abusive, and took on a large part of the WSPU's heavy workload, spending her time between 62 Nelson Street, Manchester, and London where she lived with and helped Sylvia in campaigning. As 1905 began, little had changed within the political climate of the country. The intense infighting within the Conservative Party had inadvertently united rival Liberal factions, fortifying the Liberal Party and setting the stage for their future electoral triumph.

Sensing an opportunity, the Women's Liberal Federation, which had a membership of just under 70,000 and was led by Catherine Gladstone, wife of the former Liberal Prime Minister, began rigorously testing Liberal candidates on their stance on female enfranchisement. Failure to meet their criteria meant the withdrawal of their canvassing and organisational support.

Amidst the preparations by the Conservative, ILP, and Liberal parties for the anticipated election, the WSPU sought to exert influence. In early January 1905, Emmeline met with the Labour Representation Committee (LRC), co-founded by Keir Hardie in 1900 and composed of socialist organisations and trade unions. Her aim was to persuade the LRC to champion female enfranchisement, though she knew she faced a formidable task. The trade union representatives harboured deep prejudices against women workers, believing their presence kept wages low. The proposed resolution from the ILP annual conference the previous spring endorsed women's suffrage as a step towards adult suffrage, but many LRC members believed it would only empower the property classes by giving votes to middle-class wives of mill and mine owners. They insisted, 'Adult suffrage is the only Franchise Reform which merits any support from the Labour Members of Parliament.'

Frustrated that they would not pledge to support a member's bill should it be introduced in Parliament, Emmeline travelled to London a few days before Parliament's new session was due to begin on 13 February 1905, reluctantly leaving a sickly Adela in bed with pleurisy. Along with Sylvia and other WSPU members including Isabella Ford and Harriet McIlquham, she spent her days in the Strangers' Lobby of the House of Commons, interviewing all passing MPs who had ever pledged to support a suffrage bill. Their hope was that these politicians would agree to introduce the bill should their name be called in the ballot. All but Keir Hardie refused.

At this point, Sylvia had settled into a modest two-room setup in a small house on Park Walk, Chelsea, tucked between the King's Road and Fulham Road. The house was run by a pleasant couple, Mr and Mrs Roe, who had welcomed Sylvia's two art college friends who frequently came to paint with their tenant. Ever hospitable, they now happily extended their warmth to her mother as well.

Emmeline would often arrive at the Roe household on Wednesday or Thursday afternoons, giving herself ample time before Parliament's Friday sessions, which were reserved for Private Members' Bills. Then, on Fridays, she and Sylvia would take their places in the Lobby, ready to intercept MPs as they hurried by, stopping them to make their case and press for support.

The night before Keir Hardie was set to introduce the bill (if his name was drawn), Emmeline became increasingly agitated. She lamented the plight of impoverished families, the struggles faced by mothers, the underpaid labour of working-class women, the homeless and marginalised. She worked herself up into such a feverish state that Sylvia began to feel genuinely alarmed. But when her mother saw her stricken face, she merely stopped and smiled. 'This,' she explained to her worried daughter, 'is what I call life'.

Sylvia would later reflect on this moment as a turning point, writing that her mother's words were 'an awakening to me and caused a revulsion of feeling'. For Sylvia, who had always approached life with a serious sense of duty, dedicating herself to the vital work of aiding those in need and, in her more recent London days, assisting Hardie in improving the lives of the unemployed, the idea of taking pleasure in such work was shocking. But for Emmeline, it was precisely these intense emotions that provided the fuel to drive her forward. She didn't take her mission lightly – instead, she relied on the passion that kept her focused. The unpredictability of each moment energised her, even though she was never in doubt that they would ultimately succeed. Indeed, it was this fervent conviction that attracted many of the WSPU's early members to the group. As Teresa Billington recalled, Emmeline was

> very gracious, very persuasive. To work alongside her day by day was to run the risk of losing yourself … she suffered with you and for you … She was a most astute statesman, a skilled politician, a self-dedicated re-shaper of the world … and a dictator without mercy.[1]

On the opening day of Parliament, the WSPU's worst fears were realised as Hardie's name was not drawn in the ballot. Desperation seized the group as they scoured the list of men whose names had been selected, searching for anyone who might champion the cause of women's suffrage. One faint glimmer of hope emerged through Liberal MP Bamford Slack, who had secured the fourteenth spot in the ballot. However, he was absent from the Commons that day. Hardie, sensing the urgency, immediately picked up the telephone to locate him, while Emmeline and Isabella Ford jumped into a hansom cab to track him down. When they finally found him, they successfully convinced him to introduce the measure.[2]

The Women's Enfranchisement Bill was set down for 12 May but only as Second Order of the day. This did not bode well for the women as it was widely anticipated that the anti-suffragists in Parliament would deliberately prolong the debate on the preceding bill – a slight matter concerning the requirement for carts traveling at night to display a rear light – and, in leaving no time for further discussions, would cause Slack's proposal to be pushed off the agenda. Emmeline, Isabella, Dora Montefiore, and Elizabeth Wolstenholme Elmy all journeyed to London on the 12 May and they were acutely aware of these risks, as were most of the women activists on the day. However, it didn't stop them from hoping.

That morning, the Strangers' Lobby in the House of Commons was thronged with women. Members of the National Union of Women's Suffrage Societies (NUWSS) stood shoulder to shoulder with those from the WSPU. The Women's Co-operative Guild had been led there by Australian Nellie Martel. The wool capes of middle-class women brushed against the thin cotton shawls of their working-class counterparts as women of all social strata crowded the waiting rooms or spilled onto the streets.

The air was thick with excitement, and hope surged through the gathered women, even though the chances of seeing the first suffrage bill in eight years debated on the floor of the House of Commons were slim. As anticipated, the anti-suffragists 'talked out' the women's bill, filling the time with frivolous anecdotes and jokes, much to the amusement of the attending members. The official Hansard for that morning would later record:

> Mr. Slack (Hertfordshire, St. Albans), in moving the Second Reading of this Bill, expressed his regret that the measure should

> have come on at so late an hour in the afternoon, and said that as a comparatively new Member he felt almost appalled at the extraordinary abuse of the forms of the House which that afternoon had been witnessed, manifestly and in some quarters avowedly with a view to preventing discussion of this Bill.[3]

As the news of the day's events spread among the waiting women, the atmosphere shifted dramatically. The earlier excitement and anticipation gave way to a rising tide of anger and indignation. Emmeline felt the currents of emotion around her and quickly recognised that this was a moment demanding action. Raising her voice, she urged the women gathered in the Strangers' Lobby to follow her and turning briskly, strode out the door, a stream of women flowing behind her.

Once outside, the elder Elizabeth Wolstenholme Elmy began to address the crowd. However, before she could fully express her thoughts, the police, uneasy at the sight of so many purposeful women, surged into the group, pushing and jostling them down the steps. Emmeline remained unperturbed, her demeanour calm but commanding in a way that would later be consistently written about in papers across the world. She demanded to know where she and her companions had the right to gather to express their discontent. After some tense exchanges, a police inspector grudgingly directed them to Broad Sanctuary, a stretch of land running north along Westminster Abbey.

Some of the NUWSS members, a little shaken by the police confrontation, began to disperse. Yet a determined group followed Emmeline to the designated spot, where they were soon joined by Keir Hardie. Together, they raised their voices in protest, condemning the government's cowardice in allowing their bill to be talked out of the day's agenda. As they spoke, policemen moved among them, quietly noting down names. Emmeline's mind was now alight with the possibilities that this moment had ignited within her. Just as her daughter Christabel had grasped the power of disruption and how daring to do the unexpected garnered more attention than following orders or doing nothing, Emmeline too began to see the light of a new direction – one that valued 'deeds' over 'words'.

In the months that followed, and well into the summer, the WSPU embraced this newfound strategy with fervour. They organised a series of outdoor meetings across Lancashire and Yorkshire, taking their cause directly to the people, and in doing so, they transformed their campaign into a movement of unprecedented energy and resolve. As support for the organisation began to grow, financial contributions from various backers also started to flow in. Membership steadily expanded, drawing individuals from all walks of life. As Christabel recounts:

> One recruit after another … [was] added to our band, still weak in numbers, but strong in hope and resolve. Memory here calls

> up other dear companions of that time who made their stand and played their part by our side. Mrs. Scott, our first secretary, genial and full of humour; Mrs. Harker, serious and determined; Mrs. Morrissey, lovable and all kindness, and others equally to be praised, links in a long, strong chain that reached from the earliest effort to the victory.[4]

The women worked tirelessly, active in various organisations and campaigns. Christabel, in particular, still deeply involved in the Women's Trade Union Council and the North of England Society for Women's Suffrage, worked closely with Eva Gore-Booth and Esther Roper in pressing the government to pass the Unemployed Workmen Relief Bill. When a demonstration of unemployed men in Manchester turned violent, leading to arrests, the bill was finally passed. Christabel and Emmeline observed the events with keen interest, realising the effectiveness of such actions in influencing the government.

'We must do something like that to get a Woman Suffrage Bill carried,' Christabel immediately declared, stating what she saw as the obvious: 'Militancy moved the Government to do what before they would not or could not do.'[5]

Meanwhile, Adela and Sylvia carried on their public campaigns, Adela focusing on the north of England and Sylvia on London, taking to the streets and soapboxes with stalwarts like Teresa Billington, Flora Drummond, Nellie Martel and Dora Montefiore. Their mission as ever was to underscore the necessity of female enfranchisement and to galvanise ordinary women to demand decisive action from all political parties. Both Emmeline and Christabel were much in-demand speakers at local ILP meetings focused on women's suffrage, and Women's Trades and Labour Councils. They addressed large assemblies, led demonstrations, and spoke to intimate gatherings, sharing their convictions with unflagging energy.

Unlike the NUWSS, which primarily attracted members of the middle and upper classes, the WSPU focused on reaching the very women who had the most to lose without the right to vote – the working and lower classes. This was no easy task, but it was made significantly more successful with the help of one of the most pivotal figures in the movement – a Lancashire mill worker named Annie Kenney.

Annie's journey into the suffrage movement began after she attended a meeting of the Oldham Trades Council in the spring of 1905. It was here that she heard Christabel Pankhurst and Teresa Billington speak. A mill worker from a poor family of fourteen, she recounts in her autobiography, *Memoirs of a Militant*, that at the age of 10, 'My mother announced to me that I was to work in a factory. I was to join the army of half-timers; to work in the factory half the day and attend school the other.' Although she had attended school from the age of 5, by 13 the young Annie had left entirely to endure the gruelling twelve-hour shifts as a weaver's assistant, or 'tenter' as they were more commonly known. It was in this factory role that she tragically lost the middle finger of her left hand when it was torn from her small hand as she reached to catch an errant thread.

Annie's personal experience with child labour, harsh working conditions, and meagre pay led her to embrace trade unionism, though she would later note, there were '96,000 women members of the trade union and not any women officials'. She also decided to join the ILP after being inspired by an article she read in Robert Blatchford's socialist magazine, *The Clarion.*

While trade unionism and the ILP had addressed the injustices Annie observed in her daily life, the words of the two WSPU speakers resonated on a much deeper level. Until that moment, she had never encountered the idea of 'votes for women', but when she heard Billington speak, it was as if a 'sledgehammer of cold logic and reason' had shattered the familiar, awakening her to a profound and personal truth she could no longer ignore. In Christabel she saw an admirable woman of powerful conviction, and after the meeting she and her two sisters, who were also in attendance, hurriedly introduced themselves. Christabel immediately liked Annie, describing her as 'eager and impulsive in manner, with a thin, haggard face, and restless knotted hands... Her abundant, loosely dressed golden hair was the most youthful looking thing about her...'

Impressed by Annie's enthusiasm, Christabel urged the 26-year-old to take a bold step and organise a meeting for female factory workers in Oldham and Lees to rally support for the suffrage movement. Recognising her potential, she also invited Annie to tea at 62 Nelson Street, where she was introduced to Emmeline. This encounter would not be their last, as Emmeline, much like her daughter, was immediately drawn to Annie, sensing in the young recruit a deep and unwavering commitment to the cause. The recent loss of Annie's mother, who had passed away prematurely at 53, only deepened Emmeline's compassion for her.

In the weeks that followed, Annie began returning to the Pankhurst home during her weekly half-day off, undergoing rigorous training in public speaking. Emmeline would give her leaflets on women's suffrage, which she and her younger sister Jessie – a schoolteacher who had been with Annie at the Trades Council meeting – then distributed to women workers at the Oldham mill gates. Annie proved to be an adept student, quickly mastering the skills she needed. As she handed out pamphlets, she engaged with the workers, passionately sharing everything she was learning about women's suffrage and labour rights, identifying with them as having also 'been trained in the bitter school of experience' as a factory worker,[6] and so deftly drawing them into the movement that would so profoundly transform her own life.

On weekends, Annie, in her usual 'uniform' of factory shawl and clogs, and Adela, in her practical frock and wool coat, would board the train to the factory towns scattered across the countryside, where narrow streets twisted from the smoke-spewing mills to the cramped slum homes of workers. They would mount soapboxes and speak with fervour about fair wages and women's rights. The sight of two slight young women standing in the rain, sleet, or occasional sunshine, passionately advocating for justice, was an unusual one, and the women were met as often with jeers and heckles as with surprise and embarrassment from passers-by. Yet Adela, like all the Pankhurst women, was unwavering in her convictions, and her fearless determination inspired Annie to match her in passion and commitment.

Sometimes, on weekends when he was free from school, Harry would join them, distributing flyers as the women called out to the passing workers. They spoke until their voices grew hoarse, often for hours on end, urging those who paused to listen to recognise the power they held to change their circumstances. It was a power that the Pankhurst family had themselves begun to taste, and so they chased it down, driven by the belief that even in the harshest of environments, a spark of awareness could ignite a movement.

CHAPTER

6

VICTORIES AND SETBACKS

Autumn 1905 arrived carrying with it a renewed sense of possibility for the Women's Social and Political Union. For months, they had been quietly laying the groundwork for a decisive moment, and now, with the political winds shifting, that moment seemed to be within reach. The Conservative government that had been in power for the last ten years looked set to fall as the Liberals, with the promise of several new reforms, called for a general election they were confident of winning. Across the country, Liberal representatives had been sent out to garner further support, and in Manchester, a key meeting was to be held at the Free Trade Hall on 13 October. The young Winston Churchill was part of the line-up though the event's principal speaker that evening was Sir Edward Grey, a prominent figure in the Liberal Party and soon to become the next government's Foreign Secretary.

As evening fell, hundreds of local Mancunians made their way to the hall, filling the seats, their spirits high as they awaited the arrival of those poised to shape the next government. The meeting proceeded in the usual way – speech after speech, a parade of promises and proposals. Manchester's amiable Chief Constable, Robert Peacock was on the stage and several policemen stood around the hall, but the atmosphere was one of routine optimism. Finally, Sir Edward Grey opened the floor to questions from the audience, receiving initial queries with civility and confidence. And then a sweet but firm female voice cut through the room: 'Will the Liberal Government, if returned to power, give votes to women?'

The question was met with stunned silence.

But Annie Kenney, with beating heart and calm voice, was undeterred. Standing up at the back of the hall where she sat with Christabel, she asked the question again, this time with Christabel's voice joining hers. 'Will the Liberal Government give votes to women?'

Sir Edward still refused to answer, looking everywhere but at the women. It was then that Christabel unfurled a small white banner, and raised it for all to see. *Votes for Women* it read, and the sight of those three simple words seemed to ignite the hall in cries of anger and disbelief.

Immediately the police moved in to restore order and Chief Constable Peacock left the platform, reaching the women quickly where he entreated them to write their question down. Once they had, he duly brought it back to Sir Edward who, with a stony face, took it and read the piece of paper in silence. With a tight smile, he passed it to the others on the platform, all of whom smiled in turn but said nothing. The question remained unanswered and Sir Edward stated the meeting was all but over.

Annie quickly clambered upon her chair and called out, 'Will the Liberal government give votes to women?' It was a red rag to a bull, as others in the hall jumped to their feet, shouting and snarling and hurling abuse at the small, slight woman. Almost immediately, Annie and Christabel were seized by several policemen who dragged them from the room, even as the struggling women continued to call out their question, and flung them to the street. Gathering themselves together, the two women began addressing the small crowd outside that had witnessed the expulsion. Many recognised Christabel as Dr Pankhurst's daughter. As Sylvia noted, 'There was scarcely a man or woman in the city to whom he was not a familiar figure.' However, within minutes, the policemen's rough hands were on them once again. The women writhed in defiance and Christabel attempted to spit on one of the policemen as a means of forcing their hands. It worked. Christabel and Annie were immediately arrested on a charge of obstruction and summonsed to appear in court the following morning.

The events that unfolded at Manchester's Free Trade Hall that autumn evening had not been unplanned. For months, Christabel had been calling for the WSPU to take a more confrontational form of action. Pursuing private members' suffrage bills had yielded nothing, and women's suffrage remained largely ignored by both the public and the press. In fact, the silence of the press was so pervasive that Christabel had denounced it as a force that, 'by keeping women uninformed, had so largely smothered and strangled the movement'. At the same time, she charged that the silence, 'protected politicians from criticism of their offences, emissive and commissive, against the suffrage cause'.[1]

She had seen how the unemployment bill had been passed as soon as those fighting for it used violence and arrests to bring their cause into the light. These methods were, of course, nothing new for they drew from a longstanding tradition of male-dominated radical political protest. What was revolutionary in this instance was Christabel's insistence that it should be women who would now adopt these aggressive tactics, protesting in such a way that imprisonment was inevitable. This, she was convinced, would wake up the public and the press and bring much-needed publicity to the women's cause. As David Morgan noted, 'tea parties would not do it: sensational publicity and martyrdom might. The Press would not be able to resist publishing sensational exploits.'[2]

So it had been decided among the WSPU leadership that the Liberal meeting on 13 October 1905 would serve as the debut of this new strategy. Seats were secured for Christabel and Annie who would, when the time was right, persist in asking a question about the Liberals' commitment to ensuring votes for women. Initially, Teresa Billington was to join them, but Emmeline felt it would be wiser for Teresa to oversee the WSPU's follow-up events, which were to take place after the women were released from prison after their inevitable arrest.

In addition, by utilising only Annie and Christabel in this bold new militant approach, the WSPU was also crafting a powerful visual narrative. The two women's presence together reinforced the idea that the fight for women's enfranchisement was a cross-class collaboration. It told a story of unity – of 'all women' standing together, regardless of social background. Christabel in particular, with Emmeline following her lead, insisted that the movement did not involve class at all, but rather mirrored the ideas of a new generation whereby the demand for votes represented a call for inclusion – votes for *all* women.[3]

It was, in fact, a bold strategy for the time. As Teresa Billington-Greig noted in a 1907 article in the *Aberdeen People's Journal*, the carefully planned juxtaposition of Christabel and Annie presented the WSPU as a 'new' kind of organisation:

> One of them was a mill-girl who had bitter experience of the restrictions to which working women are subjected. The other was a daughter of a lawyer, herself studying to be a lawyer. Together they represented the two forces which are the life of this new women's agitation: the need of women as typified by Annie Kenney; and the rebellion of the educated women against restrictions … represented by Christabel Pankhurst.

Given this powerful visual message, it made sense that Emmeline would also not take part. However, the reason for her stepping back was probably more pragmatic – a prison sentence could cost her the job she held as a Registrar, a vital source of income for both her family and, at times, the WSPU itself.

Originally, it was hoped that the women could secure seats in the front row of the balcony from which they would unfurl a large banner emblazoned with their critical question: 'Will the Liberal Government give votes to women?' However, when they ended up in seats at the back of the hall, it became clear that the larger banner would be unwieldy and so it was decided that a smaller one with fewer words be made. 'Thus, quite accidentally,' Emmeline observed later, 'there came into existence the … slogan of the suffrage movement around the world' – Votes for Women.[4]

With all preparations in place, Christabel and Annie stepped out into the cold night, ready to make their way to the hall, but not before Emmeline's eldest daughter had turned to her mother with a smile. 'We shall get our question answered or sleep in prison tonight,' she said and her mother, pale-faced and anxious, nodded her assent.

In the police court the following morning, Christabel and Annie found themselves standing before a local magistrate who had known Christabel's father well. Despite his familiarity with the family and his attempts to soften the inevitable outcome, neither Christabel nor Annie would let him. They remained defiant throughout until eventually the magistrate had no choice but to deliver his verdict. Annie was sentenced to pay a fine of 5 shillings or three days in prison, while Christabel's sentence was 10 shillings or a full week behind bars. Both women immediately opted for prison.

As soon as they were ushered out of the courtroom, Emmeline hurried to them, pleading with her daughter to reconsider and pay the fine instead. But Christabel, holding her mother's hand with firm resolve, responded, 'Mother, if you pay my fine, I will never go home.'[5] Emmeline relented. She knew it was the right course of action. And so she looked on, her heart torn between a mother's anxiousness and a fellow activist's pride as her firstborn was led off to Strangeways Prison.

As Christabel and Annie adjusted to the grim reality of their dank cells – enduring the discomfort of coarse prison garments and forcing down the bland, viscous gruel or thin soup that passed for food – Emmeline, true to form, stepped into the public sphere. The very next evening, she stood before a large crowd addressing the events that had transpired. The city, and indeed the entire country, were stunned by the photographs that had begun to surface in the press – images of smartly dressed young women being manhandled out of a meeting. To Victorian sensibilities, with their particular view of femininity and public decency, it was nothing short of shocking.

Thus, despite the persistent drizzle, over a thousand people assembled in Stevenson Square, on the city's northeastern edge, to hear what Emmeline, Teresa Billington and another new recruit, the working-class seamstress Hannah Mitchell, had to say. Fully aware she was risking her livelihood, Emmeline declared she was 'proud to be the mother of one of the two noble girls who had gone to prison in the endeavour to advocate the enfranchisement of women'.[6]

When Christabel finally emerged from prison on 20 October, Emmeline repeated these heartfelt words. To Annie, who had walked free four days earlier, she extended the sincere promise that she would never have to return to factory life and could consider the Pankhurst home her own.

Both women were greeted by hordes of well-wishers at the prison gates. Even more people gathered at an event organised by Teresa Billington. In a letter written by Annie only a day or two after her release to her sister Nell, who had emigrated to Canada, the young political activist claimed proudly, 'Manchester is alive, I can assure you.'[7]

Teresa chose to hold the women's victory celebration at the Free Trade Hall, the very place where they had been arrested just a week earlier. The hall was once again filled to capacity, but this time with an audience, predominantly women, who cheered as Christabel and Annie took the stage, standing on the same platform where the likely future leaders of the country had recently refused to answer their questions. Bouquets were presented, and Keir Hardie delivered a stirring speech.

The *Manchester Guardian* covered the event and all others relating to the women's arrest. Even *The Times*, long opposed to women's suffrage, felt compelled to report on the unfolding events in Manchester. It had happened: votes for women had suddenly become national news.

What Sylvia and Adela truly thought of Christabel's imprisonment and her rising prominence within the WSPU remains unclear. After her release, Christabel was instructed by her college to formally promise in writing that she would refrain from any further disruptions or risk being expelled. She wrote the required letter with Emmeline's approval and it did not for one minute diminish the pride that the girls' mother now had for her eldest child. According to Sylvia, Emmeline immediately declared Christabel the new leader of the WSPU. Christabel, she proudly claimed, would be steadfast in her emotions, unlike, the inference seemed to be, Emmeline's other two daughters.[8] Whether Emmeline said this or not is hard to prove. Certainly, while Christabel was eager to steer the WSPU along its current path, the organisation's actual leadership at the time would have had a collective say in determining its direction.

Moreover, Christabel always regarded her mother as the true commander of the movement, seeing herself as a dutiful daughter and Emmeline's loyal lieutenant. Despite their close bond, she remained in awe of her mother's unwavering determination and spirit. Similar to when they were children, Christabel more than Sylvia empathised deeply with Emmeline, recognising the sacrifices she had made as much as the potential rewards she sought. This admiration is evident in her autobiography, *Unshackled*, where she notes:

> It is not so easy now to realise the position in which she then stood. A widow, with still dependent children, risking (and eventually losing) her income and future pension in the Government service, Mother had stood firm against a world. From the blow she thus struck with her own hand at her position and fortune, there might have been no recovery, especially in those days. She faced the risk and took it – for women's sake. As history knows, she did not take it in vain, and victory was to follow.[9]

This passage reveals the depth of Christabel's admiration, as she saw in her mother's sacrifices not just a profound commitment to the cause of women's suffrage but the personal struggle behind it.

For Adela, who was still only 20, the thrill of this new strategy likely swept her up, as it did many others in the movement, and she would have been eager for her turn on the frontlines. She may have even been a little in awe of her older sister's courage; she felt her emotions hotly while Christabel always appeared cool, yet both were equally devoted, at this time, to the suffrage cause.

While excitement certainly prevailed, it would be misleading to suggest that everyone supported the more aggressive tactics the WSPU had employed. Christabel Pankhurst's infamous 'spitting' at a policeman stirred particular unease among some factions of the suffragist movement. Christabel herself later expressed dismay upon seeing the event reported in the press, insisting that she had not, in fact, spat, but merely 'gave a pout, a perfectly dry purse of the mouth'.[10] Other suffragists, including Christabel's mentors Eva Gore-Booth and Esther Roper, went so far as to suggest that the two women's conduct had done more harm than good and weakened the cause. They claimed it cast an unflattering shadow on working women and that their own group, angered by the behaviour, had now chosen to distance themselves from further public protests.[11]

Many hoped – and believed – that the events at Manchester's Free Trade Hall would mark both the beginning and the end of the WSPU's militancy. However, Emmeline and Christabel thought otherwise. They resolved that wherever a prospective member of the Liberal Government spoke, the WSPU would be there, raising their 'Votes for Women' banners and demanding answers to the question no man in government seemed able or willing to answer. To support this relentless campaign, Adela and Sylvia were enlisted to heckle alongside other determined WSPU members, taking Christabel's place while she maintained a low profile to avoid being thrown out of college.

But political events in Britain were to take another gripping turn. On 4 December 1905, Arthur Balfour's Conservative government finally resigned. A general election was swiftly scheduled for January 1906, but in the interim, Sir Henry Campbell-Bannerman, leader of the Liberals, was called upon to form a provisional government. This intensified the WSPU's plan of action and as the Liberal Cabinet Ministers stepped out for meetings in town after town, the WSPU were there to disrupt each of them.

On 21 December 1905, the interim government gathered for a grand assembly in the Royal Albert Hall in London. The WSPU had taken the bold step of writing to Sir Henry's office to tell him that one of their representatives would attend the event and they hoped he would publicly address whether the Liberals were prepared to extend the vote to women. Of course, they heard nothing back. Undeterred, the WSPU devised a plan whereby Annie Kenney would sneak into the hall incognito while Teresa Billington took a position directly above the government's platform.

At the appointed moment, Annie called out: 'Will the Liberal Government give women the vote?' Simultaneously, Teresa unfurled a 'Votes for Women' banner, letting it sway dramatically above the heads of the soon-to-be-recognised British government. For a brief, electrifying moment the hall was silent as the audience held its breath, waiting for the Cabinet's response. None came. Then, as the room broke into an uproar, the women were seized by burly ushers and once again flung out onto the street.

More than ever, the WSPU were now sure of their path. The government had been given their chance to publicly state their support of women's enfranchisement and they had chosen silence. The battle had really begun.

Though membership had grown, WSPU resources were still limited. It was decided that the group should concentrate its efforts on disrupting the meetings of the Liberal candidate closest to home. The target was Winston Churchill, whose candidature for North-West Manchester saw him staging several meetings in the area. It was nothing personal. However, as the appearance of the suffragists became more expected at each of the increasingly exasperated Churchill's meetings, it proved good copy for the local popular press who, as Christabel claimed, 'Best knew the Pankhurst name of old – that it stood for persistence in a determined course.'

In London, Sylvia continued her campaigning, directed by her mother from Manchester. Though she remained in college, she was frequently tormented by whether her art was a personal pursuit or could serve a higher purpose. She spoke at length to Hardie about her right to pursue this passion when the world was in such turmoil. Yet, despite their discussions, she found no satisfying resolution to her internal struggle. Her friends, Amy and Austin, could not help her either. For them, art was everything and would remain so throughout their lives. Yet, like many of their peers at the Royal Academy of Arts, they shared the fear that art might not provide a livelihood. It was a constant source of anxiety for the students, particularly those whose college days were coming to an end. Still, even with the looming uncertainty of their futures, Sylvia was acutely aware of their privilege. As she observed, 'They enjoyed their painting, whereas the mass of people laboured simply to keep alive.'[12]

During the Christmas break, Sylvia returned to Manchester, where her artistic talents were swiftly put to use painting 'Votes for Women' on hundreds of calico banners. She threw herself into the work of the WSPU and, once the interim government was back from its holidays, attended as many Liberal meetings as possible. As directed by Christabel, she disrupted the speakers with her pointed questions and waved her banner in defiance, even as she was being escorted out by irate male stewards. Both Sylvia and Harry went to hear Churchill at his first meeting in the Cheetham Hill schoolroom. When Sylvia challenged him with a question, Churchill ignored her, prompting Harry to shout, 'Answer her! Answer her!' Eventually, she was invited by the Chairman to mount the platform whereupon her question, 'What about votes for women?'

was put directly to the young politician. Churchill, addressing the audience rather than her, denounced Sylvia as a disgrace to her family name and declared, 'Nothing would induce me to vote for giving women the franchise. I am not going to be henpecked into a question of such importance.'[13]

Sylvia was swiftly escorted from the room, but this time, instead of being cast out onto the street, she was taken to a small side room and locked inside. Uncertain of what awaited her, she somehow managed to squeeze through the bars of the room's single small window. Emerging into the schoolyard, where a crowd had already gathered, she was met with cheers and calls for a speech, something that surely angered Churchill, who must have heard the commotion from his platform in the nearby classroom.

A few days later, it was Adela, along with Flora Drummond, who disrupted his second meeting. When both women were shuffled out by the stewards Adela felt a surge of triumph. For years, she had watched her parents stand firm against powerful politicians, and now here she was joining them in defiance.

However, Churchill's torment was far from over. As polling day inched nearer, teenager Harry came up another inventive idea to vex him. In the early hours of the morning, he and a couple of his school friends quietly slipped out, evading patrolling policemen, and plastered 'Votes for Women' posters over hundreds of Churchill's own large red-and-white campaign hoardings.

While Sylvia was in Manchester, heavily engaged in the election efforts of the WSPU, Keir Hardie had embarked on a relentless tour across the country, championing the fifty Labour Representation Committee candidates. His commitment, however, came at a cost to his own campaign for Merthyr Tydfil, which was being sorely neglected. Frank Field, Hardie's campaign manager, sent out a flurry of urgent telegrams to those he thought could help, including Emmeline, and she responded without hesitation. Hardie was an old family friend, but along with that, his presence in Parliament was a necessity if a women's suffrage measure was to see the light of day. She rushed to Wales and threw herself into the campaign, attending multiple meetings a day and passionately arguing that the Independent Labour Party was the only political force truly championing women's rights. She highlighted how closely intertwined the fight for suffrage was with the broader socialist movement, and at a large gathering of Cardiff ILP members spoke at length about why Christabel and Annie risked reputation and liberty to go to prison for the vote.

By late January 1906, the general election results were announced. It was a triumph for the Liberal Party, as expected. They won a majority of nearly 100 seats in the House of Commons, and while Churchill was among those who secured a seat, according to Sylvia, his majority paled in comparison to those of the other Manchester Liberal candidates, something the WSPU proudly took credit for. The newly defined Labour party also made significant strides with twenty-nine candidates, including Hardie, its leader, re-elected. By then, Sylvia was back in London and stood among the crowds outside the *Daily*

News offices, watching the results roll in. The atmosphere was thick with hope as the people celebrated a new government and a fresh start. For Sylvia too, the victories of Labour and Hardie seemed to signal a future full of promise.

In Manchester, Christabel was more determined than ever that 'the vote must be wrested from the unwilling grasp of the Liberal leaders', declaring bluntly that 'the Liberal Government was, in fact, the enemy'.[14] For her, this meant relocating to London, where they could repeatedly target Parliament with their demands. However, the financial burden of such a move was too great, even for Emmeline, whose job as a Registrar was already close to slipping away. 'Then only, never before and never after, did I see her flinch,' recalled Christabel. '"We can't afford it", she said with the sharpness in her tone that betrayed her pain that our new movement should, after all, be checked, and perhaps utterly thwarted, for that reason. Money, foul money, again the hindrance!'[15]

But Christabel refused to be stopped by mere shillings and pence. It was impossible for her to go, though she longed to; her final law exams would take place in June and besides the commitment she had given to the college to stay out of trouble, she knew it would be foolish to abandon her studies when she was mere months away from obtaining a degree. It was decided, then, that Annie Kenney would be sent to London to represent them, joining Sylvia. Emmeline advanced the gleeful 27-year-old £2, with strict instructions to speak to no man in the street unless he was a policeman,[16] and with that, the Oldham factory girl was dispatched to London, eager to take on the towering forces of the capital.

Annie moved in with Sylvia and the Roe family in Park Walk; it seemed that whether Sylvia agreed to it or not, her home was considered the official WSPU London headquarters. With the support of Sylvia and other London-based WSPU members like Dora Montefiore and Minnie Baldock, Annie quickly became involved in contacting groups of impoverished women in the East End. Reflecting on her experiences, she later wrote, 'I have never seen such hopeless despair, such agonising poverty, as I saw in the East End of London.'

Yet, even so, for Annie, these were also some of her brightest days, filled as they were with a deep sense of camaraderie and a purpose she had not experienced before. She had a tendency to romanticise the poverty she encountered, and in her autobiography often sentimentalises the experiences of the women she met. Though she spent her days navigating the cramped tenements and Salvation Army shelters in the soot-stained streets of the East End, preaching to women crushed under the weight of poverty, she admits she believed she was 'giving them something to dream about … How I had the courage and audacity to talk Votes for Women to those thin, sallow, pinched, pain-stricken, poverty-lined faces I do not know. Poor oppressed, unawakened East-Enders.'[17]

Almost immediately upon her arrival, she and Sylvia, guided by Hardie, set about planning an event of extraordinary ambition – the first major

WSPU gathering in London. Originally, it was to be a staged rally in Trafalgar Square on 16 February 1906, coinciding with the State Opening of Parliament and the King's Speech. However, the Square was already booked for that day. Hardie suggested booking Caxton Hall, a towering, ornate brick and sandstone building on the corner of Caxton and Palmer Streets, in Westminster, which had a capacity of 700 people. The women agreed and swiftly took action, printing flyers and posters which were distributed throughout the city. They also reached out to their allies in the East End. One of these contacts was George Lansbury, whom Sylvia had met through Hardie. Born and bred in the East End, Lansbury had a wood yard in Stephen's Row, Bow, and was an ardent supporter of women's rights. At the time he was a member of the Social Democratic Federation (SDF), though he would later join the Labour Party, leading it from 1932 to 1935. With Lansbury's help, Sylvia arranged for a group of 400 East End women to travel by train to the event.

When Emmeline arrived in London in mid-February, she was aghast at the scale of the undertaking. How could they possibly fill the huge hall or afford the train fares for the women from the East End, not to mention the 'tea and buns' Annie had promised them on arrival? She dreaded the embarrassment of standing before a vast, empty room addressing a mere handful of people.

Still, she wasn't one to dally. Funds were tight in the WSPU and Emmeline had no money of her own to spare, so she immediately set to work seeking sponsorship. Her efforts paid off quickly, as two friends, William Stead and Isabella Ford, generously donated £25 each. Buoyed by this success, the team went back to work, distributing posters, chalking details onto pavements around the city, and reaching out to journalists to drum up publicity. Many editors were happy to oblige. Charles E. Hands of the *Daily Mail* had recently coined the term 'suffragettes' to distinguish the more radical WSPU from the more genteel NUWSS. The intention of the added 'ette' was to trivialise the group, but the WSPU embraced their new nickname, and smart news editors were now quick to cover any story that involved the 'suffragettes' rather than the 'suffragists', knowing their bold antics would sell more newspapers.

The afternoon of 16 February arrived, and the hall was full to bursting, with hundreds more outside. Lansbury's East End contingent arrived, many carrying young children in their arms and waving red Labour Party banners. They sang 'The Red Flag', the anthem of Socialism, before proceedings got underway. The Eastenders mixed with wealthier classes who had also arrived, among them Lady Carlisle, a promoter of women's voting rights and a long-standing member of the Women's Liberal Federation.

Emmeline was speaking from the platform when news filtered in that the new Government had not included votes for women in its programme nor had any mention of women's enfranchisement been referred to in the King's Speech. 'There were hisses and cries of "shame", and Mrs Pankhurst proclaimed: "We have risked our reputations, our limbs, and even our lives in the cause. But there is nothing.'"[18]

Emmeline then proposed that the group take their protest directly to the House of Commons. The skies had opened up and rain was falling in sheets, but she marched with hundreds of women behind her, arriving at the Strangers' Entrance. Here, orders had been issued to the police for the first time in history that no women should be admitted. Keir Hardie, who had openly criticised the deliberate exclusion of the women's vote in programme, stepped in, negotiating with the Speaker to allow small groups of twenty women into the lobby at a time. His own party had drawn five places for private members' bills and had voted to focus these on issues related to old-age pensions, feeding schoolchildren, aiding the unemployed and protecting workmen's wages.

When Emmeline heard of the ILP's decisions, she felt betrayed. The WSPU was still closely aligned with Labour, with most of its members drawn from the party. On a more personal level, she herself, along with her beloved husband Richard, had supported the ILP from its earliest days. Yet still it ignored the issue of female enfranchisement. What Emmeline desired was for Hardie to secure the full commitment from the Labour Party to votes for women. Determined, she took her reluctant daughter Sylvia to confront him. Hardie, distressed by the confrontation, explained that his party had made its democratic choice, and though he promised that if he were given the opportunity to put forward a bill or resolution, he would champion women's suffrage, it was not enough for Emmeline. She knew nothing short of the full backing of the Labour Party could suffice. Meanwhile, outside in the pouring rain, women stood drenched and cold, waiting for their chance to speak with any MP willing to champion their cause. In groups of twenty, as the hours passed, they entered the lobby, only to return disheartened; not a single member of parliament could be swayed.

Yet Emmeline refused to see the day as a failure. Rather she found victory in all that had happened. The processions had garnered widespread media coverage, which in turn attracted new recruits to the WSPU. Not only that, but a corner had been turned. As she writes in her autobiography:

> Those women had followed me to the House of Commons. They had defied the police. They were awake at last. They were prepared to do something that women had never done before – fight for themselves. Women had always fought for men and for their children. Now they were ready to fight for their own human rights. Our militant movement was established.

CHAPTER

7

BUILDING A MILITANT MOVEMENT

From late 1905, Emmeline and Christabel referred a lot to the WSPU's new militant direction. The term has since become synonymous with the group's more violent tactics, though these were still several years away. At the time, both mother and daughter defined militancy not in terms of physical aggression, but as a form of resistance that defied society's expectations of women as submissive and accepting of their inferior status. Christabel believed women were ready to shed the 'slave spirit' imposed by patriarchal ideals, and would later tell a local journalist that 'women must banish the idea that weakness is womanliness. Women must be self-reliant and strong.'

In the WSPU, they were far from alone in embracing militancy. Flora Drummond, Minnie Baldock and Irene Fenwick Miller, whose mother, Florence, had been a member with Emmeline on the Executive Committee of the Women's Franchise League, were just some of those who eagerly took up the challenge of escalating the campaign. With the Liberal government now firmly in power at Westminster, these women saw an opportunity to intensify their efforts.

After the events of 16 February 1906, the WSPU took a significant step towards formal organisation with the formation of its Central London Committee. Sylvia was appointed Honorary Secretary and Annie was offered a modest salary of £2 per week as the group's second paid organiser after Theresa Billington. Under the guidance of Emmeline Pethick-Lawrence, a wealthy social reformer drawn into the cause through her connection with Keir Hardie, this once informal group now took on a more organised structure.

Emmeline Pethick-Lawrence had long been a supporter of women's suffrage. Born into an evangelical family in Bristol as the second of thirteen children (of whom only seven survived childhood), she was unlike other young girls of her time; her ambitions were not centred on marriage but on a life dedicated to social purpose. At 23, she became a 'sister of the people' for the West London Methodist Mission, where she first discovered her passion for enriching the lives of young girls. It was there that she met her lifelong friend, Mary Neal. They bonded over shared socialist ideals, inspired by figures like Keir Hardie and Edward Carpenter, and together they ran a girls' club at the mission. Later, they left the mission to co-found the Espérance Club, a dance and drama club for poor and working-class young women and girls that could thrive without the shackles of the Methodist religion.

During this time, Emmeline met Fred Lawrence, a younger, wealthy barrister. She did not marry him, however, until many years later, when she was 34 and he had shifted his political views from liberalism to socialism. Their union was one of equality, highlighted in a unique gesture for the era, by the combination of their surnames – Pethick-Lawrence.

When Emmeline Pankhurst first invited Mrs Pethick-Lawrence to join the WSPU, the latter hesitated. Despite her strong support for women's enfranchisement, she and Fred were deeply involved in a range of other social causes, and she feared that focusing solely on suffrage would detract from their mission of seeking broader social change. Neither was she fully convinced of the WSPU's ability to make a difference. In her autobiography, *My Part in a Changing World*, she revealed, 'I had no fancy to be drawn into a small group of brave and reckless and quite helpless people who were prepared to dash themselves against the oldest tradition of human civilization as well as one of the strongest governments of modern times.'

Yet a follow-up luncheon with Pankhurst and Annie Kenney changed her mind. 'There was something about Annie that touched my heart,' she later recalled. 'She was very simple and seemed to have a wholehearted faith in the goodness of everyone she met.' It was this sincerity, as much as the cause itself, that drew her into the movement.

As Honorary Treasurer, Mrs Pethick-Lawrence brought not only a network of influential contacts but also a much-needed talent for fundraising; up until that point, the WSPU lacked any regular form of financing beyond Emmeline's own purse. As importantly, the new WSPU member possessed the organisational skills the group had long lacked. Within days, she had hired Alfred Sayers, a chartered accountant, to audit the organisation's finances. Christabel would note in *Unshackled* that when Mrs Pethick Lawerence joined the group, 'it was a mere stirring of life, a flickering flame; she joined it at the moment of greatest unpopularity, when there was not any outward sign of the success which was to come later'.

Her own vision for the movement extended beyond logistics, however; she was, eventually, happy to embrace the WSPU's militant approach, and to help shape that in such a way as to make it appealing to others outside the organisation. As Sylvia observed, it was Mrs Pethick-Lawrence's astute understanding of the need of women of the time to have their own leaders that enabled her to craft an aura of passion and romantic heroism around Emmeline, Christabel, and other key figures in the suffragette cause.

On 9 March 1906, around thirty women marched to 10 Downing Street to demand an audience with the Prime Minister, Sir Henry Campbell-Bannerman. After waiting nearly an hour, they were asked to leave. Undeterred, Irene Fenwick Miller knocked on the door, and when it opened, Flora Drummond seized the moment, forcing her way inside. Both women were arrested, and moments later, Annie Kenney climbed onto the Prime Minister's car, addressing the crowd until her own arrest followed.

However, at Cannon Row police station, the three women were released without charge. The Prime Minister, annoyed and embarrassed by the incident, wished to avoid media attention and had contacted the police station to confirm no charges would be pressed. However, if he thought the WSPU would be thankful and discreet, he was very much mistaken. They had already alerted the press, ensuring that their newspaper contacts would be writing up an evening story about the incident by the time the women were leaving the station.

In response to the growing pressure, Campbell-Bannerman agreed to meet with a delegation from the WSPU and other suffrage societies. Preparations for the meeting began at once. At the same time, 200 members of Parliament, some supportive of the women's plight, some just wishing to get the issue dealt with, petitioned the Prime Minister to arrange an early date to discuss the matter. Sir Henry settled on 19 May 1906.

The WSPU decided to make the event as public as possible and began planning a huge demonstration that would march from the statue of Boadicea, the Celtic warrior queen, at the entrance of Westminster Bridge, to the Foreign Office where the meeting was to take place. Meanwhile, Keir Hardie had secured time for the Women's Suffrage Resolution to be debated in the House of Commons on 25 April. Though it held no immediate legislative power, a favourable vote would strengthen the women's position in their upcoming meeting with Sir Henry. Things were moving fast and it seemed that finally, the stage was being set for a pivotal moment in the suffrage campaign.

However, Hardie's resolution was to be the second order of the day and Emmeline and others feared that, like before, it would be 'talked out' by anti-suffragists. Women from several suffragist groups, including Emmeline, Sylvia and others of the WSPU, secured seats to watch proceedings of the Resolution in the Ladies' Gallery. This was an area set behind a brass grille wherein only women were permitted to listen to the debates of Parliament.

On the day, the Government and the Opposition turned out in large numbers and both front benches were fully occupied. Finally, the Resolution 'That in the opinion of this House, it is desirable that sex should cease to be a bar to the exercise of the Parliamentary franchise' was moved and seconded. However, two anti-suffragists began, as the women thought, 'talking out' the motion with well-worn jokes and drawn-out arguments about a woman's place being in the home. Emmeline gave a signal to the gathered WSPU members. Jumping to their feet, they erupted in protest, pushing their 'votes for women' banners through the grille. Their startling actions were swiftly interpreted as a breach of parliamentary decorum, prompting the police to rush into the gallery and remove them. The gathered MPs, including Hardie, whose motion had now been destroyed, were furious, while outside in the lobby, Labour Party supporters angrily accused the WSPU members of jeopardising future parliamentary support. Isabella Ford would subsequently state it was this event that led to her and Emmeline Pankhurst parting company in the ILP.

Sylvia was highly embarrassed, for she knew they had angered Hardie, their 'generous friend'. 'I felt culpable, and that I alone was culpable; for I alone understood the difficulty of his stand for us and that his rivals were taking advantage of it to aid them in decrying his whole policy.'[1]

Days passed without a word from Hardie, leaving Sylvia's distress to grow even more. When he finally spoke out, publicly defending the women and excusing their actions as a misunderstanding of parliamentary procedure, Sylvia saw it as a magnanimous gesture. Her sister, Christabel, did not. Now, more than ever she believed the WSPU's links with Labour needed to be loosened. She saw no value in maintaining the relationship, convinced that the WSPU's future lay in standing apart from any political party.

Christabel had watched events unfolding in earnest from the Pankhurst home in Manchester, where she continued her studies while overseeing the WSPU's northern operations. She had, at this stage, blossomed into a young, purposeful woman, far removed from the lazy, complaining Emerson's shopgirl she had once been. In Manchester, she was constantly distracted by the organisation's activities in London. After the March protests, she wrote to Mary Gawthorpe, a working-class teacher and radical from Leeds with strong Labour connections. Christabel hoped Gawthorpe might pressure prominent Labour politicians to clarify their stance on women's suffrage, though she harboured little optimism. 'The further one goes, the plainer it becomes that men – even Labour men – think more of their own interests than of ours,' she lamented in her letter .[2]

The warmer days of May finally arrived as did the women's meeting with the British Prime Minister. On the appointed morning, hundreds of suffrage delegates, representing a vast spectrum of women from cooperative workers and temperance activists to college graduates, socialists, and liberals, gathered to march to the Foreign Office as had been arranged. Once there, with several women squeezed into the meeting room, a passionate Emmeline, alongside Keir Hardie, presented their case to Campbell-Bannerman. The Prime Minister listened sympathetically but made it clear that while he personally supported their cause, many in his cabinet did not. He urged the women to persist in their campaign but to practice 'the virtue of patience'. To this comment, Keir Hardie responded that 'patience, like many virtues, can be carried to excess'. Annie

Kenney, in her shawl and clogs, unable to contain her frustration, leapt to her feet, crying, 'Sire, we are not satisfied and the agitation will go on.'

The meeting had not brought the breakthrough the women had hoped for, and so they left, marching to Trafalgar Square. There, before a crowd of thousands, Emmeline Pankhurst, Teresa Billington, Dora Montefiore, and other prominent female speakers addressed the gathering.

It was, in reality, the first major open-air rally for women's suffrage in London. Yet beneath the surface of the broader suffrage movement, signs of division were already showing. Most members of the NUWSS and many Liberal supporters favoured Sir Henry's cautious approach, which advocated persistence without provocation. But to the WSPU, there was only one clear conclusion from their meeting with the Prime Minister: their campaign had to intensify. As Christabel firmly put it, 'The only way for either men or women to get what they want is to interfere with the peace of mind of the Government. Men have the vote to achieve this; women, without it, must find other means to make their voices heard.'[3]

The next few months saw those 'other means' playing out on a regular basis. WSPU militancy escalated. As they had with Churchill, the organisation now intensified their campaign against Herbert Asquith, the Chancellor of the Exchequer who was likely to become the next Liberal party leader. Asquith had a reputation as being the most staunchly opposed to women's suffrage among the Liberal ministers. Wherever he went, the suffragettes pursued him relentlessly. They disrupted his meetings, followed him across the country, and even staged protests outside his home in Cavendish Square. In mid-June, Emmeline had found her way into one of Asquith's meetings on the government's education bill in Northampton. After several men had posed their questions, she calmly raised her hand. Referring to Asquith's earlier remarks on the rights of parents to have a say in their children's education, she coolly asked, 'Women are parents. Does Mr. Asquith believe that women should, like men, have the right to influence their children's education through the vote?' No sooner was the question out of Emmeline's mouth than she was forcibly removed from the meeting.

Meanwhile, more members of the WSPU were choosing to serve short prison sentences rather than pay fines imposed by the courts. Twenty-year-old Adela, who had long been eager to step into the fray, had her moment of glory on 17 June 1906. This was when she, Hannah Mitchell and Alice Morrissey disrupted a big Liberal rally for Churchill and Welsh MP, David Lloyd George in Belle Vue, Manchester. Precautions had been taken to keep the now-notorious suffragettes out of such events, but Adela, despite being well known in the area, slipped in unnoticed, disguised in her mother's 'best hat and silk coat'. As the meeting got underway, the suffragettes rose one at a time and asked their question: 'Will the Liberal Government give the vote to women?' When it was Adela's turn to stand up and put the query to the speakers, an elderly man seated behind her thumped her hard with his umbrella.

As she was being marched out, one of the policemen scolded her, suggesting she would be better off doing laundry work than agitating at political meetings. Adela, trying to loosen his grip on her arm, smacked at his hand and was duly charged with assaulting a policeman. Ten days later, she, along with her two companions, was sentenced to seven and three days in Strangeways Prison, respectively.

Hannah Mitchell's husband would later come to pay his wife's fine; she was needed at home to take care of her son and orphaned niece. Adela, on the other hand, served her full stint behind bars, and came out to her mother Emmeline, waiting with a group of cheering suffragettes. Emmeline had been filled with worry while her youngest daughter was behind bars. Adela may have been known to stand for hours in the rain on soapboxes, but she still had the weak constitution of her childhood. Emmeline's distress only deepened when she heard Adela's grim account of freezing nights spent on a plank bed under a filthy blanket, the use of slop buckets as a toilet and meals of stale bread and coarse porridge.

Moreover, Emmeline wasn't keen for her youngest daughter to lose her job. She was only a teacher, which was not a huge source of pride for Emmeline, but still, Adela's wages were a necessary contribution to a household already under financial strain. The suffragette leader's hold on her own pensionable job was slowly slipping from her grasp. The Board of Guardians had grown increasingly impatient with her frequent trips to London as an activist. In her absence, Emmeline relied on her sister Mary to step in as the Registrar for Births and Deaths. But it was a makeshift solution that couldn't last forever, and Emmeline knew it. Anxiety gnawed at her. She sought advice from her old friend Noémie, who sharply urged her to step back from politics, reminding her that her duty was to her children. 'Leave politics alone,' she wrote to her, 'and focus on securing careers for your daughters.'

It was not such a simple choice for Emmeline, however. She felt trapped between the pressing need to support her children, including Harry who was still in school, and the cause of equal rights to which she and her husband had dedicated so much of their lives. 'She was driven by a desperate heart-hunger for the ideal,' Sylvia would later write. 'Still struggling, still unsatisfied, seeking a goal of beauty for her hard pilgrimage.'[4]

Adela maintained her job for the next few months, attending and organising demonstrations at the weekend and then turning up at school the following Monday. During the summer holidays, her days of activism multiplied. She travelled to Scotland with Annie Kenney to speak in Edinburgh, Dundee and Fife. Adela also became involved in the Bolton weavers' strike, an experience she later captured in an article for Frederick Lawrence's *Labour Record*. Her decision to write on labour issues, however, did not sit well with Christabel, who insisted that the fight for women's suffrage remain the singular focus, free from competing distractions.

As autumn descended and the school year resumed, Adela intended to juggle both her teaching job in the slums of Manchester and her political work. But she had only recently turned 20 years old, and like many of the young women of her generation, she saw the romantic life of revolution spread out before her. As the days darkened, so too did her mood. Much like her mother, she craved intensity and drama. By October, unable to resist the pull any longer, Adela resigned from her teaching position to become a full-time WSPU organiser, claiming that both Christabel and her mother 'accepted it with good grace'.

Just as Adela was throwing herself fully into the movement, Sylvia was beginning to pull away. As her two years at the National College of Art drew to a close, the young artist faced growing anxiety about her future. She sought support from her mother and sisters but found little succour there. 'We were no longer a family,' she reflected bitterly. 'The movement was overshadowing all personal affections.'

Sylvia's distress grew. She was exhausted, beset with constant bouts of neuralgia and battling sleepless nights filled with worry about how she would build a proper artist's portfolio, or, more pressing, how she would pay her rent. It wasn't just that the demands of WSPU work consumed her time, it was also that her workroom had become, without any real discussion with her, the gathering space for the WSPU in London. Finally, she made a decision and gave a letter of resignation as honorary secretary of the London WSPU to Mrs Pethick-Lawrence. While the treasurer felt Sylvia had made the right choice, Emmeline was furious. Christabel, deep in her law studies with exams approaching, couldn't assist just yet, and Emmeline demanded Sylvia remain in her position until Christabel was free.

Sylvia, always stubborn, always able to decline her mother's demands, unlike her two sisters, refused and Emmeline had to appoint two new honorary secretaries, Charlotte Despard and Edith How Martyn, to take her place. Despard had been a close friend of Eleanor Marx and both she and How were committed ILP members.

However, Emmeline's anger towards Sylvia lingered. When her middle child later wrote to her, excited that her college teachers had encouraged her to apply for a scholarship to complete her five-year art course, Emmeline did not reply. Preoccupied with closing the failed business venture, Emerson's, and moving once again to cheaper lodgings at 60 Upper Brook Street, she found little time for Sylvia's news. Yet she made time to celebrate 'the clever Christabel' who, as the only woman in her class, had passed her law exams with First Class Honours, a distinction shared with just one other student, Harry Finklestone. Together with Adela, Esther Roper, and Elizabeth Wolstoneholme Elmy and her son, Frank, they had travelled to the graduation award ceremony to see Christabel conferred. When she stepped forward there was some initial booing, while someone yelled, 'Where's your banner?' But it did nothing to dampen the women's delight, particularly Emmeline and Christabel herself, who must have thought in that bittersweet moment how proud her father would have been.

The following year, the WSPU moved its headquarters to London. After receiving her degree, Christabel also transferred to the capital city where she became the WSPU's Chief Organiser on a salary of £2.10s per week. Though Sylvia had now taken two unfurnished rooms at 120 Cheyne Walk, Chelsea, Christabel did not move in with her. Instead, she took up residence with the wealthy and childless Pethick-Lawrences at Clement's Inn, where she would remain for the next six years. The snub likely wounded Sylvia. Christabel, however, justified the decision by insisting that Sylvia was already burdened by too much responsibility. In any case, Sylvia was enjoying spending time with Keir Hardie once more. He had helped her move, taking both her and Harry out to dinner that first weekend in her new place.

Harry had then returned to Manchester. Away from Sylvia and the flurry of activity that surrounded the WSPU in London, he was regularly sick. Between his bad eyesight, his poor health, and his lack of academic interest, the chances of him achieving the grades necessary for a promising career were slight. Still, even with his limited abilities, Harry did what he could to be of value to his mothers and sisters. Just as they had dedicated themselves to the fight for women's suffrage, Harry too had immersed himself in their cause. However, as a young man in a woman's cause, he was on most occasions the odd one out, and was lonely, with few friends, as a result.

Sylvia blamed Emmeline's neglect for Harry's failing health and lack of career possibilities. However, in later years, Adela would strike out at Sylvia, her old nursery-room adversary, claiming that it was her older sister who had selfishly put her own art studies before his needs. 'What he had wanted,' Adela claimed, 'was love and care beyond the ordinary. That was impossible to give him, except at the abandonment of mother's public career, unless Sylvia had made some sacrifices of her art and stayed at home to keep house and look after her brother.'[5]

And yet, beyond the resentment and blame the sisters doled out to each other, there was no lack of love for young Harry. Emmeline, his siblings, and their aunt Mary appeared to be devoted to him, even if they were generally inattentive. In those years in Manchester, Mary, in particular, kept a watchful eye over her gentle nephew, offering the care that circumstances often denied him.

CHAPTER

8

DAUGHTERS OF DEFIANCE

As 1906 rolled on, the WSPU kept as busy as ever. The Pethick-Lawrence home at Clement's Inn became the unofficial headquarters of the movement, bustling with activity. Christabel took over one main room as the WSPU's Chief Organiser while another room was used for work meetings, petition writing, gatherings, and more. The space was often loud and chaotic, and the constant presence of the suffragettes day in, day out, was occasionally difficult for the Pethick-Lawrences. Fred in particular needed space to write and print the monthly publication he had set up in 1905, the *Labour Record and Review*, and often had to fight for a quiet space where he could get it done. Yet despite the intrusion, he would go on to recall in his autobiography that the suffragettes who 'took over his flat' also 'brought with them an inexhaustible fund of logic and laughter, courage and charm, reason and raillery'.

Christabel, delighted to be in the thick of things in London, was eager to keep steering the organisation away from any alignment with a political party, including Labour. She was convinced that their cause required a more independent and strategic approach, similar to that which had been employed by the Irish nationalist, Charles Stewart Parnell – and against their beloved father, Richard Pankhurst. Parnell had urged voters not to support the governing party because of its opposition to Irish Home Rule. By adopting this same strategy, the WSPU could weaken the government's standing, sending a clear message that voters would turn against any administration that failed to uphold justice and equality for women as much as men. At the same time, Christabel believed that this approach would transform the WSPU into the organisation it had aspired to be from that autumn evening in 1903 when it was first founded – a movement by women, for women, in which they were no longer passive bystanders in the political process, dependent on the whims of male MPs, but active participants in shaping their own future.

As part of this new strategy, the WSPU's Chief Organiser also felt that the organisation needed to attract more middle- and upper-class members. This was not simply a matter of expanding membership and diluting reliance on working-class Labour women; it was about optics and influence. With her characteristic astuteness, Christabel had noted that MPs and the national newspapers were far more impressed by demonstrations led by women of higher social standing than those led by their working-class counterparts who, in any case, were regularly known to participate in labour-related marches.

This tactic was strongly supported by Mrs Pethick-Lawerence, who knew that it would also help bring much-needed money into the struggling organisation. The Honorary Treasurer helped recruit many women among her own affluent circles, as well as from her family. These included her close friend Mary Neal, two of her cousins, Jessie Lawes and Ellen Crocker, as well as her younger sister, Dorothy Pethick, who became a WSPU organiser and would later be arrested on three different occasions.[1]

Another woman who would become an influential figure in the Union and the suffragette movement was Lady Constance Lytton. She was the daughter of the 1st Earl of Lytton, Viceroy of India between 1876 and 1880, and, in that role, the man who proclaimed Queen Victoria the Empress of India. Initially drawn to the cause through her work in prison reform and her connections with Emmeline Pethick-Lawrence and Mary Neal at the Espérance Club, it took some years for her to fully commit to militant suffragism. Once converted, however, Lady Constance would become a formidable advocate, leveraging her family connections to press for women's rights in Parliament.

In the late summer of 1906, Christabel had a chance to put her new anti-government strategy to the test. A by-election was announced in Cockermouth, a quiet constituency in Cumberland traditionally held by the Liberals, but now fiercely contested by both Conservative and Labour opponents. Robert Smillie, Labour's candidate was a miners' leader who believed in adult suffrage but was ambivalent toward women's enfranchisement. Christabel travelled to Cockermouth, ostensibly to lend her support to Smillie. However, her true agenda quickly became clear during the WSPU meetings she organised in the marketplace and from the back of a truck, where she addressed large crowds of locals and the press. Her speech was direct and unapologetic. She argued that it did not matter which party held power, be they Liberal, Conservative, or Labour, if they refused to support women's suffrage. The current Liberal government, she claimed, had shown itself to be an enemy of the cause and should therefore be voted out, but all other parties should be rejected too if they didn't show their allegiance to the principle of women's right to vote. The local newspaper, taking note of her boldness, remarked that 'Miss Pankhurst, one of the notorious band of lady suffragists … had to encounter a considerable amount of interruption, but was equal to the occasion.'

The Labour Party were furious at what they saw as the WSPU's betrayal. Even Mary Gawthorpe, who had come to Cockermouth to support Smillie, was initially uncertain about this new direction. Yet within weeks, she would come around to Christabel's thinking and formally join the WSPU. Christabel, undeterred, continued campaigning alongside Teresa Billington and Marion Coates Hansen, who had also arrived in the Cumberland town, selling 'Votes for Women' literature and holding more speeches until the election result was announced on 3 August 1906.

It seemed she achieved her end. The Conservative candidate, Sir John Randles, secured the seat, while the Liberal candidate lost, and Smillie trailed far behind. Whether Smillie had ever stood a chance was irrelevant; the ILP blamed the suffragettes for the loss, accusing them of putting their cause for the vote above Labour's broader movement.

Back in London, Sylvia Pankhurst and Keir Hardie were horrified by Christabel's defiant speeches. What's more, in Christabel's anti-party election policy, Sylvia saw the growing division between the WSPU's stance and her own deepening socialist convictions. As she continued her work with the poor women of the East End, she became more convinced that Christabel – and their mother, Emmeline – were steering the WSPU away from the values their father, the Red Doctor, had instilled in them, values grounded in social justice and the fight for the downtrodden.

'It was all destructive,' she wrote of Christabel's strategy in her 1931 book, *The Suffragette Movement*. 'But how much easier to win applause by destructive condemnation than for any constructive scheme, however brilliant, however beneficent!'

While Emmeline fully endorsed her eldest daughter's bold new approach, she was nonetheless uneasy about completely breaking ties with the ILP, particularly as many of the WSPU's members were Labour members too. Thus, she made sure that she and Christabel attended a meeting of the Manchester Central Branch of the ILP on 4 September 1906. The meeting debated a motion to expel both Christabel and Teresa Billington from the party following their controversial actions at Cockermouth. However, Christabel's defence of the new strategy was so persuasive that for a finish, the majority voted in favour of keeping the women within the party, acknowledging that they were simply advancing a goal clearly aligned with the ILP's official programme. The publicity from this meeting and the earlier Cockermouth by-election brought even more recruits to the WSPU.

On 23 October, Parliament reconvened for its autumn session and groups of suffragettes, including Emmeline, began arriving at the Commons. Initially, the doorman let in a group of around thirty well-dressed women, forbidding a further group of working-class women entry into the lobby. A message was sent to the Chief Liberal Whip asking that he obtain a promise from the Prime Minister that a woman's suffrage measure be considered that session. When the Chief Whip returned to affirm that such a measure would not be considered in that session or any future session, the women immediately began to protest.

As Emmeline would later muse:

> What would a deputation of unenfranchised men have done in these circumstances – men who knew themselves to be qualified to exercise the franchise, who desperately needed the protection of the franchise, and who had a majority of legislators in favour of giving them the franchise? I hope they would have done at least as much as we did, which was to start a meeting of protest on the spot.[2]

Mary Gawthorpe, now very much committed to the WSPU cause, sprang up on a settee and began a speech, while other women gathered around her. The police raced in to stop the women and an even greater commotion ensued. In the scuffle, Emmeline was thrown to the ground. Though she was bruised but generally uninjured, several of the women near her held off the police as best they could until she was able to rise to her feet again. The police would later describe this as 'threatening behaviour'. Ten women including Adela, Annie Kenney, Teresa Billington, Emmeline Pethick Lawrence, Minnie Baldock, and Annie Cobden-Sanderson, daughter of Richard Cobden, the well-known agitator for the repeal of the Corn Laws, would later be charged at Westminster police station. Alongside the 'threatening behaviour', their charges would include the use of abusive words and 'intent to provoke a breach of the peace'.

All ten women were found guilty, and ordered to agree to keep the peace for six months or serve six weeks' imprisonment in the Second Division, a category of confinement used for common criminals. The women, bar none, chose imprisonment. Sylvia, who had not been in the lobby that day, went along to the hearing only to discover that her friends and colleagues had already been sentenced and were on their way to Holloway Prison. When she attempted a speech of protest on the court steps, she too was promptly arrested and sentenced to fourteen days in the lowest section, the Third Division. It was, at that time, the largest contingent of suffragettes to be thrown behind bars.

The treatment of the women at the House of Commons and their subsequent imprisonment shocked both press and public. These were, after all, largely middle-class women from respectable and well-connected families. In the still traditional society of early twentieth-century Britain, the notion of locking up women who had long been seen as the backbone of family virtues – modesty, propriety, and respectability – was almost unthinkable. Even playwright George Bernard Shaw wrote a letter to *The Times* condemning the Government's actions.

As public opinion began to shift, membership in the WSPU swelled as never before while donations to the overall cause surged in tandem. In the aftermath of the women's imprisonment, Lady Cook, Mrs Cobden-Unwin and Mr Cobden-Sanderson each donated £100. The wealthy Frederick Pethick Lawrence, who had in the meantime taken over his wife's duties in the WSPU, also pledged to donate £10 for every day she remained in prison.

Even the more conservative National Union of Women's Suffrage Societies (NUWSS) expressed support. At a meeting the day after the women were sent to prison, NUWSS President Millicent Garrett Fawcett, who had previously distanced herself from militant tactics, defended the suffragettes. She asserted that their recent actions had done more to propel women's suffrage into the realm of practical politics than years of more measured advocacy and she urged her members to pledge their support for their more strident sisters. She would later, upon the release of the prisoners, host a dinner for them at the Savoy Hotel. Teresa and Mrs Cobden Sanderson were invited, and toasts were made in their honour. Adela and Sylvia's names were not on the guest list, however. Sylvia would later surmise this was likely because the girls' family name was too much associated with the militant tactics the other suffragists were, at this current moment, attempting to overlook.

It had been Sylvia's first time in prison. Relegated to the worst division, she was appalled at the filth and despair of prison life and wrote at length about it in her book, *The Suffragette Movement*. In her tiny dark cell, two shelves held a tin plate, an old wooden spoon reused by the cell's long line of inmates, a tin pint pot wherein a 'skilly', a watery oatmeal concoction, would be poured daily, a piece of hard yellow soap, a small scrubbing-brush and a cloth for cleaning. The solitary furnishings included a narrow plank bed with a lumpy rolled-up mattress and blanket, an old wooden stool, a basin, and a slop pail. Cards printed with morning and evening prayers lay as grim reminders of some semblance of routine amid the bleakness.

Each morning before dawn, the prisoners would be awakened by clanging bells, and have to quickly wash, empty their slop buckets, roll up their bedding, and then clean their cell floor with the same harsh soap used for cleaning their bodies. After that, the women of the Third Division were herded into the hallway and marched to the chapel with the wardens barking insults and orders at them in equal measure. Here the chaplain's sermons against sin reverberated through the cold stone walls, causing many of the wizened old women and gaunt young girls alike to weep aloud, likely not at the remembrance of whatever crime they'd committed but at what they'd lost by being held prisoner within the wretched walls of Holloway. As Sylvia described:

> Many of them are old, with shrunken cheeks and scant white hair. Few seem young. All are anxious and careworn. They are broken down by poverty, sorrow and overwork. Think of them going back to sit, each in her lonely cell, to brood for hours on the causes which brought her here, wondering what is happening to

> those she loves outside, tortured, perhaps, by the thought that she is needed there.[3]

Not all the suffragettes endured the full six weeks of imprisonment. Two of them, Mrs Pethick-Lawrence and Dora Montefiore, fell gravely ill and agreed to keep the peace for six months in exchange for their release. Mrs Pethick-Lawrence in particular had found herself into a deep state of frightened anxiety, unable to mentally deal with the dreadfulness of life behind bars. After about a week inside, Sylvia, Adela, and the other women were moved to the First Division, thanks to the relentless efforts of Keir Hardie, Emmeline Pethick-Lawrence's father, Henry, and other influential politicians in pressurising the Home Office. The move was met with great satisfaction by Christabel and Emmeline, as being First Division inmates gave the suffragettes the powerful distinction of being political prisoners rather than common criminals.

For the majority of the women, however, prison had been a traumatic ordeal. As soon as she had been transferred to the First Division, Sylvia had claimed the right to send for drawing paper, pen, ink and pencils and immediately began documenting the grim conditions. Once on the other side of Holloway's oppressive walls, she gave interviews about the women's harrowing experience. Keir Hardie urged her to write an article about the prison conditions, which he then sold to *Pall Mall Magazine* for £10, a sum that was of real help to the now financially stricken Sylvia.

Sylvia believed her article would serve the WSPU's cause, shedding light on the brutal treatment of the suffragettes, as well as other prisoners. But Christabel and Emmeline disagreed. To them, Sylvia's focus on prison reform was, just like Adela's earlier focus on labour strikes, a distraction from their primary goal – women's suffrage.

It's also possible that Christabel resented that Sylvia had acted independently, without first consulting her. As Chief Organiser, Christabel's influence had greatly grown. Her political instincts were rapidly transforming the movement into a new and more assertive kind of suffrage party. In just a few short months, she had become the figure to whom others looked for guidance. This included her mother who, Sylvia bitterly recounted in *The Suffragette Movement*, some thirty years later, 'upheld her as an oracle', while the 'Pethick-Lawrences praised her political genius to all who would listen'. Christabel's commitment to her strategy only deepened after the events of 23 October when she saw how wealthy women such as Mrs Pethick-Lawrence and others willingly endured imprisonment for the WSPU's principles. It's feasible that Christabel, in her rising influence, expected others – including her sisters – to fall in line with this increasingly militant course.

Was Sylvia jealous of Christabel's rising star? That's possible too. After all, as she herself wrote in *The Suffragette Movement*, 'Christabel had the admiration of a multitude; hundreds, perhaps thousands, of young women, adored her to distraction and longed to emulate her.' But it seems more probable that Sylvia, as stubborn as her older sister, wanted primarily to steer the WSPU back to its socialist origins. 'As for me,' she wrote in 1931, reflecting on her feelings about Christabel at that time. 'I detested her incipient Toryism.'

After everyone's release, Mrs Pethick-Lawrence, feeling somewhat ashamed that she among all others was not able to embrace the fear, cold and solitude of prison life, retreated to her summer home in Italy to recover. Sylvia joined her a month later, grateful for the chance to rest after her own ordeal, and to spend her days sketching and painting instead. The two women found comfort in each other's company. Though Mrs Pethick-Lawrence was deeply devoted to all the Pankhurst women, a special bond grew between her and Sylvia, one that would endure for the rest of their lives. Sylvia also took the time while she was there to visit a women's prison in Milan, noting that the conditions of the Italian prisoners was considerably better than that of the poor, forgotten women she had recently been incarcerated with in England.

The WSPU's militancy continued well into the winter with four further confrontational demonstrations in Parliament Square and the Lobby of the House, where twenty women were incarcerated over the Christmas holidays. Sylvia and Mrs Pethick-Lawrence returned from Italy in time to welcome the suffragettes upon their release. The Pethick-Lawrences immediately threw a Yuletide party for the women at a Holborn restaurant. According to the prisoners, Christmas Day behind bars was the same as any other day in prison, except that the women were forced to attend mass twice. However, it bothered them little. As Sylvia noted, the women agreed that they had gone to prison for a cause they held dear and according to Mrs Martha Jones saw their incarceration, 'not as a sacrifice, but as an honour'. 'What they had seen in Holloway had more than ever convinced them of the pressing need that women should be enfranchised.'

That's not to say that the decision to risk arrest – knowing it could mean spending days, weeks, or even months in prison – was taken lightly. As the movement gained momentum, many women were shunned by their families, had their children taken from them, and saw any financial support they once relied on disappear.

On 12 February 1907, Parliament reassembled, and once more Votes for Women was left out of the King's Speech. The following day, the first Women's Parliament was organised at Caxton Hall with hundreds of women in attendance. Emmeline must have felt a quiet satisfaction as she surveyed the packed hall. Just a year prior, at the inaugural WSPU gathering in London, she had fretted for days that they would not fill the room and had to pay train fares of East End women to ensure they would attend. Now, with the hall crammed to capacity and another adjoining room equally overflowing, it was a testament to the movement's growing momentum.

After the speeches concluded, the women – Christabel and Sylvia Pankhurst among them – set out for the House of Commons, intent on delivering a resolution to the Prime Minister. However, a new challenge was to greet them. When they arrived outside Westminster, they were blocked from entering by a large group of mounted police. As the astonished crowds approached, the police charged into the women, causing them to scatter in fear of being trampled. Those who tried to reach the entrance of the Strangers' Lobby were dragged away by foot police, often thrown back into the path of the oncoming horses.

At the time in Russia, the autocratic Tsarist regime was using mounted Cossack units to crush dissent among protesting workers and peasants, resulting in the deaths of hundreds of unarmed demonstrators. The appalled British press now utilised the same language they had drawn on to describe the shocking events of the Russian unrest, calling the English mounted police 'Cossacks' and denouncing the government for adopting similar oppressive tactics against its own citizens. The public were outraged, and yet still fifty-eight women were arrested and appeared in court the next day.

According to Sylvia's later account of that morning before the magistrates, Christabel, who had decided that a second stay in prison would help push publicity for the WSPU even further, announced herself as the organiser of the march and demanded she be tried first. The magistrates duly obliged. In her defence of the women's actions, she claimed the march had been a peaceful attempt to present a resolution to the government. It was also, she further explained, part of a broader, determined campaign by the WSPU to secure the vote for women, and to that end, she concluded, 'there can be no going back for us and more will happen if we do not get justice'.[4]

Most of the arrested women received fourteen days' imprisonment. Sylvia and Charlotte Despard received three-week sentences. Of Despard's commitment to the cause, Sylvia would later write, 'She was one of our most courageous and devoted social workers. When I was in prison with her in 1907, I was impressed by her truly magnificent courage.' The two women were to spend those weeks as political prisoners in the First Division and thus have the privileges that would allow Sylvia to continue her sketches and also send and receive letters to and from Hardie.

After these violent spring events, Emmeline finally decided to resign from her post as Registrar of Births and Deaths. It was not something she did lightly. For years, she had navigated the difficult balance between Manchester and London, her public duties and private life, and the rapidly growing demands of the WSPU. Mrs Pethick-Lawrence had long urged her to devote herself fully to the cause, assuring her that the WSPU's finances were secure enough to offer Emmeline a salary of £200–£300 per annum as their lead speaker.

At first, Emmeline had hoped that their days of agitating for the franchise were close to an end. In early March, the Liberal MP, W. H. Dickinson, had agreed to introduce a women's suffrage bill and miraculously had drawn first place in the private members' ballot. But disillusionment followed swiftly. Complaints arose from MPs who objected that the Bill did not go far enough and would exclude working-class women from enfranchisement. In the end, like so many before it, the Bill was talked out.

On 20 March 1907, the WSPU organised yet another demonstration, determined to press the government for a new resolution on women's suffrage. Emmeline, still conscious of keeping her job and believing it was better for her as the de facto leader to remain out of prison, asked Lady Florence Haberton to lead the hundreds of protestors. The Belfast-born viscountess was a well-known campaigner for Victorian dress reform; as a keen cyclist, she had developed the then-famous 'divided skirt'. She was one of the founders of the Rational Dress Society, established in 1881, which campaigned against tightly fitted corsets, narrow-toed boots and shoes, and heavily weighted skirts which rendered practical movement, let alone healthy exercise, almost impossible. As such, she had been drawn to the ideas of equality propounded by the suffragettes and willingly agreed to lead the women.

Among the group were around forty factory women who had been recruited by Annie and Adela, dressed, as requested, in their everyday clogs and shawl. But the authorities were prepared. Forewarned of the demonstration, a sizable force of police officers was waiting to block the women's path. What followed was another horrifying display of aggression. The police, wielding force with little restraint, met the women head-on to prevent them from entering the Commons. The scene quickly descended into chaos, with women being pushed, struck and driven back by sheer physical force. As the violence unfolded, Caxton Hall, its doors remaining open throughout, became a refuge of sorts as injured women limped in to get their cuts and bruises tended to, before many, undeterred, ventured back out to continue their protest. The demonstration continued well into the evening by which time seventy-four women, including Lady Haberton, had been arrested. The next day, they would be sentenced to short stays in prison.

While the women were fighting in the streets of London that evening, Emmeline had boarded a train to Hexham, Northumberland, where she was needed for the WSPU's by-election campaign. The following day, with the weight of the movement's challenges pressing on her, she resigned as Registrar. Despite the growing support in Parliament, it had become painfully clear to her that there was still a strong faction that would stop at nothing to deny women the vote.

Of course, it was a bold and costly move to give up the security of a government pension and embrace the uncertainty of full-time activism. Yet Emmeline knew she had no other choice. Years earlier, she had sat captivated in a local meeting room as Lydia Becker first awakened her to the cause of women's suffrage. Now, as she travelled through the country by train, with two of her daughters in prison, each for a second time, and women around the country, some friends, some unknown to her, expressed their willingness to also cast off metaphorical shackles by taking on real ones, that same cause called to her with an urgency she could no longer ignore. This, she now understood, was a fight she was destined to lead.

Shortly afterwards, Emmeline Pankhurst packed up her home in Manchester and, like her daughters before her, moved to London.

CHAPTER

9

A SUFFRAGETTE SPLIT

Eighteen-year-old Harry did not accompany his mother when she moved to London in 1907. However, his future had become a matter of great discussion between Emmeline and her offspring. Eventually, it was decided that with all the Pankhurst women now living in London, including Harry's aunt Mary who had been to-ing and fro-ing between Manchester and London and who was now also to become a WSPU paid organiser, Harry would be apprenticed to a trade. Emmeline had met a Glaswegian builder at an ILP meeting who was willing to take him on, and so as his family moved south, the fragile Harry moved north. In Glasgow he lodged with other labourers and spent long days toiling outdoors, building barrack dwellings for the working class. He was a gentle, somewhat frail boy, but as had happened with his eyesight, Emmeline refused to recognise the physical weakness of her son, and rather hoped that by pushing him to utilise what little physical strength he had, he would, in fact, develop more. Of course, this was not to be. Though Harry enjoyed being with the other workmen, he suffered greatly from the outdoor work in the cold, wet conditions of the northern British Isles. Still, he remained in the city, and was delighted when Sylvia visited him later that winter.

Sylvia had decided to take some time away from London, and travel through the industrial landscapes of northern England. She had finally decided to put her art to social use by painting the gritty reality of women's lives in these areas. She also had another reason for wanting to escape the claustrophobia of London; Keir Hardie had taken ill and had left the city.

At the Labour Party Conference in Belfast that January, Hardie had been dismayed when women's suffrage, which was supposed to be a key measure in the upcoming session, had been struck down through an amendment that would have bound him as an MP to oppose any legislation that would extend votes to women on the basis of the existing property franchise. Hardie had made a powerful speech calling it a grave injustice to women. 'The Party is largely my own child,' he declared, 'and I cannot part from it lightly, or without pain…' But if necessary, he would resign as leader 'to remove the stigma resting upon our wives, mothers, and sisters, of being accounted unfit for citizenship'.[1]

The room was shocked. The idea of Hardie stepping down over this issue was unthinkable. Emmeline, who was among the audience, was torn between running to her old friend to urge him to stay the course or supporting his stance, which would undoubtedly highlight the urgent need for women's suffrage. Sylvia, however, swiftly penned a letter to him, pleading with him to reconsider his threat. In the end, he did not need to. The party quickly introduced a 'conscience clause', allowing members to vote according to their own beliefs, sparing him from having to follow through on his threat. Sylvia, still shaken at the sacrifice Hardie had seemed willing to make, admired his resolve, but Christabel was more cynical; she saw his pronouncement as a calculated move to consolidate his authority within the party. Perhaps she was right. Hardie was struggling. His public career had become increasingly marred by setbacks. The old-age pension, something he had fought tirelessly to achieve, had been omitted from the Budget yet again. A couple of months later, at a WSPU meeting on 8 March 1907, Hardie, as the guest speaker, declared that if a Women's Suffrage Bill wasn't passed within two years, he would personally lead a movement for full adult suffrage. This was a startling turn. It seemed to contradict his passionate defence of women's suffrage in Belfast just weeks before. And to the gathered suffragettes, it felt like a betrayal. Two more years of waiting for the vote, only to have women's suffrage potentially sidelined yet again in favour of a broader, male-dominated agenda, was unthinkable. Sylvia herself later told Hardie that she couldn't support any dilution of the WSPU's mission nor put her energy into the fight for the more ambiguous 'universal suffrage'.

Hardie was a strong advocate for the needs of poor and working-class women, but equally for their male counterparts. His life's work focused on supporting Britain's workers, but the relentless struggles were taking a toll on his health. A persistent, agonizing pain had begun to spread through the left side of his body, growing so severe that his doctor eventually admitted him to St Thomas' Hospital. Sylvia visited him regularly, though feared he might be dying. In her panic, she confided in her mother, Emmeline, who rushed to the bedside of her old friend.

Hardie did not die, but neither did the pain subside. Eventually, the 51-year-old decided to go home to Scotland and the care of his wife Lillie and daughter Nan, and then later to a hydro in the Scottish village of Wemyss Bay. It is believed that Hardy had suffered a stroke, but as his health improved, he decided to embark on a world cruise. He hoped the sea air might further aid his recovery and give him some perspective on his life's work. In the months that followed, he travelled to several British colonies and lands under imperial rule, advocating for independence. Though this was highly criticised by the

British establishment at home, his following among the poor, both in Britain and abroad, only grew.

Lonely and miserable in London, Sylvia decided the time was right for her to see if she could, in fact, make a difference with her art. She had the support of Emmeline and Fred Pethick-Lawrence. While unaware of her relationship with Hardie, they believed some time away from the city would do the serious young woman good and generously insisted on financing her travels. With Christabel's by-election campaign still in full swing, it was also agreed that the 25-year-old would continue some WSPU work as she travelled. That said, it was unlikely Sylvia realised just how often her mother would summon her to the industrial towns of the North, where the electoral battles were unfolding.

If Sylvia expected to witness the harsh deprivations of industrial life, she was not disappointed. In Cradley Heath, deep in the heart of the UK's coal and iron industries, she met women, their babies swaddled at their chests, toddlers playing close by, sweating through their work in darkened chain-making forges and workshops. For their long, gruelling hours, they earned barely 5 shillings a week. Each day, they left and returned to slums that horrified Sylvia. 'Never have I seen such hideous disregard for elementary decency in housing and sanitation,' she wrote, appalled by the decaying, poorly built hovels that served as their family homes.[2]

Sylvia spent several days with these women, chatting and listening to their stories, sketching as they spoke. Most seemed resigned to their situation, accepting also that their local trade union would always prioritise the needs of their husbands, sons and fathers over them.

From Cradley Heath, Sylvia moved on through the Black Country, connecting with ILP or WSPU members who helped introduce her to local women workers where they could. In Leicester, she was allowed to set up her easel in a small shoe factory. Here she made gouches and watercolours of the women who sat hunched along benches, stitching and 'skiving' leather or working at machines to shape toe caps. Later on in Lancashire, she was shaken by the sight of the 'pit brow lasses', women who worked in the coal mines, dragging heavy tubs of coal from the shafts, hauling them onto railways, or guiding them to sorting sheds where other women, their faces and limbs blackened with noxious coal dust, poked through the tubs, picking out stones and other unwanted detritus.[3]

As the summer moved on, so did Sylvia. She travelled to Staffordshire, the pottery capital of Britain. She sketched the ashen-skinned women who worked in the deadly lead-filled air of the factories that crafted the fine china adorning the sideboards and tables of the country's upper-middle classes. Elegantly formed and decorated, the cost of this china to the women who toiled over it was often kidney or brain disease, or the birth of stillborn babies.

When autumn deepened, Sylvia travelled to Scarborough where, in the biting cold, she sketched the hardy fisherwomen who cleaned and packed the herring brought in by the fishing boats. She lodged with an old fisherwoman who spent the evenings regaling her with tales by turns cheerful and tragic of a life shaped by the sea.

Determined to take in as much of the north as she could, Sylvia soon found herself within the farming communities of Berwick-on-Tweed. Once again, she was shocked by the gaunt bodies and ragged clothes of the women farm labourers, and the backbreaking work of picking potatoes and cutting crops by hand. In her book *The Suffragette Movement*, she described them vividly:

> Their eyelids inflamed, as though painted with blood, their faces ingrained with dirt, their garments a collection of rags. Old crones with bent backs, girls with lewd speech and hideous laughter, their faces bruised and cut from last night's levity, toiled on without pause, grubbing the tubers from the ruts.[4]

Sylvia had hoped to commit the better part of her time to living with, painting and truly understanding the lives of these working women. However, she was constantly being pulled away, summoned by her mother's urgent telegrams to speak at suffragette rallies in Rutland, Bury St Edmunds in Suffolk, and various other by-election towns.

The WSPU members needed little introduction in these places; they had already gained enough fame – and notoriety – across Britain so that hundreds of people came out to hear them talk. Not all did so in the spirit of curiosity or support, however. There was heckling that occasionally became hostile and sometimes violent. Gangs of local boys would often throw rotten vegetables at them or release mice onto the hired trucks or wagons from which the suffragettes spoke. On several occasions, smaller carts hired by the women were stolen or tipped into ponds, often with the women still on them.

Though Sylvia stood firm in her belief in female suffrage, she felt increasingly alienated by Christabel's ongoing campaign. Too often, she arrived in towns only to find that, in supporting the WSPU's anti-Liberal stance, she was unwittingly contributing to a Tory victory.[5] Throughout her travels that summer, Sylvia had become increasingly convinced that the struggles of Britain's workers were not just about gender but deeply tied to the broader economic system. Supporting a party that upheld the very capitalist forces causing this suffering felt like a betrayal of everything she truly stood for.

Her older sister's growing control over the WSPU and her push towards a more militant, less socialist agenda rankled. Particularly as it seemed their mother gave Christabel a completely free rein. But was it Emmeline's to give? Many in the Union did not believe it so. In fact, that summer, Emmeline had already made Sylvia aware that there were some grumblings among the central committee about a Pankhurst–Pethick-Lawrence dictatorship in the organisation and the direction this was taking the WSPU.

Emmeline was no fool; she was aware that these cracks had been forming for months. At the ILP Conference in Derby that spring, Emmeline attended as the sole representative of the ILP Manchester Central Branch. She knew she would have to defend the WSPU's actions at Cockermouth, and hoped that, as one of the earliest members of the party, she would carry enough influence to argue the WSPU's policy or 'part good friends' with the political party she had abandoned the Liberals for with her husband many years previously.

However, during the meeting, ILP member Margaret McMillan read out a letter from two senior WSPU figures, Charlotte Despard and Annie Cobden-Sanderson. The letter condemned the WSPU's independent stance at Cockermouth and pledged that they would never take part in election actions unless it was to support Labour candidates. Emmeline was stunned. Gathering herself, she insisted that the letter did not reflect the views of the WSPU. She argued that by opposing all government nominees, the organisation was following the proven tactics of the Irish Party under Charles Parnell – pressuring the government was the only way to win votes for women. Though her voice trembled as she spoke, her explanation was clear enough. She finished by offering to resign if her stance was found inconsistent with her membership. However, it was decided her resignation was unnecessary and instead, the WSPU policy was praised.[6]

Emmeline returned to London but said nothing to Charlotte Despard or Annie Cobden-Sanderson. However, she was well aware of the continuing discontent. Mrs Pethick-Lawrence had also noticed it, bluntly telling Emmeline and Christabel that without their strong leadership, she would need to reconsider her own position within the WSPU.

The organisation's treasurer had returned from Italy more resolute than ever in her commitment to the WSPU's cause. As a charismatic speaker and a creative fundraiser, she had begun the new year by pouring her energy into gathering support, particularly from affluent women who could financially sustain the cause. She organised fundraisers, 'self-denial weeks', and strategically courted wealthy advocates. It was she who conceived the organisation's distinctive colours – purple for dignity, white for purity, and green for hope and renewal – transforming them into a powerful symbol that would soon be recognised around the world. These hues were woven into brooches and sashes for sale to followers, ingeniously enabling any woman, regardless of her political affiliation, to show her support for the movement.

Her husband, Fred, who as a man was not formally a member of the WSPU, had nonetheless stepped up his involvement following his wife's imprisonment. He was often the person who arrived first at the police station, offering comfort to the arrested suffragette or their distraught families. During his time with the WSPU, he organised bail for over 100 women. He also shared much needed financial and legal advice to the group and wrote pro-suffragette editorials for his newspaper, *The Labour Record and Review*.

Both Emmeline and Fred fully endorsed Christabel Pankhurst's strategy of targeting Liberal MPs in by-elections. Though they still considered themselves socialists, they recognised the wisdom of not aligning the WSPU with any one party. The Union was expanding at an astonishing pace. The headquarters at Clement's Inn now occupied seven rooms, and there were forty-seven WSPU branches across Britain, run by eight paid organisers, including Adela and Emmeline's sister, Mary Clarke. For the Pethick-Lawrences, sustaining this growth required strong, strategic fundraising, and the most dependable funds would come from wealthier supporters, whose political affiliations had to matter less than their willingness to contribute.

This pragmatism was shared by Emmeline and Christabel. All four were clear-eyed in their vision of a movement untethered from any single political party, and one unafraid to embrace militancy. Together, they held tightly to the reins of the WSPU, steering it decisively in this direction.

Yet what seemed like clarity to them appeared as autocracy to others. As had been made plain at the ILP Conference, not everyone was comfortable with the consistent targeting of Liberal MPs nor the increasingly hostile stance toward Labour. The fact that no one believed they were able to question either policy only added to the alienation felt by many of the women who had been instrumental in building the Union.

A faction, led again by Despard, and including Edith How-Martyn, and Teresa Billington-Grieg (who had recently added the Greig to her name following her marriage to Frederick Lewis Greig), began to push back. They advocated for a more transparent and democratic structure, arguing that local branches should have a voice. Until then, the leadership of the WSPU had been self-appointed, with the Central Committee and paid organisers chosen at the leaders' discretion rather than through open election. Teresa Billington-Greig had hastily drafted a constitution the previous year, but it had been largely ignored by the Pankhurst–Pethick-Lawrence inner circle. Yet, with the organisation's growing size and influence, the call for coherent rules and agreed-upon regulations could no longer be easily dismissed. The frustrated women suggested that the upcoming national WSPU conference on 17 September was the right time to debate policies and hold votes on appointments to the executive committee.

Politics certainly dictated the paths these women wanted to take, but personal feelings were equally at play. Many were dissatisfied that the everyday executive control of the WSPU was held tightly in the hands of Christabel and the Pethick-Lawrences (who, as a trio, had become known as the 'triumvirate'). Despard was a true believer in radical politics. She had left the NUWSS to join the WSPU precisely because the WSPU took direct and bold action. But as a committed socialist, Despard also believed deeply in equality for everyone, and when she sensed a lack of this within the WSPU, she didn't hesitate to question its leadership.

Teresa Billington's support for Charlotte Despard's stance on the suffrage movement was also fuelled by more than just principle. It's likely she believed she had been sidelined out of a prominent role in the organisation. With Christabel's arrival in London, Teresa had been dispatched to Scotland to establish new branches of the Women's Social and Political Union (WSPU). While the mission was significant, it was hard to ignore the symbolic exile from the movement's core leadership.

Nonetheless, in Scotland, Teresa's leadership flourished. She became a key figure among the suffragettes, and her speeches were regularly reported by the local press. *The Edinburgh Evening News* remarked, 'Miss Billington is an attractive-looking young lady, whose pleasant appearance would suggest anything but the aggressive characteristics which many may have associated with one who had figured conspicuously in the agitation.' The *Dundee Evening Telegraph* echoed this, calling her 'young, charming, soft-voiced, and not devoid of a sense of humour'.

Her feminine charm wasn't her only asset, however. Her audiences were struck by her intelligence, sharp wit and firm handling of hecklers. At one gathering, when a young man shouted mockingly, 'You ought to be a soldier,' Teresa swiftly retorted: 'Evidently my friend is under the impression that when a man becomes a soldier, he gets a vote. That is a great mistake. As soon as a man becomes a soldier, he loses his vote.' The room erupted in laughter, and a sceptical crowd was won over.

Yet, despite her success in Scotland, Teresa was keenly aware of what her assignment represented. It kept her far from the WSPU's London power base, where decisions were made and influence wielded. While she built a loyal following in Britain's north, it was likely Teresa was not wrong in suspecting she had been pushed into the shadows so that Christabel could step more fully into the limelight.

There had always been competitive tension between the two young women. Both were exceptional speakers, fiercely intelligent, and equally assured of their abilities. Teresa, as the first female national organiser for the Independent Labour Party (ILP), had every reason to feel she brought invaluable skills to the WSPU. But she also suspected that Christabel saw her as a threat, and that suspicion was mutual.

Rumours began to seep into Clement's Inn that the dissatisfied women were in fact planning to oust Christabel and Emmeline from the leadership. Just before her mother had contacted her, Sylvia had received a letter from her worried elder sister asking her to investigate the rumours further. 'You, poor child, have not had much family assistance in your worries,' she wrote. 'This is more than my affairs, though it concerns the Union as a whole.' Though several women were involved in the rumoured coup, Christabel clearly believed Teresa was at the root of the problem. In her letter, she labelled her rival activist, 'a wreaker'.[7]

Hoping to calm the brewing storm, Sylvia caught a train to London. Upon arriving at Clement's Inn, she urged her mother to consider the disgruntled WSPU members' proposal seriously, arguing that, given the rapid growth of the organisation's national network, a more democratic leadership structure might be the best path forward. But Emmeline believed the opposite. Alongside the legitimate WSPU branches that had been established, other unauthorised groups had been cropping up. These were typically led by well-meaning but uninformed women who had been inspired by newspaper reports or a stirring by-election speech. For Emmeline, the solution was not more democracy but tighter control. A pared-down, authoritarian leadership would ensure that the WSPU remained focused on its singular mission: securing votes for women.

On 10 September 1907, Emmeline convened a surprise meeting in which she announced the national WSPU meeting would be cancelled and the ad-hoc constitution that Teresa had drafted the year before would be scrapped. From now on, Emmeline would decide who sat on the committee, ensuring that no one who disagreed with her would have a say. Moreover, new members would have to sign a pledge: 'I endorse the objects and methods of the Women's Social and Political Union and hereby undertake not to support the candidate of any political party at parliamentary elections until women have the vote.'

The dissenters were unwilling to accept these terms. They proclaimed themselves to be the true WSPU and announced they would hold the national meeting as planned and allow a new committee to be formed. But Emmeline was not to be outdone. As Fred Pethick-Lawrence noted, she and Christabel 'were not prepared to run the risk of having their carefully thought out policy reversed by newcomers with little political experience, or whittled down by an executive of divided opinions'. Emmeline swiftly distributed cards with the pledge to members across the country, effectively solidifying support for her restructured WSPU. By the time the dissenters took the stage at the annual meeting, the majority of attendees had already aligned themselves with the newly reformed Union. Teresa, Charlotte and around seventy other members (though this number would grow rapidly) went ahead anyway and instigated a new group, calling themselves the Women's Freedom League (WFL). There may have been a more subtle reason to the use of the word 'freedom'. After all, the irony of Emmeline's behaviour was not lost on the women. As Teresa later wrote: 'By denying votes to her followers, Mrs Pankhurst has belittled the very function which it was her desire and intention to magnify above all other rights.'

And yet, to others in the Union, including the elderly suffragette stalwart, Elizabeth Wolstenholme Elmy, Emmeline had done nothing but defuse a desperate situation and, more than anything stopped the movement from becoming a tool of the Labour Party. Emmeline and Christabel had, at this stage, resigned quietly from the ILP. In separate letters to the Manchester Central Branch of the ILP, they thanked the branch for the support it had given the women's cause but noted as, Emmeline so succinctly put it, 'until women are men's political equals my first duty is to work independently of party for the political freedom of my sex'. Now, mother and daughter were ready to make the WSPU the non-party organisation that certainly Christabel had always imagined it.

The new committee that Emmeline had mentioned included Emmeline and Mabel Tuke as joint Honorary Secretaries, Christabel as Organising Secretary, Emmeline Pethick-Lawrence as Honorary Treasurer, and Mary Gawthorpe, Nellie Martel, Annie Kenney, Elizabeth Robins and Mary Neal as the Central Committee. Their names all went on the letterheads, but committee meetings were rare and it was, as always, the Pethick-Lawrences who controlled the finances and Emmeline and Christabel who defined the policy. Even still, there was no sense of 'cloak and dagger' to this; Emmeline was upfront about it all:

> The WSPU is not hampered by a complexity of rules. We have no constitution and by-laws; nothing to be amended or tinkered with or quarrelled over at an annual meeting. In fact, we have no annual meeting, no business sessions, no election of officers. The WSPU is simply a suffrage army in the field. It is purely a volunteer army, and no one is obliged to remain in it.[8]

Interestingly, Sylvia was not a member of the new committee and her name was not on the letterhead. She had been drawn in to this incident, but she would never, in the future, be consulted on matters of policy or asked for her input on the direction of the movement. Notably, she did not sign the pledge but neither did she abandon her mother and sister. She was a Pankhurst, after all, and she would fight the Pankhursts' fight for women's enfranchisement as long as it felt right. But it was clear now more than ever that Sylvia would never be considered part of the WSPU leadership.

After the turmoil in London, she was relieved to return to the north of England where she resumed her travels and her painting. Fred Pethick-Lawrence had stopped publishing the *Labour Record and Review*; an inevitable fallout of the LRC's disappointing decision in Belfast to withdraw support for women's suffrage. That October, he had launched a three-penny monthly publication, simply called *Votes for Women*, the first publication supporting the cause since the demise of Lydia Becker's *Women's Suffrage Journal* in 1890. Sylvia was invited to write a serialised history of the movement for the publication and so took with her books and bags of family papers that had been rescued from Emmeline's move from Manchester to London.

As winter moved in, she travelled to Glasgow where she stayed in a small flat with a middle-aged couple and their daughter, and visited the cotton mills that spewed their relentless black smoke across the Glaswegian skies. On weekends, she met up with her brother Harry, and together they strolled along the Clyde, munched buns in cafés, and talked about his growing interest in Buddhism. Though their mother still hoped to see some rugged working man's strength in Harry, he was, in truth, more of a thinker, and bore all the intellectual curiosity of his father.

While in Glasgow, a letter arrived from Hardie that sent Sylvia into a downward spiral. His words spoke of an inner struggle between his passions and his need to be more morally restrained, and she took it to mean he was ending their relationship. With Christmas approaching, she was summoned by her mother to a by-election in Devon, and a few days of festive merriment and relaxation with her, Christabel and Mary Gawthorpe. Though she went, she could not escape the misery of her thoughts, and on the day after Christmas, much to her mother's annoyance, left to be on her own in London.

During this time, Adela had remained away from London, enthusiastically campaigning in the controversial by-election campaign. She travelled tirelessly, moving wherever the cause called her. By October, she had joined forces with Annie Kenney, Nellie Martel, and Mary Gawthorpe, and together they were addressing hundreds of meetings, focusing their efforts on the Midlands, the western counties, and the northern heart of Britain. Their success was such that *The Daily Chronicle*, in a piece offering Liberals ironic 'advice' on how to lose an election, cited the suffragettes as a significant and undeniable force now challenging the Government's grip on power.

But as support for the WSPU grew, so did the hostility against them. Across the counties, gangs of young men frequently disrupted their gatherings, making it nearly impossible for the women to be heard. In Devon where Adela and the others had travelled to join Emmeline, the aggression took a darker turn. Emmeline and Nellie Martel found themselves chased down a darkened alleyway by a group of young clay cutters from the nearby pits, all staunch supporters of the Liberal cause. Nellie was beaten repeatedly in the head until a local shopkeeper's wife, hearing the commotion, roared from her doorway and sent the boys scattering. Emmeline, meanwhile, had been thrown violently to the ground, twisting her ankle, and found herself surrounded by a tightening circle of men. Believing she would be thrown into a nearby empty barrel, she cried out bravely, 'Are none of you *men*?' Only the arrival of policemen running to the scene, their whistles searing through the nighttime air, stopped whatever dreadful act seemed sure to follow.[9]

Indeed, though Emmeline and Nellie shook themselves off and attempted to put the unnerving incident behind them, it was not easy for members of the Women's Social and Political Union to brace themselves against these kinds of brutality as well as the threats and insults they regularly faced. For both suffragists and suffragettes, the fear of standing up and speaking out was immense; theirs was never a popular cause, regardless of where they stood on the crossroads between peaceful protest and militant action. Margaret Wynne Nevinson, who was involved with the NUWSS, the WSPU, and the Women's

Freedom League (WFL), recalled, 'At first I refused to speak at street corners and in the open; I could not overcome my Victorian prejudices; it seemed such a vulgar thing to do, and I shrank from the rudeness and violence, the rotten eggs and the garbage.'[10]

Similarly, disrupting Liberal meetings was not done without a hammering heart and a wave of fear rising through the body. As the WSPU's Organising Secretary, Christabel meticulously planned every protest, choreographing the heckling so that interruptions were staggered throughout the event. For the women waiting silently in the audience for their cue, it was a time of 'such agonising suspense that ejection came almost as a relief'.

After all, these were women – middle class, working class – whose voices had been silenced for generations. Many had been raised to live quietly behind closed doors, tending to husbands and children, their ambitions confined to the domestic sphere. Others had no choice but to work, pouring in the same sweat and effort as men, the only difference being that they often had babies and toddlers strapped to their backs, and the pay they took home after a day's gruelling work was half of what their male counterparts received. Yet their worth was continually undermined, as much by their own men and representatives as by a government that saw no reason to give them the vote and therefore the dignity of a voice. For these women to dare to assert themselves, to defy everything they had been taught by their families, communities, and society, was both an act of extraordinary boldness and one of deep and dreadful fear.

CHAPTER

10

THE BATTLE CRY

When Emmeline returned to London, still hobbling and in pain as a result of her sprained ankle, she was surprised to find Harry staying at Sylvia's lodgings. He had been forced to quit Glasgow after the builder he was apprenticed to went bankrupt, leaving him without work. Concerned about his situation, Emmeline enthusiastically acted on an idea from Christabel: Harry should enrol in shorthand classes at a London polytechnic and train to become a secretary. But this plan didn't last. When Emmeline learned that Harry was interested in the back-to-the-land movement following an ILP lecture he gave on the subject, she arranged for him to work at a smallholding in Essex. It was owned by Joseph Fels, a wealthy Jewish American who had arrived in Britain to pioneer farm colonies and who was also an enthusiastic supporter of the WSPU. Though Emmeline believed the fresh country air would do Harry some good, in truth the conditions at the farm were deplorable. It also meant that poor, fragile Harry was forced to carry out work he found so physically taxing. However, it did solve the problem of having to find him an occupation and – an immediate worry for Emmeline – a regular place to live too.

Emmeline herself had no permanent home in London. Since leaving Manchester, she had been effectively homeless, constantly on the move as she spoke at thousands of meetings up and down the country, leading Christabel's by-election campaign. Her life was packed into two small suitcases that travelled with her from place to place. She would book hotel rooms for overnight stays, rent rooms for longer periods, and often relied on the hospitality of friends and supporters. This nomadic existence was equal parts exhilaration and exhaustion. Once she was on stage, addressing crowds of hundreds or even thousands, she was at home; swaying the listeners, keeping them spellbound with her words. Her voice was 'like a stringed instrument in the hand of a great artist, [and] put us in possession of every movement of her spirit', described the committed suffragist and composer

Ethel Smyth. '…I never heard her make a mediocre speech,' Smyth added, 'let alone one that failed to hit the centre of the target.'

Yet this small, slim, still beautiful woman whom so many admired for her strength of determination often felt isolated. She had chosen this path, driven by the belief that she was destined to achieve something significant, and the call for women's suffrage had become her life's mission. But in her quieter moments, she questioned the joylessness of it all. She spent many evenings writing letters to other suffragettes across the country, offering them encouragement and reassurance that they were not alone. But who offered the same comfort to Emmeline?

In *The Suffragette Movement*, Sylvia writes that her mother

> often resented the position, and many times unburdened her mind to me with tears. Christabel, the apple of her eye, was aloof from her, absorbed in her work and friendship with the Pethick-Lawrences … The mother was lonely and jealous for the companionship of her daughter. She who hated solitude, was alone at the Inns of Court Hotel.[1]

However, after the upheaval within the WSPU, Emmeline now found herself less on the fringes of the day-to-day running of the Union. Many of the seasoned campaigners had left, and it was up to Emmeline and Christabel to steer the organisation, guiding the wave of new, eager recruits who had joined the cause. They were shaping the WSPU like a military force; over the next year, the language and spirit of the Union became unmistakably martial. Military terminology, symbols, and even a form of uniform, woven from the WSPU's iconic white, purple, and green, became an intrinsic part of its identity.

Historians have since enjoyed likening these changes to ideas of dictatorship and ruthlessness. But to understand the shift, it makes just as much sense to see the WSPU as adopting tactics that had long been used by the patriarchy to achieve its ends. Challenge, confrontation, combat – this was the strategy they had seen work for men. They were not borrowing it to intimidate WSPU members, but instead to disrupt the expectations of what women's activism could look like. As Emmeline herself wrote in her autobiography, 'We threw away all our conventional notions of what was "ladylike" and "good form", and we applied to our methods the one test question, "will it help?"'[2]

Still, Sylvia would later present the Union's changes through a different lens, writing:

> The spirit of the WSPU now became more and more that of a volunteer army at war. It was made a point of honour to give unquestioning assent to the decisions of the leaders, and to obey the command of the officials, paid or unpaid, whom they had seen fit to place over one.[3]

She was likely referencing a secret group that emerged within the WSPU at this time. Composed of young, unmarried women who embraced the most zealous 'New Woman' spirit of the age, they called themselves the Young Hot Bloods (YHB). In truth, the YHBs were devoted followers of Christabel, born in the shadow of the eldest Pankhurst daughter's perceived courage and charisma. Pledging to undertake 'danger duty' for the cause, they operated clandestinely until the early years of the Great War.

Among their ranks were Annie Kenney's sister, Jessie, Grace Roe, Elsie Howey, and Vera Wentworth (whose given name was Jessie Spink). Membership was strictly limited to single women, which led one newspaper to later describe them as 'a spinsters' secret sect', while the name of the group itself came about from an article in the *Leicester Daily Post* that stated: 'Mrs Pankhurst will, of course, be followed blindly by a number of the younger and more hot-blooded members of the union.'

Adela, who had not been in London when the events of the WSPU's split unfolded, had nonetheless supported her mother decision. Brushing off the fact she was not included in the WSPU committee, she was, instead, one of the leaders of the YHB. Whether she admired her older sister as reverently as some of the other Young Hot Bloods remains uncertain, but in all other aspects of the secret group, she was a fitting member – young, impassioned, and part of a generation that refused to be held back, confident that by looking resolutely forward, they could sever the ties to a past that no longer served them.

The YHBs injected into the WSPU the kind of youthful energy that Emmeline had, at the time of the organisation's founding, believed was necessary in the next steps towards achieving women's suffrage. A wave of more daring militant actions swept through the organisation. Though Emmeline and Christabel were happy to be known as autocrats, theirs was not a following of passive or mindless minions. Many women joined the WSPU because its ideals resonated powerfully with their own; they were not forced into actions they hadn't themselves envisioned. So attuned was the WSPU to the restless energy of the times that most of its members instinctively understood which actions would earn Christabel's approval and advance the movement's goals.

As Christabel wrote later in *Unshackled*:

> The WSPU was organised and led in much the same way as the Salvation Army under General Booth. Our organisers and members found our leadership perfectly compatible with their own freedom to develop their activities, and indeed they often astonished themselves and their friends by their ability and initiative. They knew 'where they were' and to whom they were accountable.[4]

For example, in early January 1908, Edith New and Ada Nield Chew staged one of the movement's first iconic actions: chaining themselves to the railings of the Prime Minister's residency, 10 Downing Street. Mary Garth and Flora Drummond had succeeded in darting into the building itself, making it as far as the doors of the council chamber. Their actions were a ruse, giving New and Nield Chew their chance to wrap their chains around the railings and snap shut the padlocks. As Garth and Drummond were ejected, they joined their comrades chanting 'Votes for women!' over and over, while a large crowd of onlookers gathered round them, cheering loudly as the police, with clumsy hands, took longer than expected to break the padlocks. When the women were finally free of their chains, all four were escorted to Cannon Row Police Station.

More and more women began to follow their actions, chaining themselves to railings and vowing not to budge until they were granted the right to vote. The actions greatly irked those in power but failed to stir much sympathy. At a Liberal dinner party, when someone brought up the spectacle of suffragettes chaining themselves to railings, Winston Churchill is said to have replied, 'I might as well chain myself to St Thomas's Hospital and say I would not move till I had had a baby.'

These daring escapades, along with other suffragette exploits, were reported in *Votes for Women*, the monthly publication created by the Pethick-Lawrences. In its inaugural issue, a lead article titled 'The Battle Cry' (likely penned by Christabel, though attributed only to a WSPU 'leader') called on women 'whatever your age, whatever your class', to break from male-dominated political parties and join the WSPU. The essay made the role of members' unmistakable: 'Those who come must come as soldiers ready to march onwards in battle array… We fight for nothing less than the emancipation of one-half of the whole human race.'

Votes for Women quickly became a vital asset for the WSPU, setting it apart from other suffrage organisations. It allowed members to stay connected with the movement, fostering a sense of unity and purpose regardless of their location. Initially a monthly journal priced at three pence, within six months it had become an affordable weekly selling at one penny, with a circulation of 5,000 copies. By 1909, that number had grown to nearly 30,000 and the magazine had become essential in both rallying women to the cause and spreading the message of emancipation far and wide.

With the new structure of the WSPU now in place, Emmeline and Christabel embarked on a speaking tour across Scotland. Their mission was to update members on the recent changes within the organisation as much as to attract new supporters to their cause. Over the winter of 1907–08, Christabel had orchestrated a staggering 3,000 meetings. Both mother and daughter took the stage at many of them, the mother captivating audiences with her self-possession and passion, the daughter charming all with her sharp wit and the power of her words. Their efforts, combined with further arrests and imprisonments for obstruction, provided the WSPU with exactly what it needed – publicity, new converts, and vital funds. By early 1908, the organisation had grown exponentially, with its annual income doubling to £6,000.

At this stage, Christabel had initiated a private correspondence with Arthur Balfour, the former Conservative Prime Minister. The WSPU's organising secretary believed the Tories to be much more open to the 'women's question' than both Labour and the Liberals. She asked Balfour whether, should he return to office, he would extend the parliamentary franchise to women. Highlighting her lack of faith in any backing from Labour, she wrote, 'A favourable declaration from you will be of far greater importance and will have the effect of preventing a Labour-Suffrage alliance.'

Yet Balfour, ever the cautious pragmatist, hesitated. He claimed he was unconvinced that there was strong support among women themselves for inclusion in the electorate, and as leader of the Conservative Party, he could not endorse suffrage without consulting his colleagues. Disappointed but undeterred, Christabel thanked him for his 'kind response' and resolved to keep the lines of communication open. With the WSPU no longer tied to the Labour Party, she was adamant that they would secure the vote through whatever political support they could muster.[5]

On 29 January 1908, King Edward VII opened Parliament and once again omitted any mention of women's suffrage in his speech. The WSPU immediately called for a Women's Parliament to run from 11 to 13 February. Soon after, it was announced that a Liberal MP who supported women's suffrage, Mr Stanger, had secured a place in the private members' ballot, with the second reading of a women's franchise bill scheduled for 28 February.

On the first day of the Women's Parliament, it was decided that a deputation to carry the resolution to the Prime Minister would be organised. Most of the women present immediately volunteered, and so it was that thousands of women marched from Caxton Hall to the House of Commons. As the procession moved across the city, other citizens – women, men and children alike – came out to line the pavements and see the remarkable suffragettes.

However, even before they reached the steps of the British Parliament, the police intervened, roughly pushing back the women, hauling them off the street, or pushing them to the ground and into the back of patrol wagons. The following day, fifty women found themselves before the prosecutor for the crown, Mr Muskett, at Westminster Police Court. Each was handed down the customary sentence of a maximum of two months behind bars or a fine of £5. But the prosecutor also delivered a chilling warning that if they ever offended again, he would revive the Tumultuous Petitions Act. This law, originating from the reign of Charles II, prohibited any group larger than ten persons from presenting a petition to the King or Parliament. The penalties for violating it included a fine of £100 or three months' imprisonment. It had been passed in 1661 under the Stuarts to obstruct the progress of the then newly founded Liberal Party, and the fact that that same party appeared open to resurrecting it to impede the suffragettes as they had been impeded sent shock waves through the gathered court.

The following morning, at the second day of the Women's Parliament, there was a palpable air of excitement. Christabel, presiding over the second session of the day, immediately announced that if the government wanted twelve women or even more to be tried and imprisoned under that Act, they could be found. At the Caxton Hall meeting the next day, Emmeline put the plan into action knowing that, since she was no longer a government employee, she could risk imprisonment. Standing before the gathered women, she declared her intention to carry a resolution to Parliament demanding immediate enfranchisement. Twelve women – Annie Kenney, Gladice Keevil, Minnie Baldock among them – immediately volunteered to join her.

Emmeline walked out at the head of her group. However, still hobbling from her ordeal in Devon, the pain she was experiencing was obvious with every step she took. Flora Drummond hailed down a passing dog-cart driver and asked if he'd be so kind as to take Mrs Pankhurst to the House of Commons. Without hesitation, the driver agreed. Emmeline was carefully lifted to the seat, while her supporters formed a determined line behind the cart. They hadn't gone far before a policeman halted them, insisting they proceed in single file if they wished to continue. Emmeline disembarked from the carriage, but was so weak, she needed to be supported by two of the women. Thus, in this procession, the small group walked to the Parliament Square, flanked by crowds of onlookers, some cheering, others merely watching, but all transfixed. As they approached the square, the crowds now moving enthusiastically around them, pushing them forth, two policemen moved in, seizing Emmeline by both arms, and loudly informing her she was under arrest. Emmeline held her head high and continued to clutch the rolled petition as she was marched off to Cannon Row Police Station along with the two women still supporting her.

The women were held at the station for some hours before Fred Pethick-Lawrence was able to organise their bail. Once released, they returned to Caxton Hall to the applause from the waiting women inside. Helped onto the stage, Emmeline looked out over the crowd, triumphant. 'We shall never rest or falter,' she cried out, her voice ringing through the hall, 'till the long weary struggle for enfranchisement is won.'

The next day, the courtroom was packed to fullness, though Christabel, Sylvia and the Pethick-Lawrences managed to squeeze inside and find seats. Poor Harry, who had returned from Essex upon hearing of his mother's arrest, was left outside. Inside, Emmeline and the other suffragettes who had been arrested that day were charged with 'riotous and vulgar behaviour, knocking off policemen's helmets, and assaulting officers'. They were given no chance to defend themselves and were sentenced to six weeks in prison. The Tumultuous

Petitions Act wasn't mentioned, and Emmeline and her companions were consigned to the harsh realities of Second Division.

This was Emmeline's first experience of prison. The horror and humiliation of it all would stay with her for the rest of her life. As with all the women who endured imprisonment, she was ordered to strip out of all her clothing, including undergarments, and given rough stained replacements to put on instead, with coarse brown woollen stockings and an itchy, shapeless prison dress, marked with broad arrows, to throw over them. For shoes, she had to rummage through a basket of worn, discarded pairs, and managed only to find two mismatched ones that fit her small feet. Once locked in her cell, the exhaustion from the day and the relentless pressure of the past few months finally caught up with her, and she fell asleep on the hard, narrow bed. But the sleep was brief. Soon, the sensation of being entombed in a dark, damp cell, the stench of thousands of women who had occupied it before her, and the hollow emptiness of the hours stretching out before her began to weigh down on her, making her feel sick and anxious. A small headache turned into a throbbing migraine, and she spent the night awake, wrestling with the pain.

Each of the imprisoned women was kept in solitary confinement, allowed only one hour out of every twenty-four to step outside and walk, in silence, around a bitterly cold yard. Emmeline's migraine persisted, and by the third day, weak from pain and sleeplessness, she was moved to the prison hospital. Yet even here there was no respite. Within hours, she was woken by the sounds of a woman in labour, moaning in the cell next to her. Emmeline listened the whole night, her heart breaking, as the woman screamed through her birthing pains. Later, she discovered that the mother had been incarcerated while waiting to be tried on a charge that turned out to be false.[6]

There were no activities to fill the long days, so Emmeline asked the wardens if she could sew some prison garments. They allowed it, though her fingers, stiff with cold, made her work slow. She also translated a French book, brought to her by the chaplain from the prison library, using a slate instead of pencil and paper.

While Emmeline remained in prison, Stanger's Women's Enfranchisement Bill passed its second reading on 28 February by a vote of 271 to 92, but was blocked from progressing further. That same day, Herbert Gladstone, the Home Secretary who claimed to support women's suffrage, made a statement that rang through the movement. He declared that reasoned argument alone would never be enough to secure the vote for women. It needed, as men's suffrage had done, to 'demonstrate the greatness of their movement'. He elaborated:

> Looking back at the great political crises in the 'thirties, the 'sixties and the 'eighties it will be found that people did not go about in small crowds, nor were they content with enthusiastic meetings in large halls; they assembled in their tens of thousands

> all over the country … Of course it cannot be expected that women can assemble in such masses, but power belongs to the masses, and through this power a Government can be influenced into more effective action than a Government will be likely to take under present conditions.[7]

If Gladstone had hoped to belittle the suffragettes' efforts or intimidate them into passivity, he had underestimated who he was dealing with. Christabel and the Pethick-Lawrences seized the opportunity they saw within his words to prove that women's suffrage did have the power to 'assemble in such masses'. Within days they began organising their most ambitious demonstration yet, selecting Hyde Park as their stage. Determined to outshine the park's previous demonstration record of 72,000 attendees, they set their sights on gathering a quarter of a million people for a summer event.

Emmeline was released one day early on 19 March 1908. Though exhausted, in need of rest and the comfort of a warm hotel room, she instead slipped into a WSPU meeting at the Albert Hall that same evening. The gathering was to celebrate the close of a successful Self-Denial Week, a period when women had endured every discomfort, standing in the cold and drizzle with collection boxes, or selling WSPU literature, flowers, and all other items that might raise a penny or more. They had given up butter, sugar, meat, and sweets, donating that money to the cause instead, and hosted drawing-room gatherings and tea parties, all to raise funds for the upcoming Hyde Park rally that summer.

As the women settled in their seats, soft murmurs and the shuffling of chairs filling the hall, Emmeline waited in the wings. The women had come to find out the total they had raised (which would turn out to be an incredible £7,000), and hushed when the hall lights dimmed and those on the stage brightened. As Emmeline walked onto the stage, there were gasps of surprise before a thunderous applause erupted.

'It was some time before I could see them for my tears, or speak to them for the emotion that shook me like a storm,' she would later recall.[8] When the cheers finally softened, Emmeline gathered herself and spoke.

'They said, "You will never rouse women". Well, we have done what they thought – and hoped – would be impossible. We women are roused!' she declared, her voice ringing with pride. And once more, the hall burst into a jubilant, roaring applause.

Over the next few months, the WSPU continued their by-election campaign and Emmeline's travels around the country began in earnest once more. She gave lectures in huge halls, private parlour rooms, and from the back of lorries. She spoke of the need for the vote as being less a radical demand and more a necessary step toward legal parity for women.

For Emmeline, Christabel, Adela, who continued her activism in Britain's north, and the countless many other suffragettes who stood on stages and soapboxes across the country, the vote was about far more than political representation, it was about reclaiming control over their own lives, dismantling a legal system that treated them as second-class citizens. 'There is no department of life that you can think of,' Emmeline told one packed room, 'in which the possession of the Parliamentary vote will not make things easier for women than they are today.'

As more and more Liberals lost their seats, the suffragettes celebrated what they saw as their direct role in this. According to Emmeline, the WSPU's efforts had managed to cut the Liberal vote by 6,663. In Peckham, where the organisation had campaigned vociferously, a Liberal majority of 2,339 had been overturned, turning into a Conservative majority of 2,494 – a result the WSPU proudly took credit for.[9]

In early April 1908, Henry Campbell-Bannerman finally resigned as Prime Minister. He had been 69 when he came into office and had suffered with ill health throughout his tenure. As expected, he was succeeded by his Chancellor of the Exchequer, Herbert Asquith, a figure already in the suffragists' sightlines for his unyielding opposition to women's right to vote. The country's new leader quickly attempted to undercut the WSPU's growing momentum during by-elections. He had been particularly irritated by how Christabel's by-election campaign had successfully ousted Winston Churchill from Manchester North West (though Churchill quickly recovered, gaining a new seat in Dundee, Scotland). Asquith thus announced that his government intended to introduce a reform bill that *might* include a women's suffrage amendment – if a member of the Commons chose to propose it. The WSPU, however, greeted his statement with scepticism. Already in the thick of planning their summer Hyde Park demonstration, they were far from swayed by the dangling of an indistinct carrot. They were determined to make it clear to both Asquith and Gladstone just how widespread support for women's suffrage had become.

Under the creative direction of Christabel and Mrs Pethick-Lawrence, no effort was spared in promoting this grand event, which was due to take place on 21 June 1908. Over £1,000 was spent on advertising, with massive billboards across London and the rest of the country showcasing images of the celebrated and respected women who would take to the twenty stages in Hyde Park to speak. Posters and handbills were printed and distributed weekly in the months leading up to the event. A 'small army of women' not to mention a few men, including Harry who was back in London for the summer and eager to help, chalked pavements, canvassed door-to-door, and strode through the busy city streets with sandwich boards announcing the date, location, and cause. Sylvia did her part too, training extra speakers so that there would be a speaker at all times on each one of the twenty platforms being planned. These new speakers would join the other stalwarts, including Christabel, Adela and of course, Emmeline.

In a bold stroke, the WSPU even managed to hire and decorate a boat to sail up the Thames to the Houses of Parliament, timing their approach for when

MPs were having tea on the terrace. As politicians and their guests gathered at the water's edge, Flora Drummond's powerful voice rang out across the river, inviting them all to the rally. 'You shall have police protection,' she assured them. 'And there will be no arrests, we promise you.' The Thames boat police were quickly dispatched, but by the time they arrived, the WSPU's boat had already sailed away.

Flora, now known affectionately as 'The General' due to her penchant for wearing an officer's cap and, later, for masterfully leading marches on horseback, was in charge of the procession to Hyde Park. Several new trains had been laid on for the day, bringing marchers from all corners of Britain. The General thus decided that there would be seven processions in total leaving from Trafalgar Square, Kensington High Street, Paddington and Marylebone Stations, Euston Road and the Albert Bridge. Each procession was to be led by a Chief Marshal, supported by a Group Marshal, a Banner Marshal, and a Group Captain. Emmeline Pethick-Lawrence had urged everyone attending to wear the WSPU colours of purple, white, and green, now easy to find as major department stores had already begun to stock the fashionable 'suffragette clothing'. In fact, as Lisa Tickner notes in her book, *The Spectacle of Women: Imagery of the Suffrage Campaign*, reports showed that over 10,000 scarves in suffragette colours were sold in the two days before the event.

When the day finally arrived, the sun broke through the clouds, shining down on Emmeline Pankhurst as she, accompanied by the venerable Elizabeth Wolstenholme Elmy, led the colourful processions of more than 40,000 demonstrators. Among them were famed suffragettes (including the three Pankhurst daughters), known suffragists, and men and women of all political parties, including socialist Viscountess Ethel Snowdon, Hanna Sheehy-Skeffington, founder of the Irish Women's Franchise League, and Keir Hardie, who had returned to London that April. Famed male literary figures marching alongside the women included H.G. Wells, George Bernard Shaw and Thomas Hardy. The stunning spectacle of these marchers glorious in their rich purple, green and white colours flowed towards London's largest royal park, dazzling the thousands that had come out to support or just get a look at the daring suffragettes.

'The Women Suffragists provided London yesterday with one of the most wonderful and astonishing sights that has ever been seen since the days of Boadicea … It is probable that so many people never before stood in one square mass anywhere in England,' said the *Daily Express*.

On the twenty platforms, dozens of suffragettes delivered impassioned speeches to the crowds that had gathered to listen. By the end of the day, a resolution calling on the government to introduce a women's suffrage bill was unanimously passed. The entire park then erupted into three resounding cries of, 'Votes for Women!'

The WSPU had hoped for a turnout of 250,000, but according to a report in *The Times* the next day, it was likely that over half a million people had come out to witness this historic event, though as the journalist wrote, 'it would be difficult to contradict anyone who asserted that it was trebled. Like the distance and numbers of the stars, the facts were beyond the threshold of perception'.

Emmeline herself was astounded. 'Never had I imagined that so many people could be gathered together to share in a political demonstration. It was as gay and beautiful as it was awe-inspiring.'[10]

The WSPU believed that they had more than met Gladstone's challenge of proving that if power belongs to the masses, then the women fighting for suffrage did indeed hold that power. Buoyed by hope, they delivered a resolution to the House of Commons. But Asquith would not budge. His formal response was a reiteration of his earlier pronouncement that if at some later date, an MP chose to propose a general reform bill that could be amended to include women's suffrage then, and only then, would such a possibility be considered.

The call of half a million British women and men had been ignored. For the WSPU, it was a critical crossroads. As Emmeline would later write, they had 'exhausted argument'. They had accomplished more than most male-led movements before them, yet the government remained unmoved.

'We either had to abandon our agitation altogether, as the suffragists of the eighties had done,' Emmeline declared, 'or we must continue to act, and go on acting until the government's selfishness and obstinacy were broken down – or until the government itself was overthrown.'

CHAPTER

11

BREAKING LAWS TO MAKE LAWS

Despite Prime Minister Asquith's indifference to the record-breaking crowd drawn by WSPU at Hyde Park, Emmeline, Christabel Pankhurst and the Pethick-Lawrences were determined to emphasise the undeniable public support behind their cause. They promptly called for a new demonstration in Parliament Square for the evening of 30 June. This assembly was a bold move, as gathering near Parliament was against government regulations. The Commissioner of Police quickly issued a warning to discourage public assembly, though he also noted that access to Parliament itself must remain open.

On the afternoon of the demonstration, WSPU members gathered at Caxton Hall. Emmeline, with a determined band of twelve women that included Mrs Pethick-Lawrence, marched toward Parliament, carrying a resolution on women's suffrage. Meanwhile, Christabel addressed the remaining audience in the hall, passionately asserting that sometimes one must be 'a law-breaker before one could be a law-maker'. She drew upon the words of the great Victorian radical, John Bright, who, in 1866, had urged men to crowd the streets from Westminster Bridge to Charing Cross to get Parliament's attention in their fight for enfranchisement. Now, she declared, women were following that same advice.

When the marching women reached the House of Commons, unsurprisingly they were informed that Asquith would not receive them. The women returned to Caxton Hall. But as dusk fell, small groups of suffragettes slipped back into Parliament Square, mingling with a growing crowd that was now heavily monitored by 2,000 foot and mounted police. As Christabel later observed, 'Parliament was guarded by police as against some dangerous and terrible enemy.'[1] Some women made it inside the House, only to be roughly seized and marched back out to the street. Others, prepared to be arrested, began to address the crowd on the need for women's votes. Sylvia recalled in *The Suffragette Movement* that:

> Women spoke from the steps of the Government buildings and offices in Broad Sanctuary, they lifted themselves above the people by the railings round the Abbey Gardens and Palace Yard or raised their voices standing among the crowds on road or pavement. They were torn by the harrying constables from their foothold and flung into the masses of people.

While many of the gathered crowd cheered on the suffragettes, others were less supportive. Groups of men taunted them, attempting on more than one occasion to drag some of the women down side streets. Yet, bruised and frightened, the suffragettes pressed on, bolstered by bystanders who tried to help them reach the House of Commons doors. Time and again, however, the women were forced back by the police. Several MPs including Winston Churchill, Herbert Gladstone and David Lloyd-George came out to watch the women's struggle, which lasted until midnight.

Two of the suffragettes present, Edith New and Mary Leigh, appalled by the violence that had been meted out to their suffragette sisters by those under orders from the powers that be, resolved to retaliate in kind. Hailing a taxi to 10 Downing Street, they hurled stones at Prime Minister Asquith's official residence, shattering two windowpanes. It was a move that would go down in history as the WSPU's first act of deliberate property damage. Of course, the women were promptly arrested and appeared in Westminster police court the next day alongside twenty-five others, all sentenced to two months in prison. New and Leigh, realising they had acted on impulse, sent a message to Emmeline while still in the cells of the police court. They assured the suffragette leader that the WSPU could publicly disown their deed if necessary.

However, Emmeline would do no such thing. Quickly making her way to the cells, she commended them instead, remarking that 'the smashing of windows is a time-honoured method of showing displeasure in a political situation'. Following the women's imprisonment, she would later remark on the double standard found even here: 'Window breaking, when Englishmen do it is regarded as an honest expression of political opinion. Window breaking, when Englishwomen do it, is treated as a crime.'[2]

As the judge passed sentence, the two women, no doubt bolstered by their leader's support, cheerily informed him they'd repeat such acts if needed. 'We have no other course but to rebel against oppression,' Mary Leigh declared. 'This fight is going on.'

And indeed it was. From this point onwards, the suffragettes' tactics became bolder and more defiant. NUWSS leader Millicent Fawcett would later reflect that this first instance of window-breaking marked the moment she withdrew her support for the WSPU's militant methods. Yet for many suffragettes, the shift toward more aggressive militancy came from a mounting frustration. As academic Kerry McInnery observed,

> The suffragettes had forcibly inserted themselves into masculinised political space through political techniques like marches, pageants, public speaking, and petitioning the king. Through these protests, the suffragettes resisted the gendering of space into masculine and feminine spheres of influence and the gendered division between the public and the private realms. They used their bodies to lay claim to public space, and, in doing so, rejected the exclusion of women from politics on the grounds of their gendered embodiment and the gender-based violence used to police the border between public and private.[3]

They had tried everything. Public demonstrations, imprisonment, sensational publicity – and still, the government refused to budge on the single demand: that, as half of the population, women should have a say in their own governance. What else, they wondered, was left to try? The next twelve months would answer that question.

July and August 1908 were months of unrelenting heat. Many of the suffragettes still wore the restrictive fashions of the day – corsets over bodices or chemisettes, heavy skirts cascading to the floor. These layers only added to their discomfort as they stood on the back of lorries, chained themselves to railings, tirelessly walked the streets distributing suffragette flyers and handbills, or snuck into Liberal meetings to heckle the speakers. And yet still they did it. At every opportunity, the suffragettes challenged cabinet ministers who arrived at city assembly halls, community centres, universities and schools, standing up to interrogate them on their position on women's suffrage or waiting outside to present them with a petition and a copy of *Votes for Women*.

Christabel, known for her own sharp wit on the stage, encouraged the women to use humour in their speeches and while haranguing cabinet ministers. This clever approach not only unsettled frustrated politicians and members of the public but, as Annie Kenney pointed out, could also transform a hostile audience into a sympathetic one.

At one Liberal meeting, for instance, when Winston Churchill, the chief speaker, asked, 'What have our Dominions done?' a suffragette chimed in from the crowd: 'Given votes to women, which you have not.' Her response sparked hearty laughter throughout the audience.[4]

On another occasion, an elderly man persistently interrupted a suffragette speaking to a large crowd, declaring, 'If you were my wife, I'd give you poison.' Undeterred, the speaker finally replied, 'Yes, and if I were your wife, I'd take it.'

At the WSPU headquarters in London, the heat was no match for the boundless energy of the movement's leaders, however. Emmeline, Christabel, and Mrs Pethick-Lawrence bustled about undeterred, keeping the wheels of the WSPU in constant motion. Every Monday, they hosted lively 'At Homes' at Clement's Inn, drawing packed rooms of enthusiastic supporters. Mrs Pethick-Lawrence kept track of the more well-to-do attendees, contacting them sooner rather than later for financial support, a request many were more than willing to meet.

Throughout the week, Emmeline travelled up and down the country, joining her fellow suffragettes in their fight on the by-election campaign trail. Energised by the success of the Hyde Park rally, Christabel set about organising similar demonstrations across the provinces. On 18 July, a crowd of over 50,000 in Nottingham turned out to hear Emmeline and other WSPU leaders speak. The following day, in Emmeline's hometown of Manchester, over 150,000 people enthusiastically applauded her, Christabel, Adela, Annie and Mary Gawthorpe as they took the stage. Later, on 26 July in Leeds, another vast gathering of over 100,000 braced the oppressive heat to hear the message of the suffragettes.[5]

As the cooler days of autumn finally rolled in, a further demonstration was planned for Trafalgar Square, London, on 13 October, with Emmeline, Christabel and Flora Drummond due to speak. In a smaller demonstration before that, a handbill had been handed around rallying the public with the words: 'Men and Women – Help the Suffragettes to Rush the House of Commons'. Unbeknownst to the Suffragettes, Lloyd George had been in the audience with his 6-year-old daughter and had taken the handbill back to the Cabinet. The word 'rush' had been suggested by Mabel Tuke in place of other commonly used words such as 'raid' or 'storm', but it was a word that instantly raised the government's hackles.

On the morning before 13 October, the three Trafalgar Square speakers received a summons to appear at Bow Street police station at 3.00pm. The charges were of 'Conduct likely to provoke a breach of the peace by inciting the public to a wrongful and illegal act' through their published handbill. Instead of appearing at Bow Street, however, the women chose to attend the WSPU's weekly gathering at Queen's Hall that evening. Word of the summons had spread quickly, and the packed hall buzzed with excitement. Emmeline addressed the crowd with calm defiance, saying, 'We are here, and we shall not go to Bow Street until they come and take us.' Christabel, meanwhile, had sent a note to Inspector Jarvis, letting him know they would not be available for arrest until 6.00pm the following day and inviting him to send police to the WSPU office, where the ladies would then be 'at their complete disposal'. This open defiance infuriated Jarvis and arrest warrants were issued immediately. However, despite an extensive search of WSPU headquarters, the trio was nowhere to be found.

In fact, the women had retired to a rooftop apartment at Clement's Inn, preparing for the possibility of a long prison stay. The following afternoon, refreshed and with preparations in hand, they made their way downstairs to the WSPU offices. At 6.00pm police officers duly arrived and read out the warrants for arrest amid the flashing cameras of the photo-journalists who had earlier been called by the publicity-savvy Christabel to the suffragettes' HQ.

Hauled off to Bow Street police station, the women were told they'd have to stay the night in holding cells, as the hour was too late to request bail. There's little doubt that the authorities intended to keep the women from attending the political 'rush' they'd organised that night. Seeing the cold, dirty cell with nothing but a narrow bench to sit or sleep on, Christabel later recalled their collective disgust that 'we or any persons charged but not found guilty of an offence should suffer the ordeal of a night in such conditions'.[6]

Luckily, relief came in the form of Sir James Murray, a Scottish Liberal MP and father of a young WSPU member, who had received an earlier telegram from Emmeline. Arriving at the prison, the formidable though friendly politician insisted that beds from the Savoy Hotel be brought to the cell along with a table of nourishing food. The police meekly followed the order.

Once the women's cell had been so elegantly furnished, the cheery politician gave the women 'hearty good wishes for the coming trial', so that, as Christabel claimed, 'With thankful hearts we fed and slept, and awoke refreshed and ready for all that might betide…'

The following day the three women appeared before the magistrate, Mr Curtis Bennett, in a courtroom packed to capacity. It had been decided that Christabel, who though legally trained as a lawyer was barred on condition of her sex from practising, would nonetheless represent the trio, making this her first legal case. Immediately, she requested a jury trial, hoping to present their case to ordinary citizens. The suffragettes had long suspected that judges were quietly influenced by the very authorities the women challenged. The request was swiftly denied. The magistrate set a date, 21 October, giving Christabel a week to gather evidence and call witnesses. In a masterful publicity stroke, she immediately subpoenaed two government heavyweights, Home Secretary Herbert Gladstone and Chancellor Lloyd George, both of whom had attended WSPU demonstrations earlier that month.

On the first day of the trial, the courtroom was once again packed to bursting. Sylvia was there with her art college friend Amy Browning, carefully taking notes so she could report the proceedings in *Votes for Women*. Any ill feelings she may have had towards her sister were absent from the finished article. In it, she portrayed Christabel with admiring detail, describing how her 'soft brown hair was uncovered, the little silky curls with just a hint of gold … [and] her rose-petal cheeks even more exquisitely flushed'. Yet it was not her charming appearance that won over the crowd, Sylvia insisted, it was her older sister's command in the courtroom. 'She triumphed not by her grace and freshness,' she wrote, 'but by the force and depth of her arguments.'[7]

Indeed, Christabel tackled her reluctant witnesses with remarkable poise. Lloyd George, one of the nation's most powerful men and speakers, found himself flushed when the young woman questioning him quoted back his own militant statements. As she pressed him further on the peacefulness of the suffragette demonstration he had attended on 13 October, he stumbled, offering evasive replies. Knowing that Lloyd George had brought his 6-year-old daughter along to observe that day, Christabel seized the opportunity. 'You thought it was safe enough for a child of such tender years to be in the crowd?' she asked pointedly. As a few chuckles rippled through the room, the flustered Chancellor of the Exchequer retorted sharply, 'I was not *among* the crowd.'

For a finish, Christabel drew powerful comparisons between the dignified tone of the women's protests and the harsh tactics police had employed against suffragettes at a recent public meeting in Swansea, under Lloyd George's direction. As her words landed, and a few aghast whispers ran through the room, the renowned debater sat tight-lipped and fuming, unable to find a response.

The ruddy-faced and visibly sweating Herbert Gladstone faced similar treatment, embarrassed by Christabel's reminders of his parliamentary speech urging women to 'take action'. She even quoted his father, the famed statesman William Ewart Gladstone, on the necessity of resistance in political struggle: 'I am sorry to say that if no instructions have even been addressed in political crises to the people of this country, except to remember to hate violence and love order and exercise patience, the liberties of this country would never have been attained.'

The court and press were mesmerised by Christabel's command on the courtroom floor. While Emmeline and Flora Drummond also questioned witnesses like Lloyd George and Gladstone, it was 'Portia in the Dock' – as some of the more poetic journalists had dubbed the eldest Pankhurst daughter – who drew the most attention. The well-known English essayist, parodist and caricaturist, Max Beerbohm, who like many other leading journalists of the day had secured his seat in the courtroom, described Christabel as 'A most accomplished comedian', with a 'charmingly melodious' voice.

He wrote: 'Her whole body is alive with her every meaning…' and in her interrogation of Lloyd George noted that 'the contrast between the buoyancy of the girl and the depression of the statesman was almost painful. Youth and an ideal on the one hand and on the other, middle age and no illusions left over!'

Interestingly, Amy Browning later confirmed to the press that the serene, collected Christabel had been enduring excruciating period pain throughout the trial. She and Sylvia had spent hours running back and forth to the chemist, searching desperately for anything to relieve Christabel's agony as she stood for hours, questioning witness after witness.

In addition, as the trial progressed, worries grew in both Christabel and Emmeline that if both were put behind bars for a long time, as seemed likely, who would lead the WSPU? It felt like too much of a burden to place solely on Emmeline Pethick-Lawrence's shoulders. Eventually, after much worried discussion, it was decided that Sylvia would step in to take Christabel's place with the charming American-born actress and playwright, Elizabeth Robins, to help her.

After three intense days, the trial was at an end and the defendants gave their summing-up speeches. Christabel spoke first, and her assertion that a jury would have acquitted them visibly infuriated the magistrate.

'[T]hey dare not see this case before a jury … they have removed this case to what we can only call a Star Chamber of the twentieth century,' she boldly declared.[8] The Star Chamber was the judicial arm of the King's Court established under the first Tudor King, Henry VII, to obtain justice where common-law courts failed. However, it quickly became beset by corruption, and though it had been abolished in 1641, in 1908 it still evoked the unchecked power wielded by the state.

Christabel further accused the Government of 'practically tearing up' the Magna Carta, England's cornerstone of individual liberty, declaring that women were being denied both their legal and constitutional rights. Taxation and representation, she argued, were inseparable under the law, and the suffragettes sought only to enforce this fundamental principle. Women had a constitutional right, she insisted, to bring their grievances directly to the House of Commons – a right they had peacefully exercised. Several newspapers reported that Christabel broke down in tears, either from the strain of the proceedings or from the realisation of the sheer injustice that women had endured in the courts over the years. Her sister Sylvia later wrote that it was the latter that had driven Christabel to weep with rage.

Flora Drummond, who was, in fact, in the first trimester of pregnancy, kept her summing-up short, which gave more time to Emmeline to address the judge and court. Where Christabel had delivered a fiery denunciation of government oppression, Emmeline took a different approach. She knew she had to temper her daughter's passionate but logical argument with something more personal and resonant. Rising to address the court, she appeared calm and composed, though she later admitted this serene exterior was but a cover for the acute inner turmoil she was truly feeling.

An experienced strategist, the suffragette leader acknowledged Curtis Bennett in a respectful, measured tone, addressing him as 'Sir' before offering a carefully crafted account of her life and values. She described her upbringing by a father who instilled in all his children – sons and daughters alike – a sense of duty to their country. 'I married a man whose wife I was, but also his comrade in all his public life,' she noted, reminding the court that her late husband had been a distinguished lawyer committed to justice and social progress. It was a commitment she shared, and so she had also done whatever was in her power to help her fellow countrywomen. In this capacity, she had served as a Poor Law Guardian and School Board member, both of which had exposed her to the harsh realities faced by many of her sex who found themselves 'in a deplorable position because of the state of the English law as it affects women'. It was here more than at any time, she revealed, that she recognised the urgent need to change the laws affecting women and children and to secure for women the rights of self-governing citizens. Emmeline explained how, as a widow, she had shouldered the responsibility of supporting her family, fulfilling roles traditionally reserved for men. For a decade, she had worked under the Registrar, ultimately resigning only when her commitment to women's rights forced her to choose between her career and the cause.

In presenting herself this way – as a wife, mother, and hardworking widow – Emmeline managed to root her passion for women's rights to values of feminine duty and honour that the courtroom, which many of those present, still imbued with the Victorian values of late, could respect.

'I have tried, with other women,' the poised suffragette leader explained, 'to get some reform of these laws.' They had petitioned, held vast public meetings, and exhausted every peaceful avenue, yet still, still the vote had been held from them.

> [I]f you decide against us today, to prison we must go, because we feel that we should be going back to the hopeless condition this movement was in three years ago if we consented to be bound over to keep the peace we have never broken.

In the hush that had fallen over the courtroom, Emmeline's voice held all present spellbound as she implored the magistrate with her final words.

> I want you, if you can, as a man, to realise what it means to women like us. We are driven to do this; we are determined to continue this agitation because we feel honour-bound. Just as it was the duty of your forefathers, it is our duty to make this world a better place for women than it is today.
>
> If you had the power to send us to prison, not for six months, but for six years, for 16 years, or for the whole of our lives, the Government must not think that they can stop this agitation. It will go on. … We are here not because we are law-breakers; we are here in our efforts to become law-makers.[9]

Emmeline's impassioned plea had left many in the courtroom visibly moved. Even Curtis Bennett, with his hands pressed over his face, seemed stirred – though not enough to acquit the women. Emmeline and Flora Drummond were given fines of £50 each or three-month sentences, while Christabel faced a £50 fine or ten weeks' imprisonment, all in the Second Division.

'We will go to prison,' Emmeline said calmly – and upon her words the packed court erupted into cheers.[10]

As they were led from the courtroom crowds surged around them, some jeering, some shouting support, while newspapermen hurried back to their offices to file what would become front-page stories. It was remarkable to think that just five years earlier, the WSPU had begun as a small gathering around a kitchen table in Emmeline's modest Manchester home. In those short years, the Pankhursts and their allies had transformed the movement, lifting it from obscurity and into the heart of public debate. However, as they stepped beyond the courthouse doors, the time had arrived when their mission would demand more than ever before.

CHAPTER

12

WE CANNOT ALWAYS CONTROL OUR WOMEN

In prison for the second time, Emmeline immediately insisted on a meeting with Holloway's Governor. When he arrived, she informed him that every suffragette, many of whom were coming and going through Holloway while the trio were incarcerated, would no longer accept being treated as common criminals. They would refuse to submit to searches or undress in the presence of wardresses. As prisoners in the second division, Emmeline and her fellow suffragettes were held under strict silence, confined to their cells. Emmeline insisted that, as a political prisoner, she must be allowed to speak with her fellow suffragettes during exercise or at any other permitted time.

The Governor, taken aback but cautious, agreed to waive the search and allowed that she and other suffragettes could change their clothing in the privacy of their cells. However, her request for the right to speak freely, he explained, would have to go to the Home Secretary. Undeterred, Emmeline immediately sent a formal petition to Herbert Gladstone. She requested to be treated as a political prisoner, with the right to read books and newspapers of her choosing, to work on her writings and needlework, to meet with her secretary and handle correspondence related to her public work, to converse with Christabel, Flora Drummond, and the other suffragettes in confinement, to wear her own clothing, and to arrange her own meals. But her appeal met with silence.

The Governor eventually returned, uncomfortably relaying that the Home Secretary had denied her request. Emmeline was undeterred. The next day, during the prisoners' single hour of silent exercise in the bleak, windswept yard, she strode over to Christabel and linked her arm with her daughter's, whispering to her as they walked. Immediately, the attending wardress ordered her to stop talking. Emmeline refused. Several more wardresses soon rushed over, grabbing Emmeline roughly and hauling her back to her cell. She later informed the Governor, unrepentant, that she would never stop trying to speak to her daughter. As a punishment, the 51-year-old Emmeline, now declared a 'dangerous criminal', was left in solitary confinement for a period of two weeks, and refused her daily walk or her daily visit to chapel.[1]

While her mother was harassing the system, Flora and Christabel were not faring well. Flora had collapsed and, given her fragile health and pregnancy, was released for hospital treatment. For Christabel, however, the fight seemed to have drained out of her. Out of the glare of the public spotlight and her busy daily routine, she was at a loss of purpose. Her health declined, and she spent long hours listlessly lying on the narrow plank bed in her cell. When Emmeline was finally released from solitary confinement and learned of her daughter's worsening condition, the news triggered an excruciating migraine of her own. Trapped within the cold, gloomy walls of Holloway, both mother and daughter battled with waves of illness and the seemingly endless lonely days so alien to them both.

Meanwhile, Sylvia was rising to the occasion, ensuring the WSPU remained active and visible. In December, when Lloyd George extended an olive branch by agreeing to address a Women's Liberal Federation (WLF) meeting at the Albert Hall, Sylvia saw an opportunity. She secured all the front-row seats for WSPU members, positioning them for maximum impact. The WLF pleaded with the WSPU not to disrupt the Chancellor's speech. But Sylvia made it clear that they would only remain silent if he confirmed that the government would support women's suffrage in the next parliamentary session.

Knowing that WSPU members would likely be violently ejected for heckling, Sylvia had them remove their coats beforehand so that any rough treatment would be more obvious. Once the women were thrown out, they were directed to immediately return to Clement's Inn, where Sylvia had arranged for photojournalists to capture their bruises, torn clothing, and visible injuries. The next day, newspapers published these photos under headlines like 'Nauseating Brutality' and 'Unnecessary Violence'.[2]

Flora Drummond, newly discharged from the hospital, wasted no time in sharing news of Emmeline's defiance and the rebellious acts of other suffragette prisoners, which had led many of them to solitary confinement. Inspired, a group of suffragettes quickly organised a march to Holloway. They gathered outside the prison walls, singing songs and shouting words of encouragement to lift the spirits of those inside. 'Faintly, the sound came to our ears,' Emmeline later recalled. 'It lightened our burden of pain and loneliness in ways we could hardly describe.'[3]

As the women's sentence continued, the strict rules began to loosen, however. Allowed back out to the yard for her one hour a day, Emmeline was finally given permission to walk and talk quietly with her daughter. To the other suffragettes imprisoned, she passed on encouragement when she could, especially to those enduring the shock and fear of being behind bars for the first time. 'Mrs Pankhurst was absolutely lovely to me in Holloway,' Kathleen Brown, a Newcastle suffragette imprisoned for throwing stones at Whitehall, wrote to Una Dugdale, 'whenever she could, she spoke to me – or pressed my hand'.

Christabel was due to be released on 22 December. Though Emmeline had been charged with an extra two weeks, orders came through that she too would be released. Along with Christabel and Mary Leigh, all three were actually given their freedom on Saturday 19 December. A grateful Lady Constance Lytton, who had joined the WSPU that autumn, immediately wrote to Gladstone thanking him for the group's delightful early Christmas gift. As news of the women's impending release reached Clement's Inn, joyful improvisations were immediately made to the welcome breakfast that had been arranged for Christabel on 22 December at the Inns of Court Hotel. Over 500 women crammed into the hotel hall that morning, greeting the released prisoners with rapturous applause.

Once the breakfast was finished, a large procession of about 200 WSPU members marched through the West End. The procession was led by Charlotte Marsh who carried a flag with the suffragette tricolours. Behind her Emmeline Pethick-Lawrence, Flora Drummond, and Annie and Jessie Kenney led the way in front of a band. After them, dozens of marching suffragettes were flanked by four suffragettes on horseback, while behind them a wagon, drawn by four white horses, and bearing a banner emblazoned with the words 'To Victory', carried a beaming Emmeline, Christabel and Mary Leigh, all waving to watching passersby.

As Christabel would later recall:

> One of the happiest days in the whole movement was this. Confidence, unity, and enthusiasm were complete. A great year had ended. The beloved WSPU had winged its way through storm and stress, further and higher towards its great aim. Each woman in our army of justice had done, had given, had been her best. All had known the pure delight of a self-regardless service and a self-transcending purpose.[4]

While events were unfolding in London, Adela, who had succeeded Helen Archdale as WSPU Organiser in Yorkshire, had remained outside the capital. She continued the relentless work of rallying support in the provinces, a task as gruelling as it was exhilarating. She would later claim that during these years, there was hardly a town or village in the UK she hadn't visited, standing on the back of lorries in the summer heat, on soapboxes in the winter rain, speaking in halls and on village greens. She faced hecklers, endured taunts, and batted back jeers as deftly as she put forth argument after argument for women's suffrage. Alongside countless young women recruited to the cause, Adela sold

WSPU literature on street corners, raised funds at meetings, liaised with press and police in each town, chalked meeting details on pavements, handed out flyers, and barely had time to sleep or eat before she and her comrades were on to the next town and the next meeting. But they were heady days, and it was women like Adela who kept the WSPU's pulse strong across the country. Despite her punishing schedule, she was one of the few who also managed to visit Emmeline in prison before her mother was confined to solitary; others, including Sylvia, Keir Hardie, and Annie Cobden Sanderson, had applied for visitation and been denied.

With the WSPU's leaders now out of prison, and young women like Adela daily joining up for the cause, the organisation had been instilled with a new sense of vigour. The year 1909 began with the usual lack of mention of votes for women in the King's Speech, which prompted a small WSPU deputation to march to 10 Downing Street on the day of the first meeting of the Cabinet Council. Refusing to leave until they had handed their resolution to the Prime Minister, the women were almost immediately arrested on the charge of obstruction. Among them was Emmeline's sister, Mary Clarke, who was sentenced to a month in the Second Division. Emmeline, away on a speaking tour in Leicester, Torquay, Plymouth, Brighton, and Eastbourne, visited her sister in February and was disturbed to find her visibly unwell. The next day, Mary was moved to the hospital wing, though she remained in solitary confinement.

Concerned, Emmeline wrote to C. P. Scott, the influential editor of the *Manchester Guardian* and Liberal Party member, hoping he might sway Gladstone to grant Mary certain allowances, like exercise with her fellow prisoners and access to newspapers.

Scott, who was sympathetic to the women prisoners, contacted Gladstone, only to be met with indifference: 'It is the old story,' Gladstone insisted. 'These ladies make a great fuss about going to prison, and as soon as they get there, they wish to be relieved of its main inconvenience.'[5] Though Scott's intervention led nowhere, Emmeline wrote to thank him, noting that while her sister's health was fragile, Mary was resilient – able to 'endure better than anyone I have ever known'.

The WSPU leader could do nothing but return to the by-election circuit, campaigning vigorously in Scotland. There, she was joined by WSPU members including Christabel, Flora Drummond, Adela, Mary Leigh, Nellie Crocker, Hertha Ayrton, Elsa Gye, Ada Flatman, and Gertrude Conolan. Adela, who had been sent to Aberdeen that winter to organise a six-month campaign, had been met at the station by Helen Fraser, who was alarmed to see her struggling to breathe. Fraser quickly arranged for Adela to see a doctor, who diagnosed her with pneumonia. Believing Emmeline had knowingly sent her daughter to Scotland in this condition, the doctor was quick to voice her disgust.[6] But Emmeline had been unaware of Adela's health issues and was as shocked as

Fraser to hear of them. Still, it did not deter Adela. She had said nothing of her illness, hoping not to worry her mother and within days, was back on the campaign trail.

A short time later in July, Adela was arrested in Edinburgh for attempting to break in to a meeting where Churchill was speaking. The following month, she and American suffragette Alice Paul were arrested together outside St Andrew's Hall in Glasgow. Alice, inspired by a lecture from Christabel Pankhurst at Birmingham University, had joined the WSPU, writing excitedly to her mother, 'I have become a suffragette!' The two activists had attempted to disrupt a speech by Lord Crewe by climbing onto the hall's roof, but were spotted by workmen at nearby Mitchell Library. Descending, they addressed a supportive crowd of thousands before being taken into custody. Released without a prison sentence, both women quickly resumed their activism.

In October, Adela faced charges in Dundee for disorderly conduct, along with fellow suffragette Laura Evans and two local male supporters, Owen Clarke and William Stewart Carr. From an attic on Overgate Street, they had hurled objects while shouting, 'Votes for women!' The police found various tools, including axes, hosepipes, and cooking utensils, suggesting the group had been camped there for days without permission. Adela admitted to throwing stones but claimed that stewards on the Kinnaird Hall roof had thrown them first, smashing the glass windows so that the shards flew into the small group's faces.

Adela's exploits are not so well documented as those of her mother and much-admired sister Christabel. She was, at this stage, one of thousands of fearless WSPU demonstrators who kept the militant spirit alive across the country. And though Scotland was a stronghold for the movement, being distant from London's power centre, the exploits of the women there often failed to reach the wider British press.

Sylvia, in the meantime, had resumed her discreet friendship with Keir Hardie. Over the preceding months, she had blossomed in her role as both an artist and an organiser for the WSPU. Her participation in the Hyde Park demonstration that summer had been thrilling for her – as much for the chance to work alongside her family in harmony and excitement as for the role she had as a speaker to thousands. As the WSPU's 'unofficial' artist, Sylvia designed and oversaw the mass production of banners and posters that appeared all over London, promoting the event and decorating the stages on the day itself. Her artistry also appeared on the WSPU's flyers, badges, postcards, tea towels, and other merchandise sold to raise funds for the movement.

In the spring of 1909, Sylvia was entrusted with organising the next major suffragette project, which was the Women's Exhibition to be held 13–26 May 1909 in the Prince's Skating Rink in Knightsbridge. The project was immense, and as planning got underway, Sylvia found herself with barely a moment to rest. To help, she recruited her friend Amy Browning and six other young artists from their student days. The men were paid the current decorating rates of 10d an hour, while the women were given 30 shillings a week.[7] Though these were modest wages for the work they were undertaking, the aim was to keep costs down, and the artists embraced their duties with enthusiasm. The results were astonishing. Huge paintings highlighting the work of suffragettes adorned the exhibition hall's walls. Images of angels, doves, and vibrant flowers, all layered with symbolic meaning, left visitors in awe. Above one door was a 13-foot-high figure of a woman sowing grain while mirroring her on the far end of the hall was a similar figure reaping the harvested corn. Alongside a variety of colourful stalls and entertainment from bands, singers and Edith Garrud, an expert in jiu-jitsu, the exhibition also included two replica prison cells. There were several talks to be held over the three days, with Emmeline chairing the opening ceremony at which Dr Elizabeth Garrett Anderson, the only woman mayor in England, having been elected mayor of her childhood hometown of Aldeburgh in 1908, gave the address. Years later, Sylvia would recall her involvement in the exhibition as one of her proudest endeavours as part of the movement.

In June of that year, the WSPU, having already been threatened the year previously with the Tumultuous Petitioning Act, decided to test whether the government would allow them their right of petition. This was an act which had been written into the Bill of Rights in 1691 and which allowed every citizen the right to petition the King, who had absolute authority at the time. Now that the power of the King had passed firmly into the hands of Parliament, the WSPU sought to see if that right would be respected by the Prime Minister. On 29 June, a delegation of women gathered to go to the House of Commons, where, at 8.00pm, they planned to petition the Prime Minister directly. Emmeline Pankhurst had sent Asquith a note informing him of their intentions. And while he had quickly declined the meeting, the women prepared nonetheless.

To avoid violating the Tumultuous Petitioning Act the group limited itself to eight members. Emmeline, the elderly Georgina Solomon – the widow of a former Prime Minister of Britain's Cape Colony – and Dorinda Neligan, an Irish suffragette and vice-president of the Association of Headmistresses in Britain, were among the delegates. When they arrived at the Strangers' Entrance, Chief Inspector Scantlebury met them with a note from Asquith's secretary, formally refusing to meet. Emmeline tossed the note to the ground, declaring, 'I stand upon my right, as a subject of the King, to petition the Prime Minister, and I am resolved to stand here until I am received.'

Of course, the police cared little for Emmeline's words, and when they attempted to move her, Emmeline lightly struck Scantlebury on the arm, the aim being, as both she and the Inspector knew, to be arrested. All eight women were swiftly taken into custody, but events continued to escalate.

More groups of suffragettes and supporters arrived at the House, insisting on their right to meet the Prime Minister. They were refused, again and again, both verbally and physically, and by the end of the night, 108 women and fourteen men had been arrested.

However, alongside these gatherings, a smaller group of women appeared outside the Home Office, Treasury and Privy Council buildings. Wrapping stones in brown paper, so as to avoid causing harm to anyone inside, they hurled them at the windows, shattering the glass. In all, fourteen of these women were also arrested.

The WSPU later asserted the action was unsanctioned, with Emmeline stating, 'We cannot always control our women.' Mrs Bouvier, one of the stone-throwers, claimed the idea had come from miners in Staffordshire who had recently thrown stones to demonstrate their displeasure, and men in the recent Winchester riots who had similarly hurled stones without punishment, leading instead to the redress of their grievances. Even Sylvia stepped in to support the stone throwers, condemning the ever-increasing police violence by writing in *Votes for Women*, 'Since we must go to prison to obtain the vote, let it be the windows of the Government, not the bodies of women which shall be broken.' Christabel would also later defend the action as 'essentially right, appropriate, and fitting'.

Yet, as the trial of the fourteen window-breakers and over a hundred other suffragettes unfolded, another dramatic step was taken by an individual suffragette. A few days earlier, Marion Dunlop, a Scottish artist and children's book illustrator, as well as a confirmed suffragette, had been arrested for stamping an extract of the Bill of Rights on the wall of St Stephen's Hall in the House of Commons. Sentenced to a month in the Second Division, she immediately requested political prisoner status. Her request was denied. On 5 July, acting entirely on her own initiative, Dunlop began a hunger strike to demand political offender status. She held firm for ninety-one hours before her release and thus became the first WSPU member to adopt such a drastic measure. She would not be the last.

The fourteen women convicted of stone-throwing on 12 July were inspired by Dunlop's courage. When their request to the Home Secretary to be transferred to the First Division was rejected, they refused to wear prison clothes or clean their cells. In the oppressive summer heat, they broke the glass of their cell windows, letting in some much-needed air. Their defiance was met with swift retaliation as they were quickly rounded up and marched into dark, isolated punishment cells. Undeterred, they too launched a hunger strike. Once again, the authorities, faced with women determined to hold firm to their demands and prepared to risk their health in the process, decided to release them.

Although Emmeline and Christabel had not initially encouraged Marion Dunlop or other suffragettes to adopt hunger strikes, they were hopeful that such a tactic would lead swiftly to the release of the fasting prisoner. Fred Pethick-Lawrence and the legal team had assured them that this would be the likely step taken, adding that force-feeding would be unlawful. Yet they were

Emmeline Pankhurst. (Source: Library of Congress, Washington, DC)

Christabel Pankhurst (c.1905–1 910). (Source: London School of Economics (LSE) Library)

Sylvia Pankhurst working on a painting (c.1900–1906). (Soure: London School of Economics (LSE) Library)

(L-R) Annie Kenney and Christabel Pankhurst (c.1908). (Source: Wikipedia)

Right: A portrait photo of Adela Pankhurst taken by Col Linley Blathwayt at Eagle House in Batheaston (1910). Adela wears the WSPU brooch given to those who have been to prison for the cause.

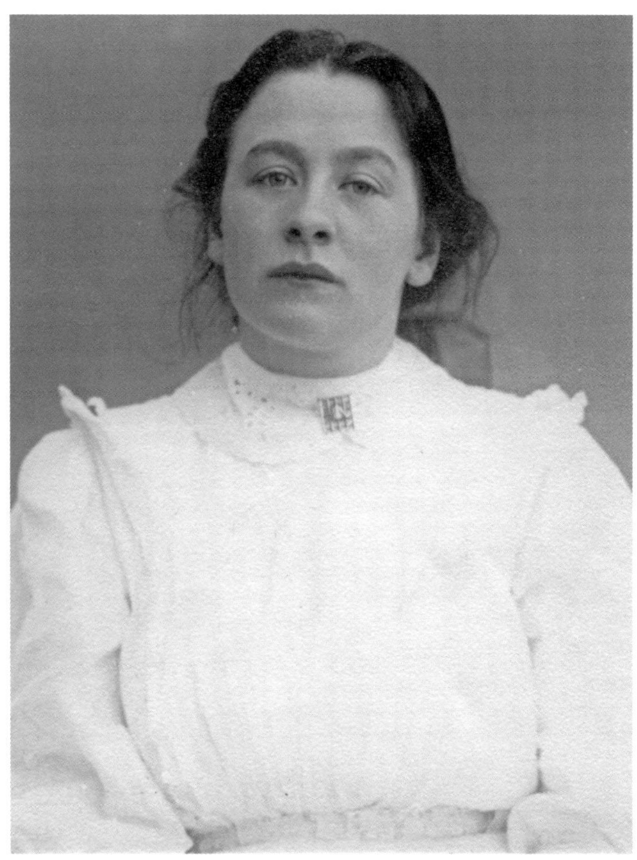

Below: Leaders of the Women's Social and Political Union (WSPU) work around a kitchen table (c.1907–1907). (L-R): Flora Drummons, Christabel Pankhurst, Annie Kenney, unknown woman, Emmeline Pankhurst, Charlotte Despard and unknown woman. (Source: London School of Economics (LSE) Library)

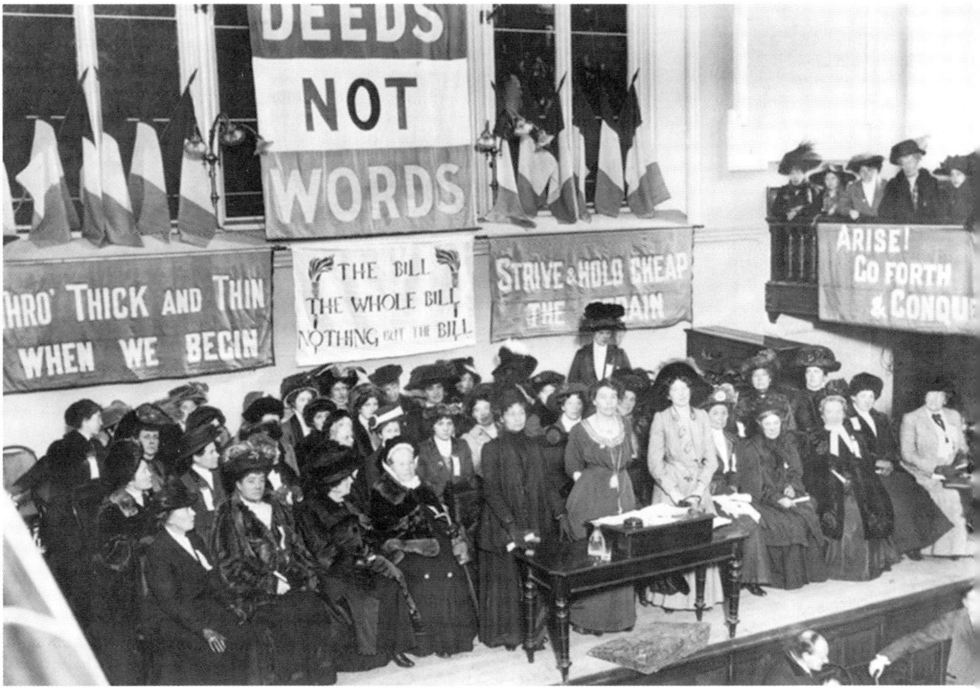

A suffragette meeting in Caxton Hall, Manchester, England (1908). Standing in the centre (L-R): Emmeline Pankhurst, Emmeline Pethick Lawrence and Christobel Pankhurst. (Source: *The New York Times* photo archive)

A suffragette chained to a railing. (Source: London School of Economics (LSE) Library)

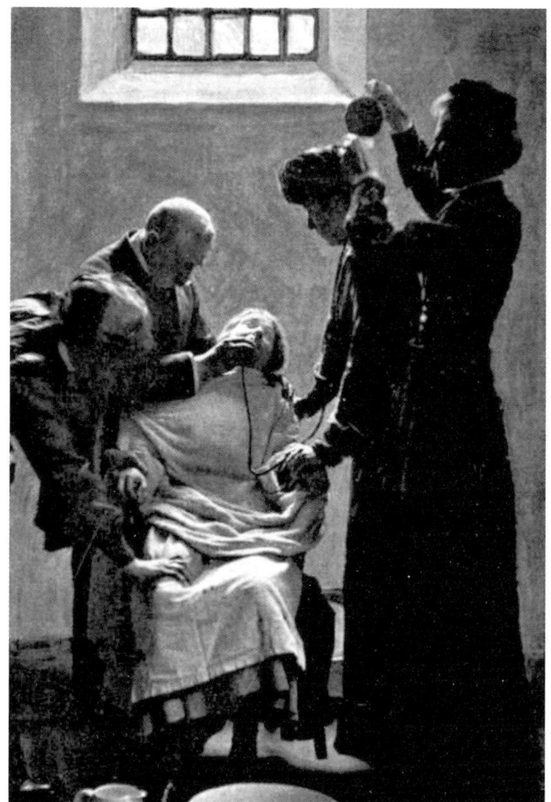

Force-feeding: A suffragette on hunger strike being forcibly fed with a nasal tube. (Source: Wikipedia)

Emmeline Pankhurst is arrested by police outside Buckingham Palace while trying to present a petition to George V in May 1914, from the collections of the Imperial War Museum.

Hunger-striking Sylvia Pankhurst being carried on a stretecher by supporters in Old Ford Street, Bow, London in June 1914. (Heritage Image Partnership Ltd./ Alamy Stock Photo)

Emmeline Pankhurst addresses a crowd in New York City in 1913. (Hulton Archive—Getty Images)

soon to discover that the authorities were more than willing to stretch the law to suit their purposes.

In response to the WSPU's escalating activism, attempts were made to restrict or outright ban women from attending Liberal public meetings. For many of the suffragettes, this only encouraged them to come up with even more creative ways to disturb the Liberal speakers, jumping out of bushes as the men made their way into halls, shouting through windows and even lowering themselves through skylights to interrupt with cries of, 'Votes for women!'

But as heckling grew more difficult, breaking windows with bricks and stones became more widespread. On 20 August, as Prime Minister Asquith spoke at the Sun Hall in Liverpool, a series of stones shattered the glass of the windows, and the voices of women chanting for votes and demanding political status for suffragette prisoners could be heard outside.

Less than a month later, the protests escalated when Mary Leigh and Charlotte Marsh led a daring attack as Asquith arrived at Birmingham's Bingley Hall. Climbing onto a nearby rooftop, they dislodged slate tiles and hurled them onto the Prime Minister's car – carefully avoiding Asquith and his driver but smashing the car's windows and headlamp.

Hoses were turned on the women in an attempt to force them down, and they were eventually led away, wet, bruised, and barefoot, their shoes having been lost in the struggle. Leigh and Marsh were sentenced to hard labour – three months and two months, respectively, in Winson Green Gaol – while the other women involved received shorter sentences.

Though the WSPU leadership had not sanctioned such direct property damage, Emmeline, Christabel, and Emmeline Pethick Lawrence found themselves having to endorse it. Pethick Lawrence wrote a piece in *Votes for Women* condemning the government's ban on women at public meetings, and Christabel followed with a letter to *The Times*. Responding to those who publicly condemned the act as a tactic of the WSPU, Emmeline declared, 'The women in this movement are here not at my behest, but because they feel a burning desire to promote the cause of votes for women.'

But worse was yet to come. At Winson Green Gaol, Leigh, Marsh, and the others went on hunger strike, refusing food until they were granted political prisoner status. This time, however, they were not released. Instead, the authorities began to use forcible feeding. This practice involved inserting a rubber tube up the nose or, after a steel gag had been used to force a mouth open, down the throat. Milk, eggs, or watery gruel were poured directly into the stomach, and women had to be physically restrained during the process. Mary Leigh, who had been force fed through the nose later reported how, when, the tube was withdrawn, 'It felt like the back of my nose and throat were being torn out with it.'[8]

The WSPU leadership reacted with disbelief and outrage, denouncing the government for what they saw as the ultimate violation of passive resistance.

The WSPU leadership was not alone in its horror – many observers, including sympathetic politicians, were appalled, though it seemed their shock did not translate into government action.

At the first opportunity, Keir Hardie demanded answers in the House of Commons regarding the forcible feeding of the Winson Green prisoners. Speaking for the Home Secretary, Mr Masterman dismissed concerns, calling the brutal practice 'ordinary hospital treatment' for prisoners who refused food – a response that elicited supportive laughter from some members.[9] Yet, while Parliament responded with indifference, the public response was furious. Letters of protest flooded the press, with journalists like Henry W. Nevinson and H. N. Brailsford, long-standing supporters of the suffragettes and founders in 1907 of the Men's League for Women's Suffrage, resigning from the *Daily News* in outrage. 'We cannot denounce torture in Russia and support it in England,' they insisted. Meanwhile, a petition signed by over 116 prominent British doctors was sent to the Prime Minister, urging him to end the abusive practice.

As the government refused to act, the WSPU took legal action, initiating a case against the Home Secretary and Winson Green prison officials, alleging assault against Mary Leigh, one of the first militants to be force-fed. Should the case succeed, they were prepared to file on behalf of all suffragette prisoners. However, when the case finally reached court two months later, it was dismissed. The ruling upheld the forcible feeding as necessary to 'preserve her life' and insisted that only minimal force had been used.

The dismissal of the case confirmed that the government was not simply turning a blind eye – it was willing to endorse any measures it saw fit to suppress the suffragette movement, no matter how brutal or inhumane. As for the suffragettes, what had begun with Marion Dunlop's solitary act had ignited a powerful and – to them – unavoidable new tactic. The hunger strike would soon become one of the most compelling symbols of suffragettes' militancy.

CHAPTER

13

AMERICA, A TRUCE AND TWO TERRIBLE DEATHS

As public tensions flared between the government and the suffragettes, Emmeline was also dealing with private turmoil. Harry, who had returned to his job at Joseph Fels's farm in Essex, had developed a serious inflammation of the bladder. He was brought to a nursing home run by two WSPU supporters, Catherine Pine and Gertrude Townend, at 3 Pembridge Gardens in London. Initially, Emmeline was distressed when told that Harry needed an examination under anaesthetic. However, her fears eased somewhat when the procedure showed signs of relieving his symptoms, and she decided that, once he was well enough, he should return to the Essex farm. To help him regain his strength, he, she, and Christabel would spend a weekend at Margate under the kind invitation of Emmeline Pethick-Lawrence.

Emmeline hoped that the sea air would do her son some good, but her concerns about Harry's health did not subside. In particular, she worried how she would pay for his ongoing hospital bills. She was, after all, a widow whose income from the WSPU was modest and barely covered essentials, let alone costly hospital fees. As such, when Harry returned to his work on the farm commune, Emmeline, who also returned to her work campaigning in Sheffield, decided to write to an old American friend from her Women's Franchise League days. Harriot Stanton Blatch, the daughter of US suffragist Elizabeth Cady Stanton, had hinted before at the possibility of a US lecture tour for Emmeline and the WSPU leader wanted to explore whether this was still feasible. It was. Blatch helped connect her to lecture organisers, and a tour was soon arranged for the following autumn.

Emmeline was set to leave from Liverpool on 13 October aboard the *Oceanic*, accompanied by Mrs Pethick-Lawrence's sister, Dorothy Pethick. But days before her departure, she received alarming news that Harry had been struck down with inflammation of the spinal cord. Paralysed from the waist down, he had been transferred once again to Nurse Pine's nursing home under the care of Dr Mills. The illness was poliomyelitis, today more simply known as polio. In the early twentieth century little was known about the disease and it would be another fifty-five years before a vaccine for the deadly virus would be readily available.

Emmeline rushed back to London to be by her boy's bedside. Sylvia, who had been spending time painting in Cinder Hill, Kent, had also received a telegram informing her of her brother's illness and was at the nursing home by the time Emmeline arrived. Seeing her youngest child bedridden and in such pain was devastating to Emmeline and no doubt brought back memories of the unbearable pain she had felt years earlier when her beloved 'Little Frank' had died. Now, however, Emmeline faced a harrowing choice: should she stay by Harry's bedside, or travel to America to secure the funds for his treatment? As a single mother with limited resources, this high-paying tour seemed essential, and so she decided to go. Years later, Sylvia would criticise her mother's decision, writing bitterly, 'So ruthless was the inner call to action… there was never a moment of doubt as to where she should be substituted – on the platform or by the bedside of her son. The movement was paramount.'[1]

However, in her 1935 biography of Emmeline, Sylvia offered a softer perspective, writing that her mother 'steeled herself to persevere with her journey, declaring that he would recover as before. Her mission must come before personal considerations; moreover, the fees to be earned by her lectures would be of utmost value in providing for the boy's need.'[2] Sylvia never wavered from her belief that, at this stage, the movement was Emmeline's priority, and thus coloured all decisions. Yet she allowed for the fact that Emmeline had to find the cost of Harry's medical care somehow.

Thus Emmeline set off for America, entrusting Harry's care to her sister Mary and her daughters. But Mary, already a WSPU organiser in Brighton, and Christabel, as the WSPU's Organising Secretary, could only manage from afar. Adela, meanwhile, was campaigning in Scotland and was not told by Sylvia or anyone else just how critical her brother's health was. This left Sylvia to shoulder the weight of Harry's care alone.

Sylvia kept Emmeline updated on Harry's condition, and for a brief time, there was hope. Harry managed to wiggle his toes and could even raise himself slightly using a pulley. Yet he often asked Sylvia when he would walk again – a question the 28-year-old dreaded, knowing in her heart that he likely never would.

In the meantime, Emmeline's six-week tour of America was a triumph. She spoke to packed halls across New York, New England, Maryland, the Midwest and Toronto in Canada, winning over audiences who had expected a much more strident figure. While the press had initially been poised to criticise her, they found themselves charmed by the graceful presence of this still beautiful woman.

The *New York Times* noted her 'small, gentle-looking' appearance and observed that, 'wearing a grey checked travelling wrap and a grey fur hat encircled with a mauve veil, she looked younger than her photos … more like a warm, home-keeping mother than a political leader'. Emmeline's speeches tended to fold personal reflections through her political mission. She often spoke of her family, mentioning her beloved Harry and her worries for his health. This unexpected softness, so unlike the shrill antagonist many had imagined, quickly endeared her to the American public. She was motherly, feminine, and deeply moving, and at many times brought her audience, men and women alike, to tears with her descriptions of what British women were prepared to go through to gain their simple right to vote.

She was also a masterful orator, blending humility with a quiet boldness. At Carnegie Hall, she surveyed the packed room and introduced herself with a wry smile: 'I am what you call a hooligan.' Instantly, the hall erupted in hearty, supportive laughter. The *New York Evening Sun*'s Arthur Ruhl noted how this poised leader of Britain's suffragettes then proceeded to speak for two hours without notes, without repetition, radiating confidence and holding her audience rapt. F. L. Bullard, meanwhile, marvelled at how such a cultured, graceful woman could be the very 'hooligan' she so wittily claimed to be.

By the time Emmeline boarded the ship back to Britain on 2 December 1909, she had made the cause of Britain's suffragettes known across American soil and had drawn a new wave of international support for the movement.

Her trip home was not without worries, however. Her 'right of petition' case was being heard in London at the same time she sailed across the ocean. As such, it was likely another prison sentence awaited her once she was back in her home country. However, as it transpired, some unknown friend paid her fine of £5 in her absence,[3] allowing a grateful Emmeline to go directly to her son Harry's bedside rather than back to Holloway Prison. This reprieve was especially welcome as Harry's health had severely declined, and his mother was told definitively that he would never walk again. Concerned for Emmeline's own wellbeing, Christabel had urged Dr Mills to break the news gently, but little could ease Emmeline's distress. Determined to see her son improve, she decided Sylvia would care for him, putting aside her artistic ambitions for as long as necessary to become his nurse.

Without delay, Emmeline returned to her WSPU duties. The very next day, on 9 December 1909, she spoke at an 'At Home' event at Albert Hall, held partly in honour of Charlotte Marsh. Marsh had just been released from Winson Green Gaol after enduring 139 force-feedings over her three-month sentence, and in front of a rapturous crowd was awarded the WSPU Hunger Strike Medal. Designed by Sylvia, this medal was a silver bar hanging on a length of ribbon in the suffragettes' purple, white and green colours and engraved with 'For Valour' in imitation of the Victoria Cross. It was an addition to the single silver bar that many WSPU prisoners also received in recognition of their 'gallant action'.

As the Pankhurst family waited for Harry's health to improve, Emmeline received a generous offer of a home from suffragette friends bound for India. Grateful for this kindness, Emmeline immediately began organising her son's move. However, it was not to be. Harry was unable to leave the nursing home as the familiar bladder illness had returned. Dr Mills, increasingly concerned, consulted other specialists who confirmed the worst: Harry had mere weeks left to live. Emmeline was stunned and, grappling with the news, could not bring herself to break it to her son. Wretched and subdued, 'she hovered about his bedside, the savour of life, the thrill of the movement, dull as spent ashes'.[4] On the few rare occasions she had to, Emmeline gathered herself to attend or speak at WSPU events.

Sylvia, in Emmeline's absence, had learned from her brother of a young woman he'd fallen in love with, a fellow suffragette named Helen Craggs. They had met in 1908 when Harry was helping Christabel campaign against Winston Churchill in Manchester. He spoke of Helen often, even in the delirium of his drugs, longing to see her once more. Moved, Sylvia reached out to Helen, who agreed to come to the nursing home.

Ever reserved, Sylvia never questioned Helen's true feelings, but she implored the 21-year-old to pretend if necessary and return Harry's affections so as to give him comfort in those final days. However, as Sylvia watched Helen tend to Harry with gentleness, she came to believe the younger woman's feelings were sincere. Years later, Helen would confirm this, confiding to Grace Roe that Harry had been her first love.

However, an angry Emmeline felt Sylvia's actions, taken without consulting her first, robbed her of what precious time she had left with her young son. Yet even while her mother railed against her, Sylvia stood by her choice, happy to see the comfort Helen's presence gave Harry. With Christmas approaching, she listened as Helen created the dream of a future for her rapidly dying younger brother. She held his hand, mopped his brow, and spoke of trips they would take together to a wintery Venice for his recovery. She spent the yuletide season at the nursing home along with the Pankhursts, even as tensions thickened between Emmeline, Sylvia, and Adela, who had arrived late, furious that she hadn't been told of Harry's condition sooner.

Eventually, on 5 January, Harry slipped into unconsciousness and died. Emmeline was distraught. 'Broken as I have never seen her,' Sylvia described. Emmeline's brother Herbert stepped in, covering the cost of the funeral on 8 January. Harry was laid to rest beside his younger brother in Highgate Cemetery. Seeing the coffin being lowered into the ground, a grief-stricken Emmeline told Sylvia, 'Remember, when my time comes, I want to be put with my two boys.'[5]

Each Pankhurst daughter carried her own grief privately. Christabel, crushed, could barely speak of it. In her book *Unshackled* she only briefly mentions their last days together: 'He was no better. We had Christmas together. He had grown so like his father, in his support of the women's cause, in his way with his mother and sisters, and in his attitude towards all women. In the New Year, he left us.'[6]

Sylvia, having spent the longest time with Harry in his final days, may have been the most prepared for his death – or perhaps not. After all, this was the second time when she had been left to stand helplessly by as a beloved family member passed away before her eyes. However, she mustered the strength to pen Harry's obituary for her mother in *Votes for Women*: 'Harry Pankhurst was courageous in action, unselfishly devoted to the public good, a fighter in the cause of women. Happy, even in her grief, must be the mother who had borne such a son.'[7]

For Adela, Harry was really the only sibling with whom she had had a close connection. He had been her childhood companion, her confidant, her ally in the early days of the suffrage struggle. She never forgave Sylvia for not revealing to her sooner the extent of her brother's illness.

The evening of Harry's funeral, Emmeline caught a train from London to Manchester where she was due to address a meeting. Over 5,000 people had turned out for it, including a strong force of Liberals who had planned to disrupt the meeting just as Emmeline's soldiers in the suffrage field had so often disturbed theirs. Yet, upon hearing that Emmeline had just buried her 21-year-old son, the hall fell silent, every eye fixed on her. Against the weight of her loss, she rose to speak, her voice filling the room with its calm intensity. 'Surely every mother here knows that I would rather be quiet tonight, by my own fireside with my sad thoughts. But it is only a sense of my great responsibility and duty in this campaign that has urged me to appear,' she said.[8]

After that, Emmeline threw herself wholly into her work. Christabel did likewise, and the Liberals felt the brunt of their commitment. Parliament had been dissolved on 15 December, with a general election set for the following January. Confident of victory, Prime Minister Asquith expected the Liberals would retain power, and indeed they did, but only narrowly. The Liberals secured 275 seats – only two more than the Conservatives' 273. With the backing of 82 Irish Nationalists and 40 Labour members, including Keir Hardie and, for the first time, George Lansbury, they managed to hold their slim grip on power. Of course, nothing could prove that the Liberals had not been able to gain a larger majority as a result of the suffragettes, and in many regards, the WSPU and its Organising Secretary now faced a conundrum: for the organisation to continue to appear to have influence over any election results, tactics would need to continue escalating. However, this would mean more women facing prison, hunger strikes, and the harsh brutality of force-feeding.

Just before Christmas, Lancaster suffragette, Selina Martin, and Leslie Hall had harangued the Prime Minister on the subject of votes for women just as he was leaving his motor car. When he ignored them, Martin hurled an empty ginger beer bottle into his empty car. Both women were swiftly arrested and charged with disorderly conduct, leading to their imprisonment in Walton Gaol, Liverpool. In protest, the two suffragettes went on hunger strike, with Selina barricading herself inside her cell. However, prison officials forced their way in, dragged Selina from her bed, threw her to the ground, and handcuffed her. After a night spent in a 'punishment cell', she was carried face-down to the doctor's room, where she was subjected to the degrading ordeal of force-feeding. This brutal treatment continued for weeks; Selina and Leslie spent the next two months in solitary confinement, bound in straitjackets and regularly force-fed, until their release on 3 February.[9]

When details of their ordeal were leaked by fellow women prisoners, public outcry was swift. Home Secretary Gladstone attempted damage control with a letter to *The Times* denying the allegations, but the news had already stirred national anger. Alongside the general disgust at the practice, was a bubbling fury among many that it appeared that mainly working-class women were treated so badly. In contrast, Lady Constance Lytton, a highborn activist arrested in October 1909, was released instead of being force-fed after beginning a hunger strike. Deeply embarrassed by this preferential treatment, Lady Constance, now hearing about Selina Martin's treatment, decided to disguise herself as a working-class seamstress named 'Jane Wharton' to see if she would then experience the same treatment as her fellow activists.

In January 1910, she was arrested after throwing rocks at an MP's car. She was imprisoned in Walton gaol for fourteen days 'hard labour'. This time, she endured eight force-feedings before her true identity was discovered. Upon her release on 25 January, she shared her ordeal with the public, sparking widespread horror.

Lady Constance described how she was held down as a steel gag forced her jaws open and a large tube was pushed painfully down her throat. Food was poured in, but in her distress, she vomited almost immediately, only to be held down and fed again. When the ordeal ended, she was left lying on the floor in her vomit-stained prison clothes until the doctor and wardresses returned the next morning to force-feed her again.

Christabel would write in *Unshackled* that: 'Lady Constance had made a stand for real democracy. She had taken a desperate risk for votes for women.'[10]

Unfortunately, though the affluent rebel's experiment had exposed the class prejudices within the prison system, the experience left her in severe bad health. She suffered a heart attack later that year, followed by a series of strokes that left her partially paralysed.

Hunger striking had now become the standard protest after arrest for the suffragettes. As WSPU leaders, Emmeline and Christabel had been forced to endorse the strikes. Yet these and other increasingly violent tactics, often launched independently of Union headquarters, seemed to signal that control was slipping from the grasp of Emmeline and the 'triumvirate'. Not only that, but the escalation in violence, though devastating to the women's health, was also something of an admission that previous efforts were not forcing the change they sought.

Of the Pankhursts, it was actually Adela who was first to go on hunger strike, something she did while imprisoned in Dundee with fellow suffragette Laura Evans. However, the Scottish authorities were reluctant to force-feed her, particularly given her slight, fragile frame; at the time she weighed a mere seven stone. Like all hunger strikers in Scottish prisons, she was also given a psychiatric evaluation, and it revealed her to be 'of the degenerate type' – a diagnosis that, in their view, made her especially unfit for the harsh procedure.[11] After five days of fasting, she was quietly released.

Meanwhile, the government insisted that force-feeding was a medical procedure, denying its risks and ignoring the suffragettes' claim that it was illegal, performed without consent. When Emily Davison, arrested in October alongside Lady Constance Lytton, resisted force-feeding on this basis by barricading herself in her cell, prison staff responded with shocking force, hosing her with icy water through a small window. After breaking down the door, they wrapped her in hot blankets – only to restrain her for another forced feeding. Davison later sued the wardens of Strangeways, and while she received only a small settlement, she successfully won the case, proving her treatment had been abusive.

Sadly, Davison's treatment was not unique. In a 1961 BBC broadcast, suffragette Mary Richardson recalled how she was thrown to the ground, a sheet pulled over her, and three heavy wardresses lay across her body as the doctor administered the watery food up her swollen nostril.[12]

All of this was enough for Henry Noel Brailsford, the former *Daily News* journalist. His suggestion of forming a Conciliation Committee for Women's Suffrage following the results of the general election was widely accepted. The Committee would work on a Bill aimed at securing a limited measure of women's suffrage based on their property holdings and marital status. Lady Constance's brother, Victor Bulwer-Lytton, 2nd Earl of Lytton, became the chair, while MPs from all the different parties made up the committee. Although initially doubtful about this new venture, the WSPU leaders shrewdly saw it as an opportunity to regroup and so have time to plan a return to the safer tactics of old. As Christabel later wrote: 'Mild militancy was more or less played out. The Government had, as far as they could, closed their door to it … a pause in militancy would be valuable, for it would give time for familiarity to fade.'[13]

On 31 January 1910, at a meeting at the Queen's Hall, Emmeline announced a pause in militancy in support of the work of the Conciliation Committee. This 'truce' meant the suffragettes would still oppose Liberal candidates at by-elections, but only through constitutional methods. It was, of course, a controversial decision, and one that may have not been accepted by many of the more aggressively militant suffragettes. After all, they may have wondered whether their sacrifices were made in vain. However, for many others, it was a welcome relief. After many gruelling years of protests, arrests, and now hunger strikes, hundreds of suffragettes were exhausted and in poor health, worn down as much by the relentless travel and cold weather as by prison and forced feeding. With violence suspended, they seized the chance to recuperate.

Christabel travelled to the Channel Islands with Annie Kenney, while Sylvia later joined Annie and the Pethick-Lawrences for a holiday at Innsbruck, Germany. Many wealthy supporters of the WSPU opened their homes to suffragettes in need of rest. Henry Harben and his wife, Agnes, invited them to Newland Park in Buckinghamshire. Recently released hunger strikers found care at the Pembroke Gardens nursing home, run by Catherine Pine and Gertrude Townsend. Hilda Brackenbury and her daughters opened their London and Surrey homes, while the Pethick-Lawrences' estate near Dorking and Eagle House in Bath, the home of Colonel Linley Blathwayt and his family, became regular retreats for the movement. These homes became havens, not only for recovery but for building deep friendships and, in some cases, romantic connections.

Annie, in particular, seemed to have had a magnetic presence, attracting friends and admirers alike, and some diaries from the time suggest she may have had romantic relationships with several other suffragettes. There has been speculation about a possible romance between Annie and Christabel, but it's more likely they simply shared a devoted friendship. While Christabel had her fair share of besotted admirers, she tended to keep her distance. As a publicity mastermind, she recognised the importance of protecting her reputation from salacious gossip (not, of course, that female homosexuality was accepted as real in these pre-war years). More importantly, her passion was utterly poured into the movement. It was, to her, not just about securing the vote, but about dismantling the patriarchal systems that suppressed women's freedoms on every level. She was a part of a new generation of independent women – brilliant, bold, and ambitious; frustrated with a world built by and for men. Despite graduating at the top of her class in law, she had been denied a career simply because of her gender. For Christabel, then, this was more than a single fight; it was a life's purpose, a push for political, structural, and moral freedom for women. And with such dedication, it's unlikely she had emotional space for romantic dalliances, certainly not with men, and probably not with women either.

Around this time, however, Emmeline developed a deep and meaningful bond with the composer Ethel Smyth. Ethel was nearly always dressed in plain country tweeds, a tie in the suffragette colours of purple, green, and white, and a distinctive porkpie hat. This near-androgenous look personified the independent, 'man-hating' suffragette stereotype popularised by anti-suffrage propaganda of the late Victorian era. But Ethel was anything but a caricature;

as Sylvia put it, she was 'individualised to the last point'. Introduced to the WSPU by Lady Constance Lytton, Ethel felt an immediate and overwhelming admiration for Emmeline, and claimed that upon meeting her, she had 'been swept off her feet at once'. Though Ethel had been in relationships with men, she was open about her feelings for women and saw in Emmeline a match to her spirit and strength.

The women embarked on a deep, enduring friendship that lasted for the next four years. Ethel made no secret of her affection, calling Emmeline 'my dearest Em' and writing ardent letters to her while Emmeline travelled for the WSPU. In one she claimed: 'It is the crowning achievement of my life to have made you love me.' For Emmeline, the relationship likely brought a much-needed comfort. The recent loss of her son Harry, still unbearable, would also have rekindled the sorrow from Richard's death and the grief for her late son, Frank. While her connection with Christabel was a constant, her favoured daughter's close relationship with the Pethick-Lawrences often left Emmeline feeling deeply lonely – a feeling she had confided to Sylvia.

Ethel herself noted this, writing in *Female Pipings in Eden*, 'From intimate friendship, she had hitherto held aloof, her boundless love and admiration for her eldest daughter satisfying all the needs of her heart.'[14] Thus in Ethel, Emmeline may have found a connection that, at least for a time, offered solace and joy amidst the trials of her public and personal battles.

Several historians have suggested the relationship was a romantic one. Yet this seems improbable. Just as with Christabel, Emmeline would not have risked such a scandal. Moreover, this suggestion overlooks the very real, deeply human need that Emmeline – a steadying hand and source of strength for so many of the young WSPU members – would have had for a friend of similar age and intellect that she could turn to for support and succour.

Emmeline's daughters were aware of the deep friendship between the two women. While Sylvia and Adela chose not to read anything too meaningful into it, Christabel took a different view, seeing Ethel as a rival for her mother's affections. This tension would finally be resolved, though it would take Christabel some years to see the importance of this friendship to Emmeline. Ethel would later have a deep romance with Virginia Woolf, twenty-five years her junior, and their relationship would last through the end of Woolf's life.

Meanwhile, as the suffragettes awaited the outcome of their 'truce' with the government, hoping Parliament would support the Conciliation Bill being developed by Lord Lytton and his multi-party allies, they kept their movement active in public life and the media. On 7 May 1910, King Edward VII died, succeeded by his son, George V. Christabel published a lengthy tribute in *Votes for Women*, bordered in black, and announced that all WSPU activities would be paused until after the royal funeral. Adela and Sylvia were aghast at this, their strong socialist beliefs at odds with Christabel's apparent royalist views. Sylvia, referencing her sister's upbringing as the daughter of the 'Red Doctor', later wrote scathingly about Christabel's stance, stating, 'It was as though she knew nothing of the struggle convulsing the groups of political thinkers through which she had passed…'

By the following month, activities had been reignited. On 18 June, the WSPU organised a procession of 10,000 women under the banner 'From Prison to Citizenship'. Emmeline, dressed entirely in white, led the march to Albert Hall, where speeches resounded in support of the Bill. There was renewed optimism on 11 July, when Labour MP David Shackleton presented the Bill, which comfortably passed to a second reading. On 23 July, the WSPU staged another massive rally in Hyde Park, with 150 speakers across forty stages voicing hope that the vote would soon be granted.

But, once again, political delays emerged. Tensions between Conservatives and Liberals in the House of Lords triggered another general election, and Asquith announced that parliament would be dissolved on 28 November. Against this backdrop, Foreign Secretary, Sir Edward Grey, dropped the shocking announcement there would be no time for the Conciliation Bill. Appalled and outraged, the suffragettes and their supporters were forced to accept that the Bill had been abandoned, leaving them right where they had been nearly a year earlier.

A ninth Women's Parliament was swiftly organised for 18 November, and during it, Emmeline called an end to the truce. Over 300 suffragettes marched to Parliament from Caxton Hall and found themselves facing the usual wall of armed police. Emmeline was allowed to lead a delegation that included notable figures such as Dr Elizabeth Garrett Anderson, Dr Louisa Garrett Anderson, the physicist and engineer Hertha Ayrton, and Indian princess Sophia Duleep Singh in through Parliament's St Stephens entrance. Reaching the Prime Minister's offices, they were told, unsurprisingly, that he would not meet with them. As they were being escorted back outside, the brutal reality unfolding on the streets rose to meet them.

The police had turned on the protesters. Truncheons and whips had been unleashed and were being used to knock the women to the ground. Many were kicked, fielding punches to their faces and chests. Several women later reported that the assaults had a disturbing sexual element: police twisted their breasts, lifted their skirts, and exposed them to the jeering male crowd.

Christina Richardson, an older protester, recounted seeing 'policemen grab women by the collars, shake them, and fling them aside like rats. I saw them take women up and fling them on the crowd as many logs on a woodpile…' Sixty-six-year-old Georgiana Solomon, the widow of South African politician Saul Solomon, described how she was 'gripped by the breasts', noting that younger women were 'assaulted in this and other repellent ways'.[15]

The violence raged on for six hours, with police arresting 115 women and four men for a finish. The next day, the media coverage was split. Most newspapers condemned the suffragettes' 'aggressive' behaviour and praised the police's 'restraint'. *The Daily Mirror*, for example, claimed the police showed 'good temper and tact', even while its front page bore a photograph of a beaten Ada Wright lying on the ground. *The Times* reported that officers had suffered in the line of duty, with helmets knocked off and injuries sustained. Yet other reports, including a later piece in *The Daily Mirror*, highlighted the disturbing pleasure some policemen seemed to take in their violent treatment of the suffragettes.

In the aftermath of the brutal protest, now referred to as 'Black Friday', answers were demanded by concerned individuals and organisations. Many called for a public inquiry, which was flatly rejected by Winston Churchill, who had been promoted to Home Secretary earlier that year. The Conciliation Committee took it upon themselves to investigate the police violence, gathering 135 statements from women involved and bystanders alike. Among them was the harrowing account of May Billinghurst, a disabled suffragist, who described being thrown from her wheelchair and beaten by police. 'At first, the police threw me out of the machine onto the ground in a very brutal manner … my arms and back were so badly bruised that for two days I could not leave my bed,' she reported.

Other accounts confirmed similar brutalities, while a few attempted to paint a different picture. One handwritten note asserted that, in the case of May Billinghurst, the police showed 'extreme forbearance' and accused the disabled woman of deliberately steering her hand-tricycle toward police ranks. However, while such inconsistencies abounded, twenty-nine statements documented disturbing instances of sexual assault.[16]

The next day, the arrested women and men were brought before Bow Street Police Court. However, all charges were dismissed after Winston Churchill decided that 'no public advantage would be gained by proceeding with the prosecution'. To the WSPU, this decision was clearly an attempt to avoid further scrutiny into police conduct. Many suffragettes believed Churchill had intentionally instructed the police – reportedly drawn from London's East End and Whitechapel – to 'manhandle' the women. Christabel Pankhurst voiced these suspicions in a written piece for the 25 November edition of *Votes for Women*, claiming, 'The orders of the Home Secretary were … that the women were to be thrown from one to the other.' Her article was cited by *The Times*, prompting Churchill to angrily deny the accusation in Parliament and even consider suing Christabel and the newspaper.

Just days later, on 22 November, Prime Minister Asquith announced that if the Liberals won the next election (which he was sure they would), they would allocate time for a Conciliation Bill in Parliament. But for the WSPU, this promise – vague and relegated to a future Parliament – fell far short. Another protest ensued outside Downing Street, leading to more physical confrontations with police and 162 arrests, including Emmeline Pankhurst.

Hearing of Emmeline's arrest, her sister Mary, who was back in Brighton, recovering from the ordeal of Black Friday, which she had also taken part in, rushed to London to see her. However, when she was denied access to her sister at Cannon Row Police Station, she defiantly threw a stone through one of the station windows, shattering the glass, and was immediately arrested. The next day, both sisters appeared in court. Yet, while Emmeline was discharged due to lack of evidence, Mary, pleading guilty to breaking a window, was sentenced to one month in Holloway Prison along with seventy-five other suffragettes.

With another election approaching, Emmeline threw herself back into campaigning. Though exhausted, she often delivered up to five speeches a day, subsisting mainly on hot beverages, according to Grace Roe, the local WSPU Organiser at Wisbech. Two days before Christmas, Emmeline's sister Mary and several other suffragettes were released from Holloway Prison. The WSPU leader returned to London to welcome them, presiding over a luncheon at the Criterion Restaurant. Shocked at her sister's gaunt appearance, she later recalled, 'It was clear to those who knew her best, that her health had suffered gravely from the terrible events of Black Friday and her time in prison.'

Mary, worn down and weakened, stayed with their brother Herbert at his home in Winchmore Hill, where Emmeline joined them for a subdued Christmas dinner. The year had been exhausting, marked by yet further personal grief when, in April, their mother, Sophia Goulden, had passed away from a prolonged bout of pneumonia. The losses weighed heavily on the siblings, and the holiday gathering was quiet. During dinner, Mary complained of feeling unwell and went to rest. Concerned, Emmeline checked on her a while later and found her sister unconscious. Mary had suffered a brain haemorrhage and died shortly afterwards.

For Emmeline, this new loss was devastating. Her sister had been her confidante, the one who had shared nearly every chapter of her life from girlhood onwards, who had cared for her children like a second mother. Nor could Emmeline accept her death as mere misfortune; she saw it, rather, as a grim casualty in the fight for women's suffrage. Mary, she believed, was the first martyr of their cause.

She shared this conviction with Sylvia when she visited her on Boxing Day to tell her of her aunt's death. Sylvia had spent Christmas alone in her flat at Linden Gardens, a place she had moved to after Harry's passing. Emmeline expressed her sorrow and anger to her sympathetic daughter, lamenting that the struggle had claimed Mary's young life. She communicated these same feelings in a letter to C. P. Scott, the editor of the *Manchester Guardian*, shortly after: 'We who loved her and knew her selfless heart struggle to contain our desire for vengeance,' she wrote, 'though we know that had she foreseen her fate, she would have been proud to give her life for freedom. She is the first to die. How many more must follow before the men of your party recognize their responsibility?'[17]

Emmeline was not just venting her anger to Scott. Wearied by the seemingly endless battle and the suffering it had caused for so many, her words were an exhausted plea. She urged Scott to intervene: 'I write to you not only because you saw her in prison, but because you – more than any man outside the Cabinet – have the power to help bring this dreadful struggle to an end.'

However, this 'dreadful' suffrage struggle was far from over. The fight had already claimed Mary's life, but many other women were suffering, their health and strength irrevocably damaged. Behind the headlines of protests and victories countless women already bore the scars of brutal attacks, imprisonments, hunger strikes, and forced feeding. As Emmeline Pethick-Lawrence had written in her appreciation of Mary in *Votes for Women*: 'How many more lives must be laid down … before an elementary act of justice and reparation is done to the womanhood of the country?'

Henria Williams, a governess and schoolmistress, who had also taken part in the Black Friday demonstration, tragically died two months later. Her death was likely caused by the violent treatment she suffered that day, which was believed to have exacerbated an existing health condition. She had been rescued from the demonstration's chaos by a man, Frank Whitty, who demanded of the policeman who beat her, 'Are you going to arrest her or kill her?'

Mary Gawthorpe, one of the movement's most dedicated voices, had joined the WSPU after much deliberation, devoting herself as a full-time organiser in 1906. By 1911, however, she was forced to step back entirely, her body broken by injuries sustained during a violent political meeting. Minnie Baldock, who alongside Annie Kenney had founded the first London branch of the WSPU, withdrew from the organisation that same year. Illness forced her out, though the WSPU's increasingly militant tactics deepened her disillusionment. Many others, attempting to recover from the effects of hunger strikes and forced feedings, also often found themselves too frail to return to the front lines. In November 1911, Cecilia Wolseley Haig died at her home in Brook Street, London, after a year-long illness that Sylvia later claimed arose as a result of the brutal beatings she received at the hands of the police on Black Friday. In *The Suffragette Movement*, she noted:

> I saw Cecilia Haig go out [on 18 November] with the rest; a tall, strongly built, reserved woman, comfortably situated, who in ordinary circumstances might have gone through life without receiving an insult, much less a blow. She was assaulted with violence and indecency, and died in December 1911, after a painful illness, arising from her injuries.[18]

CHAPTER

14

NO VOTE, NO CENSUS AND A 'TORPEDOED' BILL

What began as a campaign for freedom and equality had exacted a devastating cost, and as Emmeline faced the new year she must have felt the weight of all this grief bearing down heavily on her.

Yet, as 1911 dawned, a small ray of light broke through the gloom, bringing good news for the Pankhurst family: Sylvia had been invited to embark on a tour of America. Christabel had long left her dancing days behind and Adela had put her storytelling dreams away. However, Sylvia had nurtured her artistic side, using both paint and pen to capture the world she saw unfolding around her. Visual arts gave voice to her private emotions, but it was through writing that she found an audience. Both Emmeline and Christabel had been approached by publishers to pen a detailed account of the WSPU, but they were too entrenched in their daily activities to have time to do it. Sylvia, on the other hand, was used to applying herself to creative endeavours and was available. She had also already been crafting a chronicle of the suffrage movement and was able to shape this writing into a book simply titled *Suffragette: The History of the Women's Militant Suffrage Movement*. However, more than a dry history, it was an insider's account of the WSPU's journey, detailing its growth, its fierce ambitions, and the ideals that bound its members together. Selling well in Britain, her publishing agent arranged an American tour to bring her voice to a wider audience. For Sylvia, it was an exciting time, and for Emmeline, it must have been a source of pride as she watched the Pankhurst name gain further recognition across the Atlantic.

As with her mother before her, Sylvia was warmly welcomed in America by the press and public alike when she arrived in the US in early January 1911. Reporting on a speech she gave in New York, *The New York Times* described her as 'a little rosy-cheeked slip of an English girl [who] held the attention of a distinguished New York audience for over an hour and a half'.

While she was in America to promote her book and the suffragette cause, Sylvia could not resist the opportunity to experience a wider America. During her three-month tour, which spanned Pennsylvania, Michigan, Illinois, Wisconsin, Ohio, Indiana, Tennessee, Missouri and Arkansas, she took it upon herself to visit factory towns, the 'Socialist city' of Milwaukee in Wisconsin, and, to many of her American hosts' horror, the Indian University in Arkansas and the Negro University in Tennessee. In Tennessee, she also visited a prison and was repulsed by the grim conditions. Pitch-dark cells included a macabre 'cage within a cage' system where prisoners in small, barred enclosures with a narrow wooden bench to huddle on, were only allowed into the outer cage for a brief daily respite, like animals in a zoo.[1]

The everyday racism she encountered among white Americans was shocking to her. In one of her many letters to Keir Hardie, she described the desolate conditions of Native Americans forced onto barren lands, where they lived in simple earthen huts, along uncultivatable grounds, wearing nothing but ragged clothes. Her empathy was instinctive and profound, and in many ways revealed a mind decades ahead of its time in its grasp of systemic injustice. In a letter to Hardie, she wrote, 'It is here that they have driven the poor Indians, and now they say they are lazy and will not work! Small wonder that they are fast dying off. Soon, like the buffalo that once roamed here, they will be gone.'[2]

But Sylvia's letters to Hardie were not solely filled with the injustices she encountered on her journeys. They also overflowed with tender declarations of her feelings for him. 'My Darling, I am longing to be in your arms, away from it all,' she confided in one letter. In another, she mused on the idea of thought transference: 'As much as I love my Darling's arms about me, sweet as kisses are, I rather think it will tend to make us less dependent on those things.'[3]

Hardie's responses were just as effusive. In reply to her musings, he wrote, 'Don't you think the satisfaction which comes from the pressure of my arms around you must be the transference of something from one to the other?'[4]

While Sylvia was wading through the strange and unfamiliar world of American society, Adela, back in Britain, was dealing with her own set of challenges. Over the last four years, the youngest Pankhurst daughter had been working tirelessly in the provinces, particularly focusing on Scotland throughout 1910. There, she had forged friendships and garnered a dedicated following. Despite this, Christabel was critical of her sister's work.

The WSPU's organising secretary was, in truth, generally distrustful of the Scottish WSPU branches, perhaps as a remnant of the strong support they had given Teresa Billington-Greig during the days before the Union's split. This tension only intensified with the publication of a scathing article by Teresa that appeared in the *New Age* on 12 January. In it, Teresa announced her resignation from the post of Secretary of the WFL but took the opportunity to launch a fierce critique of the WSPU. The former Union member condemned the organisation's leadership – Emmeline, Christabel, and the Pethick-Lawrences – for fostering what she termed an 'emotional yoke' that exploited the very virtues of its members. This, she argued, created a system of mental and spiritual slavery. Teresa's article painted the WSPU as not only suppressing free speech but also as increasingly exclusive, prioritising social standing over the working-class involvement that had once been its hallmark. The national newspapers gleefully picked up the story, giving it more column inches than it likely deserved. The *Daily Express* even published it as a front-page story, though they did mention that there was a rising number of working-class members alongside the influx of women from privileged backgrounds.[5]

The WSPU leaders did not respond publicly to the article, hoping the controversy would fade. However, the article struck a chord with several of the members who were already questioning the organisation's direction. A small but growing faction, including Mary Gawthorpe and Dora Marsden, was increasingly dissatisfied with the leadership style. Tensions were also surfacing between the London headquarters and local organisers. Emmeline and Christabel had recently clashed with Helen Fraser, their Scottish organiser and a close friend of Adela's, ultimately dismissing her from her post.

Adela had written to Mabel Tuke at WSPU headquarters expressing her concerns that militancy was not as readily embraced outside London and often alienated those who sympathised with votes for women. In fact, Adela, who had never dropped her socialist leanings, had confided to Helen as early as 1909 that she was unhappy with the WSPU's increasingly violent tactics and its disconnect from the grassroots movement. Her letter to Mrs Tuke was brusque, noting her frustration over receiving orders from London that ignored local conditions. Mabel was furious, likely seeing Adela in the light that her sister, Christabel, had so often put her – not as a Pankhurst leader but rather just one of the provincial rank and files. Though Adela apologised for any offense she may have caused Mabel, she was quick to note that she had obviously 'not yet learned it was a crime to have an opinion'. Adela was summoned to London and accused of disloyalty. In fact, Christabel, who, according to Sylvia, saw Adela as 'a very black sheep among organisers because [of] the warmth of her Socialism',[6] went so far as to accuse the shocked Adela of wanting to form a rival suffrage group with herself as leader.

Adela, still mourning the loss of her brother, and worn down after years on the WSPU frontlines, was already on the brink of breakdown. These surprising accusations prompted her to immediately hand in her resignation to Mrs Pethick-Lawrence. However, the older woman, ever empathetic, persuaded her to stay a little longer while encouraging her to take a much-needed rest. Adela, still only 26 years old, agreed and took some time to relax, recover and reflect on her place in the world.[7]

At the time, Emmeline was concerned about her young daughter's health and relieved that she had been urged to take some time away to recuperate. Though she had not joined Christabel in openly criticising Adela, Emmeline assumed Christabel's suspicions were correct; she remained, as always, steadfastly loyal to her 'darling Christabel'. To Emmeline, her eldest daughter was a political genius. In contrast, she tended to stick to the belief that Adela had taken on too much too young, burdening herself with responsibilities she could not handle emotionally or otherwise. Sylvia would later argue that Adela, whom she had had little fondness for as children, was a remarkable speaker and an exceptional organiser. She claimed that Emmeline and Christabel judged Adela more harshly than she deserved and that Christabel, in particular, was threatened by Adela's political views and insights.

Meanwhile, in January and February of 1911, the WSPU agreed to another truce with Prime Minister Asquith's Liberal government, which had returned to power. Although the King's Speech yet again made no mention of women's suffrage, there was cause for cautious optimism. Three MPs from the Conciliation Committee secured the top spots in the private members' ballot, and Sir George Kemp, who drew first place, pledged to sponsor a new women's suffrage bill.

With the Conciliation Bill back on the table and scheduled for a second reading on 5 May, the WSPU mobilised its members for a dynamic campaign. Despite her reservations about the bill, Emmeline saw the necessity of supporting it and threw herself into the effort. She now had a new chauffeur and car, so was able to drive across the country to the various meetings. Irish-born Aileen Preston, the first woman in history to qualify for the Automobile Association Certificate in Driving, was the woman behind the wheel, while the car itself, a large Wolseley, was a gift from wealthy American supporter, Mary Dodge.

Alieen was paid £1 a week and loved her job. She herself had put an advertisement in the classified columns of the *Morning Post* and *Votes for Women* looking for work as a 'Lady Chaffeuse' and qualified motor mechanic. Her family, however, were horrified to hear that Aileen's new boss was 'that dreadful woman' and claimed their daughter was going 'straight into the dark arms of Hell'.[8] But their daughter took immense pride in her work. As she explained:

> We would start off about half past ten in the morning and then we'd have a puncture. Mrs. Pankhurst never got out of the car, she never moved from her papers, so I used to jack her up with the car. I took that for granted. She was always absolutely absorbed in working out her speech for the next meeting or reading some book on social welfare. In my mind, all the time was, 'Mrs Pankhurst's got to be there.' That's all that mattered. Her meeting was the only thing that mattered, and we always got there in time.[9]

As part of the campaign, Emmeline spoke at a large WSPU gathering held at the Albert Hall on 23 March. Here, guests included the Australian suffragist

Vida Goldstein, who had been at the forefront of obtaining the vote for Australian women in 1902. Ethel Smyth was also celebrated at the event for her composition of 'The March of the Women'. With words composed by actress, journalist and suffragette, Cicely Hamilton, the powerful song would become the anthem of the movement from that day forth.

Though Christabel and Emmeline were still smarting from Teresa Billington-Greig's scathing article earlier in the year, they did not see this as a reason to completely ignore the WLF. In fact, the overlapping goals of both organisations tended to create significant moments of collaboration. One such occasion arose that April when the WSPU joined forces with the Women's Freedom League (WFL) to support a bold, non-violent boycott of the 1911 Census. The rallying cry for the campaign, 'If women don't count, neither shall they be counted,' resonated with both militant and constitutional suffragists. It was a clever act of defiance aimed at drawing attention to the government's refusal to grant women full citizenship. However, several of the more conservative newspapers sharply criticised the protest, with *Punch Magazine* mockingly declaring that women had finally 'taken leave of their census'.[10]

On the evening Britain's 1911 census was due to be taken across the country, all-night events had been organised so that women could leave their homes during the hours census enumerators were making their rounds. In London, suffragettes picnicked under the stars on Wimbledon Green, while Trafalgar Square came alive with the songs and laughter of the thousands who gathered there. The WSPU had put together their own packed programme of events, which included a late-night concert at Queen's Hall followed by a night of entertainment at the Scala Theatre, carrying on until 3.00am. Following that, festivities continued at the Aldwych Roller Skating Rink, which had been booked until 8.00am.

Emmeline attended all the WSPU events, but as the night faded, she and Ethel left the merriment of the skating rink and returned to Emmeline's hotel room. The room was dark but they stood at the window and watched the sunrise over the Thames. In that still, profound moment, Ethel wrote of an overwhelming sense of connection, a feeling of oneness with the movement, all that they loved, and with the world:

> Our foreheads pressed against the window pane staring silently into the dawn, gradually we realised that her love for down-trodden women … her hope of better things for them … my music … our friendship … that all this was part of the mystery that was holding our eyes. And suddenly it came to us that all was well; for a second we were standing on the spot in a madly spinning world where nothing stirs, where there is eternal stillness.[11]

Not all women could leave their homes on census night, but many employed creative ways to get the 'No Vote, No Census' point across. For example,

Miss Davies, a suffragette in Birkenhead, completed her census form by giving the name of a male servant and then adding 'no other persons, but many women'.

Others chose to hide in creative locations. Radical suffragette, Emily Wilding Davison, hid in a broom cupboard in the Houses of Parliament for up to forty-six hours. By doing so, she ensured that the Palace of Westminster would be recorded as her residence. Discovered by a cleaner, she was arrested though later released without charge. However, as she planned, she was officially recorded in the Census with the note: 'Found hiding in the Crypt of Westminster Hall, Westminster.'

Decades later, in 1991, a plaque was put up in that very cupboard, honouring Davison's bold stand. Installed by Labour MP Tony Benn, with the support of Helena Kennedy QC, and Jeremy Corbyn MP, the inscription reads: 'A brave suffragette campaigning for votes for women at a time when Parliament denied them that right.'[12]

The months of 1911 rolled on with the belief growing that the second Conciliation Bill would, in fact, achieve the vote for women. On 5 May, during its second reading, it won a comfortable victory of 255 votes to 88. In a gesture of encouragement, the government promised an 'elastic' week in 1912 to move the Bill through all its stages. Optimism surged among women everywhere.

That summer, on 17 June, the Women's Coronation procession was organised. It was a response to the King's Coronation celebrations, planned for later that month, which would celebrate the 'manhood of the Empire'. The procession drew an astounding 50,000 participants. Militants and non-militants united in a vibrant display of solidarity, with Flora Drummond leading the way on horseback, followed closely by colour bearer Charlotte Marsh. Among the marchers was Marjorie Annan Bryce, gallantly dressed as Joan of Arc. The leaders of the WSPU, Christabel, Emmeline, Mrs Pethick-Lawrence and Mabel Tuke, followed after that.

The procession also featured various contingents, each representing diverse areas of the movement. In the International Contingent, women from the USA, Russia and Romania were among those marching shoulder to shoulder. In addition, the Women's Freedom League, the Church League for Women's Suffrage, the Catholic Women's Suffrage Society, the Men's Political Union for Women's Enfranchisement, as well as the National Union of Women's Suffrage Societies all took part. The 7-mile-long procession marched along St James's Street, where Elizabeth Wolstenholme-Elmy, now 78 years old and proudly dubbed the 'oldest suffragette', stood on a balcony and took the salute as nearly 1,000 former prisoners, including the Pankhursts, all clad in white, marched by.

At the Albert Hall, the leaders of the WSPU took to the stage. Christabel, filled with optimism, surveyed the eager faces and declared, 'We stand today speaking with a most certain hope than we have ever had before of the early triumph of our cause. It is the first time in human history that politicians have made a pledge to women and undertaken to fulfil it in the spirit!'

The whole event was, as the *Daily Telegraph* hailed it, 'a triumph'. The next couple of months moved forward in that happy vein. While the WSPU remained active in campaigning, there was a palpable sense that the long-awaited vote was finally within reach.

For Emmeline, however, personal worries still dogged her. Adela, now back in the field as the organiser for Sheffield and its district, was struggling with nervous exhaustion. She was under the care of Helen Archdale, an older WSPU member who had two children but was estranged from her husband, an army officer stationed in India. Worried about Adela's well-being, Emmeline confided in Helen, saying, 'I feel that Adela may not be able to continue her organising work in Sheffield, and given her condition, there couldn't be a better time to end that arrangement.' Adela herself had told her mother she wanted to enrol in a college course. Emmeline wholeheartedly supported this ambition, but to fund her education, knew she would likely need to return to America for another lucrative speaking tour.

Sylvia, fresh from her own tour across the Atlantic, described life in the States as a whirlwind – 'harsh and rude', yet brimming with opportunity for young people. She found it a place more open to new ideas than the more traditional countries of Europe. She had toyed briefly during her tour of emigrating there. However, in 1912, she would undertake a second tour of the vast country and on this occasion would come to a different conclusion. The reality of America felt too harsh and unforgiving, far removed from the dreams of equality that she held dear.

Emmeline departed for New York on 4 October aboard the White Star liner, *Oceanic*, accompanied once again by Emmeline Pethick-Lawrence's sister, Dorothy. This second three-month trip proved to be less frenetic than the first, although Emmeline still managed to address hundreds of thousands of women across New York, Kentucky, Kansas, Montana, Seattle, Montreal, and Winnipeg. By this time, she had become something of a celebrity. A Women's Political Union (WPU) had been established by Harriet Stanford Blatch, modelled after the Women's Social and Political Union (WSPU), down to the use of purple, white and green as its colours. When Emmeline delivered her inaugural speech at the Brooklyn Academy of Music on 17 October, flags of these colours hung from the rafters and adorned the stage. Blatch herself introduced Emmeline as 'the woman who in all the world is doing the most for suffrage'.[13] As Emmeline travelled across the country, this introduction was repeated frequently, accompanied by bands playing 'See the Conquering Hero Comes'.

While the tour was a resounding success, and once again brought in both private funds and more money for the UK movement, when she returned home in January 1912, the hopes of Britain's suffragettes had once more fallen apart.

Not long after Emmeline had set off for America, Parliament reconvened and delivered the devastating news that the Conciliation Bill would not be passed. Instead, a government-sponsored suffrage bill to enfranchise the four million men currently excluded from voting was announced. Emmeline was in Minneapolis when she was telegrammed the devastating news. She thought to return immediately to British shores but decided against it. However, she did return a telegram with the words, 'Protest imperative!'

In Emmeline's absence, Emmeline Pethick-Lawrence took the lead and organised a deputation to meet with Asquith. She was joined by Christabel, Sylvia, Annie Kenney, Lady Constance Lytton, Mabel Tuke, Elizabeth Robins, and other leaders from the Women's Freedom League and the NUWSS. Asquith agreed to meet with the women on 17 November. The confrontation was heated but fruitless. The deputation made it clear that it was an insult to respond to women's passionate demands by extending voting rights to men who had not even campaigned for such reforms, but Asquith could only suggest that there might be a chance for women if an amendment could be made to the new bill including them. The suffragettes knew this was a hollow possibility; Asquith had never wanted the bill to pass. Lloyd George had criticised the Conciliation Bill for excluding thousands of working-class women. But Asquith understood that adding these women through an amendment would be anathema to the Conservatives, who stood firmly against the idea. As the *Evening Standard*, a Conservative newspaper, pointed out at the time: 'When it comes to throwing ten million in at one stroke – giving the franchise to every labourer's wife, every scullery maid, matchbox-maker, and street flower-seller over twenty-one – they [the Tories] will draw back.'

Following the encounter, Mrs Pethick-Lawrence announced plans for another deputation to Parliament and called for a mass demonstration outside the House of Commons on 21 November. Handbills were quickly printed rallying men and women alike to gather in Parliament Square. The words on the handbill, signed by Emmeline Pethick-Lawrence herself, called on supporters 'to protect women from being brutally victimised by police, both in uniform and plain clothes, as they were on 18 November 1910, when one woman lost her life and many others were injured'.

On 21 November she and Christabel addressed crowds at Caxton Hall before Mrs Pethick-Lawrence led the supporters towards Parliament. At the same time, another group of 150 women set out from Clement's Inn with a more dramatic plan in mind. Armed with bags of stones and hammers, they moved methodically through the city, targeting not just government offices but a surprising array of other establishments, including the National Liberal Federation, the Guards' Club, the offices of the *Daily Mail* and *Daily News*, Swan and Edgar's department store, Lyon's Tea Shop, Dunn's Hat Shop, two hotels, and several small businesses. In a well-coordinated campaign, they smashed windows across the city. By the end of the night, 223 women had been arrested, including Mrs Pethick-Lawrence.[14]

It's not known whether Christabel had directly planned or approved the window-smashing attacks, but in the days that followed, she staunchly defended what had happened. She also published an article in the following month's issue of *Votes for Women*, titled 'Broken windows', outlining the WSPU's new policy of attacking public and private property. Her article was a fiery response to a speech given by the Chancellor of the Exchequer, David Lloyd George, or 'oily George' as he was known in Suffragette circles, in Bath on 24 November.

Addressing the fallout over the Second Conciliation Bill, he claimed it had been 'torpedoed' by the introduction of the Manhood Suffrage Bill. This new bill, he stated, could pave the way for a broader and more inclusive amendment for women's suffrage – not merely for a select class of well-to-do women, but for working-class women as well.

Christabel was incensed by what she saw as political posturing and wrote in her article:

> The Government's latest attempt to cheat women of the vote is, of course, inspired by Mr. Lloyd George. The whole crooked scheme is characteristic of the man and of the methods he has from the first employed against the Suffrage cause … We shall never believe that Mr Lloyd George is a genuine supporter of a democratic franchise for women until he secures that it be made a Government measure.

As another year came to an end, the Women's Social and Political Union (WSPU) was once again engaging in militant activities. Protests were being organised, windows were being smashed, and women were being arrested. However, the escalating violence left the press and public divided. Some continued to support the suffragettes, others felt it was time to abandon such extreme measures, particularly as they were now extending to the destruction of private property. A steadfast opposition also clung to the belief that granting women the vote would spell disaster for the nation. The *Evening Standard* claimed that the WSPU was nothing more than 'a little band, of notoriety-seeking and misguided females … drawn almost exclusively from … an upper class of more or less well-educated and well-to-do women'.

Even within the suffragette movement, further cracks were beginning to show. A new journal, *The Freewoman*, launched by former WSPU members Mary Gawthorpe and Dora Marsden, delivered a stinging critique of Christabel Pankhurst's leadership in its inaugural issue. The editorial accused her of lacking both political acumen and common sense. 'Does she truly believe,' the writers mocked, 'that militancy – no matter its form – will force the Government under Mr. Asquith to introduce a women's suffrage bill? Or that the Liberal Party will demand Mr. Asquith's resignation?'

Christabel was stunned. She had considered Mary Gawthorpe a friend. While outraged supporters of the WSPU flooded the journal's letters page with rebuttals, Christabel chose not to respond publicly.

Meanwhile, on 15 December, the women's militancy took yet another dangerous turn. Emily Wilding Davison was arrested for attempting to set fire to a post box outside the Parliament Street post office. Earlier that day, she had already ignited two other post boxes using linen soaked in paraffin. In court, Davison claimed her actions were partly a protest against the unjust two-month imprisonment and poor treatment of fellow suffragette Mary Leigh. However, it was not the only reason. She went on to explain that 'In past agitation for reform, the next step after window-breaking was incendiarism', and claimed she was now employing that militant action, 'in order to draw the attention of the private citizen to the fact that this question of reform is their concern as well as that of women'.[15]

Her act of arson had not been initiated by the WSPU leadership. However, Emmeline, upon her return from the United States, would later defend the actions taken by Davison, who had been given a six-month prison sentence. A new, almost inevitable, and more perilous path had now opened up for the suffragettes. While criticisms against this path continued to intensify, for the WSPU, the direction it was taking them seemed unavoidable. As Emmeline would later write in her biography, 'We had reached a stage at which the mere sympathy of Members of Parliament, however sincerely felt, was no longer of the slightest use.'

CHAPTER 15

I INCITE THIS MEETING TO REBELLION

So began the most violent era of the suffrage movement in Britain. On 18 January, Emmeline finally returned to England, determined to lead the Women's Social and Political Union (WSPU) into an even more militant phase. Days later, on 22 January, she was welcomed back by a jubilant crowd of thousands at the London Pavilion. Christabel gave her a warm introduction, though in her address also took the opportunity to give a direct challenge to the Labour Party. She urged them to fight for an equal franchise that included women, especially as many Independent Labour Party (ILP) branches were already condemning the Government's proposed Manhood Suffrage Bill. It was daring of Christabel to make such a demand. She had worked hard to sever the WSPU's ties with the ILP and was no longer a member herself. Yet her gamble paid off. Just four days later, at the Labour Party Conference in Birmingham, a resolution was passed by a large majority, calling for both adult men and women to be included in the upcoming reform bill.

The impact of this move rippled beyond the militant wing of the suffrage movement. Millicent Garrett Fawcett, leader of the National Union of Women's Suffrage Societies (NUWSS), decided to bet on Labour's newly declared stance and shifted her group's strategy. Abandoning her organisation's nonpartisan approach, Fawcett sought an electoral alliance with Labour. The NUWSS pledged their support for Labour candidates, launching what became known as the Election Fighting Fund.

In the meantime, both Emmeline and Christabel began their relentless meetings up and down the British Isles, urging the Government to scrap the Manhood Suffrage Bill and replace it with legislation granting equal voting rights to men and women. In their speeches, they also passionately defended the suffragettes' increasingly violent militant tactics. At a meeting in Northern Ireland, Christabel opened her speech with a wry observation that brought the house down with laughter: she doubted she needed to apologise in Ireland for the militant methods they used against the British government. Some days later, on 16 February at a dinner being held for released suffragette prisoners – held shortly after the King's Speech had made only a vague reference to universal franchise – Emmeline delivered one of her most famous defences of political violence.

She laid bare the grim double standards of the government. Smashing windows, she noted, provoked such outrage that women were arrested and subjected to the horrifying abuse of forced feeding while imprisoned. Yet, when women were beaten in Parliament Square or other public spaces, there was no evidence of concern. 'We submitted for years patiently to insult and assault. Women had their health injured. Women lost their lives,' she declared.

> We should not have minded if that had succeeded, but that did not succeed, and we have made more progress with less hurt to ourselves by breaking glass than ever we made when we allowed them to break our bodies … [but] … is not a woman's life, is not her health, are not her limbs more valuable than a pane of glass?[1]

The room, which had earlier been ringing out with shouts and cheers now fell silent, the women gathered deeply moved by her words. The WSPU leader concluded with the stark realisation that in a world where a pane of glass seemed to hold more worth than a woman's body or life, 'the argument of the pane of glass is the most valuable argument in modern politics'.

This speech had been agreed upon by Emmeline, Christabel and Mrs Pethick-Lawrence, who days earlier had met to discuss the new roadway for a women's revolution. Mrs Pethick-Lawrence had initially been reticent but, for a finish, all three leaders agreed that attacks on private as well as Government property were now necessary, despite the fact that such attacks and their incitement would inevitably court arrest. All three also agreed that if this threat loomed, Christabel, as the key strategist, should avoid arrest so she could continue to lead the movement. Emmeline had told the released prisoners and guests gathered at the dinner that those who joined her on the next protest, organised for 4 March, would be attacking private property on a much larger scale than previously. She insisted, however, that 'We only go as far as we are obliged to go in order to win.'[2]

These weren't just words chosen to rouse her audience. Emmeline, more than most, was acutely aware of the danger and suffering many of her fellow suffragettes endured due to the extreme tactics they felt compelled to use. In that speech and others, she often drew attention to the toll these actions had taken on the health of so many women. What she did not highlight, however, was how much her own health had deteriorated. Years of relentless campaigning and imprisonment had left their mark on the 53-year-old leader of the WSPU. She was plagued by a persistent cough and recurring spells of exhaustion.

As plans for the next wave of militant action were being finalised, Emmeline, with Christabel's blessing, decided to take a brief but much-needed rest. She retreated to the peaceful surroundings of Ethel Smyth's country cottage known as 'Coign', at Hook Heath in Surrey. There, in the warmth of the cosy home and her good friend's company, Emmeline slowly began to regain the strength she would need for the battles ahead. She spent her days resting, strolling through the fields, and, under Ethel's enthusiastic guidance, learning a skill she had urged others to adopt: throwing a stone with precision.

In the meantime, Christabel had decided to move out of Clement's Inn into a flat of her own. The 31-year-old wanted more independence. However, her decision was also fuelled by a growing weariness of life at the Pethick-Lawrences', which included several weekly dinner parties. Though these gatherings often secured new supporters or financial donations for the WSPU, Christabel found them draining. She had also begun to question Fred Pethick-Lawrence's role within the organisation. Over the years, Fred had taken on more speaking engagements, and while Christabel found him an uninspiring orator, he had gained a loyal following in the Men's Political Union. This, however, concerned Christabel even more; she worried that his increasing prominence within these circles might reignite calls to open the women-only WSPU membership to men.

She spoke privately to Emmeline once her mother had returned from America. Emmeline, always jealous of her daughter's relationships with the Pethick-Lawrences, had long harboured a dislike for Fred too, calling him 'the Godfather' behind his back. She eagerly supported her daughter's decision to create some distance. As if by fate, an opportunity soon arose. Jessie Stephenson, the organiser in Manchester, had a flat in Staple Inn, close to Clement's Inn, and agreed to sub-let it to Christabel. By mid-February, Christabel had moved in.

Emmeline returned to London in late February, better rested and with a new skill under her belt – she was now a semi-competent stone thrower! The WSPU headquarters were in a flurry of activity. Flyers had been printed up and distributed highlighting the 4 March protest. While the details of the planned attacks were deliberately vague, one sentence did warn members of the public who joined the demonstration that they might not 'altogether escape the uncomfortable consequences of the warfare between women and the Government'.

However, the WSPU now planned a covert attack on the government. Until now, they had always warned the authorities in advance of their protests, a practice that offered a degree of predictability. But a hastily written letter from Emmeline Pankhurst to Ethel Smyth, found later in a police raid, hinted at a dramatic shift. Dated Friday 1 March, the letter revealed a secret plan:

> There will be an unannounced affair, a sort of skirmish, in which some of our bad, bold ones will take part, an unadvertised affair.

> I shall take part, but not in the way I told you of – that is off. On Monday [4 March] there will be the affair as originally planned. C. and I have talked it over. My cough is troublesome. I must take care, or I shall not be very fit for the fray at the end of the week. There may be a long trial. I will meet your train on Monday.[3]

True to her word, that Friday, the suffragettes struck without warning for the first time. Emmeline Pankhurst, Mabel Tuke and Kitty Marshall took a taxi to 10 Downing Street and broke two windows. Meanwhile, well-dressed women armed with hammers concealed in their pockets and hand muffs spread out across London's West End. They targeted the plate-glass windows of fashionable shops and department stores, wreaking havoc that totalled around £5,000 in damages.

This sudden and organised outburst of destruction sent shockwaves through London. Emmeline herself was arrested alongside 120 others. In Bow Street Police Court the following day, she revealed to the magistrate that she and all the other arrested women were only following a path laid out and well-trod by men. She referenced recent remarks by Mr Hobhouse, a government official, who claimed that women had failed to demonstrate their desire for the vote as men in the past had. Hobhouse had pointed to dramatic actions such as the destruction of Nottingham Castle in 1832 and the tearing down of Hyde Park railings in 1867 as proof that real protest required a certain fervour.

On 4 March, the suffragettes escalated their campaign with another round of window-smashing, resulting in ninety-six arrests, including Ethel Smyth and Dr Louisa Garrett Anderson, daughter of the pioneering Dr Elizabeth Garrett Anderson and niece of Millicent Garrett Fawcett. A planned meeting by the Women's Social and Political Union that evening, promoted through handbills signed by Emmeline, aimed to rally support for a protest in Parliament Square. However, a heavy police presence transformed the gathering into a series of scattered incidents instead.

For the suffragettes, these sudden strikes were a declaration that they would no longer follow the rules of engagement as dictated by their oppressors. It was a message received loud and clear by the government. On Tuesday, 5 March, the authorities summoned Scotland Yard to raid the WSPU headquarters. They arrived armed with warrants for the arrest of the Pethick-Lawrences and Christabel. The Triumvirate, along with Emmeline and Mabel Tuke, were to face charges of 'conspiring to incite others to commit malicious damage to property'.[4]

However, only the Pethick-Lawrences were to be found at Clement's Inn. Christabel was in her new flat, working on an editorial for *Votes for Women* and was unaware of the unfolding events when a frantic Evelyn Sharp arrived with the message that the police had a warrant for her arrest. Evelyn also carried a cheque from Fred that needed Christabel's signature to transfer WSPU funds to Hertha Ayrton's bank account, keeping their money safe from police hands.

Just as Evelyn left, another suffragette arrived, breathless and clutching a hastily scrawled letter from Jessie Kenney. The letter informed her that the Pethick-Lawrences had been arrested and that, as had been discussed, Christabel was now to evade capture so as to keep the WSPU leadership intact.

Quickly, she packed a small suitcase. With no policemen in sight, she dashed out to hail a cab. Unsure of where to go, she had finally decided to make her way to the nursing home at 3 Pembridge Gardens where, a year earlier, her brother Harry had passed away. At 11.00pm, Nurses Catherine Pine and Gertrude Townend opened the door, surprised to find a distraught Christabel standing there. They ushered her inside, offering her hot milk at the kitchen table while arranging for her to spend the night with a supportive friend nearby.[5]

Grateful for their help, Christabel also appreciated the extra day of hiding – it gave her time to think. As a lawyer, she understood her status as a political offender might allow her to escape to a foreign country, making extradition difficult for the government. With this in mind, she resolved to go to Paris, where she and her mother had connections with several French suffragettes. In Paris, she could continue to maintain her leadership and the WSPU's strategy, albeit from afar.

On the morning of 6 March, disguised in long grey coat and a black cloche hat, Christabel prepared her escape. With £100 in gold sovereigns tied securely around her waist, she left her anxious hosts behind and took a cab to Victoria Station, where, using the pseudonym Amy Richards, she boarded the boat train to France.

Before she left, Christabel wrote a note for Annie, emphasising the urgency of the situation. If she were caught during her flight, Annie was to take charge of the WSPU and continue its militant campaign without hesitation. Christabel had absolute faith in her close friend's abilities, describing Annie as someone 'marked out for command' because of her unwavering strength of character, single-minded determination, sharp intuition, and perfect loyalty. For a finish, however, a tense and tired Christabel arrived safely in Paris. The leadership of the WSPU had not been crushed and the fight would go on.

In the meantime, Scotland Yard agents had seized dozens of boxes of letters and documents from Clement's Inn that would be painstakingly read in preparation for the state's conspiracy case against the WSPU. Included in these were several of Emmeline's own private papers, including photographs of her children in infancy, and private letters exchanged between her and her husband long ago. 'Some of these I never saw again,' she lamented later.[6]

Emmeline, who was now already in Holloway on charges of stone throwing, was brought before the Bow Street Court on 6 March, along with Mabel Tuke and the Pethick-Lawrences. All four were formally charged with having 'wantonly conspired and combined together, unlawfully and maliciously, to commit damage and injury to an amount exceeding £5 to plate-glass windows' and also with 'unlawfully aiding, abetting, counselling, and procuring the commission of offences against the Malicious Injuries to Property Act'.[7]

Emmeline's health had worsened once more and, as she stood in the dock, she gripped its rails for support, her voice faltering as she inquired how to secure resources to prepare her defence. Once back in her damp cell, away from all other suffragette prisoners, her condition deteriorated and she was soon moved to the hospital wing. Though she was more comfortable here, she had little energy or focus to ready herself for trial. At 53, Emmeline was already enduring the more taxing symptoms of menopause, but the cold, damp conditions of her cell had also left her battling bronchitis. Plus, while she was permitted to see her solicitor, Alfred Marshall, the fact that a wardress remained with them at all times, recording their conversations, meant that whatever was said in those meetings would likely hold no surprises when echoed in court.

By 17 March she had recovered sufficiently to be discharged from the hospital wing. However, to her surprise, she found herself transferred to the wing housing her fellow suffragettes, her new cell adjacent to that of her friend, the composer Ethel Smyth. Here, the austere monotony of Holloway became a little more bearable; thanks to the quiet kindness of a sympathetic head wardress, Ethel was often allowed to enjoy a prolonged tea-time in Emmeline's cell. Such stolen moments of friendship, however modest, brought unexpected warmth.

The suffragette block had a freer, and as such, a more defiant, spirit. Ethel later recalled the creative mischief that helped to brighten their days. The women somehow got their hands on large scraps of brightly coloured material, and with pens and chalk, scrawled across them 'designs and mottoes, brimming with insult and defiance [that] would adorn the courtyard walls for hours before being discovered and torn down'.[8] Though these moments were few, it allowed the prisoners to delight in their rebellion.

On 28 March, however, the political struggle that had resulted in their imprisonment returned with full force. The Second Conciliation Bill was scheduled for its second reading. That morning, *The Times* published a letter from Sir Almroth Wright, a respected doctor and Fellow of the Royal Society, which argued that women were fundamentally unfit for the vote, citing physiological differences and claiming that many militant suffragists suffered from mental instability. He suggested that this instability arose from the surplus of single women who, in his view, 'had better long ago have gone out to mate with its complement of men beyond the seas'.[9] The argument was nothing that the suffragettes hadn't heard before but it dampened spirits so that when word of the Bill's defeat by fourteen votes came through they were not surprised.

Several MPs later claimed they had voted against the Second Conciliation Bill due to the escalating violence of the WSPU. But the militants knew better. This explanation was, at best, a convenient excuse. The reality was more political: many Liberal and Labour members opposed the bill because they prioritised the universal manhood suffrage bill, while Irish Nationalists feared the bill's success might destabilise Prime Minister Asquith's government at a critical moment in their own long and weary push for Home Rule.

Blaming suffragette violence, however, offered a simpler, more publicly palatable narrative, even while the suffragettes were not alone in resorting to such tactics at this time. In truth, this was a time of profound unrest across Britain. In 1911, Liverpool's dockers, railway workers, sailors, and other tradesmen staged a massive strike demanding a minimum wage, leading to violent clashes. The miners' strike in South Wales, which began in 1910, had devolved into years of brutal confrontations, including hand-to-hand fighting between rioting miners and police. Yet while such violence from men was considered dreadful it was also deemed legitimate, whereas women resorting to similar tactics was seen not just as shocking but immoral.

Following the West End window-smashing campaign, Mr Lasenby Liberty, whose store had been targeted, voiced the indignation of many in a *Times* letter. He demanded Mrs Pankhurst explain 'the mental process by which they deem the breaking of the very shrines at which they worship will advance their cause'.

Just as with Mary Gawthorpe, others once sympathetic to the cause also began to distance themselves from the WSPU with the excuse of the women's horrifying lack of social decorum. Among them was Dr Elizabeth Garrett Anderson, the pioneering feminist who had once marched alongside Emmeline Pankhurst. Despite her own daughter enduring a prison sentence for suffrage activism, or perhaps, because of it, Dr Garrett Anderson now turned her back on Emmeline, writing to her sister Millicent Fawcett:

> Katie Thompson sent me rather a large cheque today for the Cause. I have written to ask if I may hand it to you. I certainly do not mean to give it to Mrs. Pankhurst. I think she and the P. Lawrences have shown very little fortitude or dignity.

Towards the end of March, Emmeline and her fellow WSPU leaders appeared in the dock for their conspiracy hearing. Mabel Tuke was acquitted, but Emmeline and the Pethick-Lawrences were committed for trial at the Central Criminal Court, the Old Bailey. Fred was required to pay £2,000 and provided two sureties for £1,000 each; Emmeline was required to pay £1,500 and to find two sureties at £750 each. As Emmeline was already serving a sentence, she was returned to Holloway. On 4 April, just before Good Friday, the trio returned to court to discover when their trial would happen. Set for May 1912, they had a month for preparation. In addition, Emmeline was unexpectedly released on bail, her prison sentence for window-breaking deferred until after the conspiracy trial.

That Easter, Emmeline sought refuge with Ethel in Coign. Ethel, too, had been released early after serving only three weeks of her two-month sentence. Emmeline longed to spend the Easter break with her eldest daughter, Christabel, but she took solace in her daughter's continued leadership of the WSPU from afar. Christabel, who continued to successfully evade arrest, was orchestrating the movement with remarkable ingenuity. Anonymous articles continued to appear in *Votes for Women*, and the campaign of window-breaking remained in full swing. Only a few, including Emmeline, knew Christabel's exact location.

On arrival in Paris, her eldest daughter had booked herself into a cheap hotel near the Arc de Triomphe. From there, she quickly set about establishing lines of communication with her team back in Britain. Still using her pseudonym Amy Richards, her secret missives to London were routed through trusted intermediaries, often the servants of wealthy suffragettes who would travel discreetly to London, delivering Christabel's letters to the staff at Clement's Inn. These letters kept Annie Kenney and, eventually, Emmeline herself, informed of Christabel's whereabouts and strategies.

Emmeline had entrusted Ethel with the details regarding Christabel's new address and Ethel immediately reached out to contacts she had in the arts world in Paris. One of these was the influential Princesse Winnaretta Singer de Polignac, the American-born heiress to the Singer sewing machine empire and widow of Prince Edmond de Polignac. The Princess was a patron of the avant garde arts scene in Paris and had sponsored Ethel among other composers. She and Ethel had also embarked on a short-lived passionate affair, but had remained friends thereafter. Winnaretta's renowned salon was a hub of French cultural life, with writers such as Colette and Marcel Proust, composers including Maurice Ravel, and the Impressionist artist Claude Monet all attending them regularly. The Princess happily agreed to take Christabel under her wing, introduce her to several important political and cultural figures, and help her establish a foothold in the French capital.

In the meantime, ensuring that she could keep links with the WSPU back in London, Christabel and Annie came up with a system whereby the latter would travel incognito to Paris every Friday. Here, she would spend the weekend with Christabel, who would give her the instructions she needed to implement during the following week.

Annie grew to cherish these clandestine trips. Not only did her friendship with Christabel deepen, but her own confidence as a key figure in the suffrage movement flourished. Reflecting in her memoir, Annie fondly described these Parisian weekends:

> Christabel's vitality was good for me. She was fresh, virile, energetic. I would arrive sick, tired to exhaustion, and yet on Sunday morning I felt refreshed and ready for the labour awaiting me. She has the most vitalising personality that I had ever met … The Saturdays in Paris were a joy. We would walk along the river or go into the Bois, or visit the gardens … [with] stacks of newspapers, pockets stuffed with pencils, and always a knife to sharpen them … arm in arm, talking incessantly.

Initially, Christabel resisted becoming too involved in the exciting cultural whirl of the Princess's salon. Having just left behind the lively social scene of the Pethick-Lawrences, she was determined to rest and remain anonymous until she could be sure her safety in France was secure. She was also, like so many of her colleagues in arms, exhausted. 'I had been working very, very hard, and when I stepped ashore in France I was on the verge of a nervous breakdown,' she later explained. Thus, to recuperate, she retreated to a quiet hamlet near Boulogne on the northern coast, close to England.

Once she felt safe and well enough to return to Paris, she did so, making the capital city her base of operations. By this time, her circumstances had improved significantly. Likely with financial support from the Princesse de Polignac, Christabel moved into a larger apartment in a more fashionable district and from there continued her WSPU work.

That April, Sylvia returned to Britain following a second tour to the United States. She arrived to find her mother newly released from prison, her elder sister a fugitive in Paris, and her younger sister, Adela, recuperating from severe mental and physical ill-health at a retreat for sick suffragettes in Bath.

Sylvia's American tour, coming so soon after Emmeline's, had not gone well. Once again, she had difficulty dealing with the blatant racism of American society but she had also been met with little sympathy for the suffragette cause. Headlines in *The New York Times* like 'Suffragists Smash London Shop Windows' framed the British movement as one of 'wanton terrorism', alienating many. Disheartened and a little disgusted by her American compatriots, Sylvia had been glad to return to England.

Determined to support her family and, perhaps, as historian June Purvis suggests, seeing this as a ripe opportunity to steer the WSPU back toward its socialist roots in their physical absence, Sylvia decided to visit Christabel in Paris. The press at the time was full of headlines eagerly querying 'Where was Christabel?', while articles claimed supposed sightings of the fugitive suffragette filled the pages. Sylvia knew she needed to be cautious when crossing the Channel and was helped in her disguise by Nurse Pine. Then, travelling undetected, she arrived safely in France and sought out her sister. Christabel was delighted to see Sylvia, bringing her on shopping sprees and visits to galleries. However, when Sylvia suggested she could be of help in the WSPU, Christabel dismissed her offer. Instead, she advised her younger sister to stay out of sight: 'Behave as though you were not in the country … When those who are doing the work are arrested, you may be needed and can be called on.'

Sylvia later reflected that such advice to do nothing as yet was 'ludicrous', given the dire state of the movement and their mother's impending conspiracy trial. 'The movement was limitless in its need,' she noted.[10] However, it's possible that Christabel, acutely aware of the dangers faced by their mother, herself, and countless other suffragettes at the time of this increased militancy, was trying to protect Sylvia from further harm. To Sylvia, though, the exchange was a painful snub. Christabel's casual disregard of her struck home just how unimportant Sylvia was to the WSPU. She was not one of its leaders, and had never been invited into such a role. Instead, her role, as she believed she saw through the eyes of Christabel, consisted of little more than producing banners and artwork for the cause.

Interestingly, Sylvia contends that at this time her older sister also made her feelings about Adela plain. 'I would not care if you were multiplied by a hundred,' Christabel is said to have remarked. 'But one of Adela is too many.'[11]

Indeed, the issue of Adela had remained a concern for both Christabel and Emmeline. It seems certain that Christabel wanted her youngest sister out of the movement. Perhaps this was due to Adela's popularity in Scotland or her untempered left-wing ideals, which increasingly diverged from the WSPU's more conservative views. Adela later claimed her break with the WSPU was as a result of the organisation's escalating violence, and while others back this up, it's still true that, regardless, she wasn't slow to contribute to that violence by throwing stones on several occasions and enduring hunger strikes.

For Emmeline, the situation may have been more complicated. While she deferred to Christabel's negative judgement of Adela, her younger daughter's frequent health problems likely weighed heavily on her mind. Emmeline had already endured the devastating losses of two sons and her husband to illness. Could she face the possibility of losing another child? These unspoken fears may have helped shape her treatment of Adela, though most historians prefer to think maternal love played but a small part. The quote from an early suffragette supporter is often used to highlight Emmeline's feelings towards her daughters: 'Mrs Pankhurst would walk over the dead bodies of all her children except Christabel and say "See what I have done for the cause."' Certainly, as a daughter, Adela had never felt her mother's warmth even though she adored Emmeline and craved her approval. Her contributions to the movement were also consistently overlooked. While Christabel and even Sylvia were lauded for their input, Adela's work seemed to vanish into the background. The erasure was so complete that Emmeline didn't even mention Adela in her later autobiography, *My Story*.

Whether it was Adela's health, her political ideals, or her perceived inadequacies that led to Emmeline's increasingly harsh treatment of Adela over the next few years, it's impossible to say for certain. However, in those unstable months for the WSPU, Emmeline encouraged Adela to pursue the horticultural studies the young girl had recently decided upon – but with one significant condition: Adela was never to speak in public in Britain again. It wasn't an official expulsion, but the message was clear enough. For Adela, it must have come as a shock. It was, after all, the end of a role she had held since the age of 18, when she sat in the kitchen listening to her mother and others of the newly formed WSPU dream of a better future for women. The movement that had shaped her life was now slipping away, and her relationship with her mother – strained and uneven – had been dealt another blow. For Emmeline, the decision may have been motivated by love, fear, or necessity. For Adela, it was simply another wound in a relationship full of them.

On 15 May, Emmeline and the Pethick-Lawrences' Old Bailey conspiracy trial began, presided over by Justice Coleridge. It would last for six days, and be covered in length by the national press. Emmeline chose to represent herself, confidently cross-examining witnesses and challenging evidence. Fred Pethick-Lawrence also acted as his own lawyer, while his wife was defended by Tim Healy KC, an Irish politician who would later serve as the first Attorney General of the Irish Free State.

Emmeline was as eloquent and sharp-minded as ever. At one point, she highlighted the irony of the situation that had led her and Emmeline Pethick-Lawrence to be punished under the law, while they had no say in shaping the laws they were accused of breaking. As she proceeded with her defence, she once more stirred the hearts and minds of many in the gallery with her recollection of her time as a Poor Law Guardian. She described how witnessing the appalling conditions endured by poor women and children had inspired her to fight for change. Emmeline went on to explain how after years of trying to secure the vote for women through common constitutional ways, she had come to realise those methods were futile. It was this realisation that had led her to found the Women's Social and Political Union in 1903.

In her closing arguments, Emmeline defended the WSPU's militancy, stating: 'No step we have taken forward has been taken until after some act of repression on the part of our enemy, the Government.' And she emphasised, 'It is the Government which is our enemy – it is not the Members of Parliament, it is not the men in the country; it is the Government in power alone that can give us the vote.'[12]

The all-male jury deliberated for less than half an hour before delivering a guilty verdict. However, they appealed to the judge to exercise leniency, believing the defendants had acted out of pure motives. Judge Coleridge was unmoved. Moreover, he dismissed the defendants' request to be treated as political prisoners, instead giving them a much heavier sentence of nine months in the Second Division. He claimed it was the trio's complete lack of remorse that had led to this decision. In addition, Emmeline and Fred were ordered to cover the prosecution's costs.

As the judge departed, there was hissing and cries of 'Shame! Shame!' from the courtroom. This quickly changed to cheers as the prisoners were led away, Fred to Wormwood Scrubs (though he would later be transferred to Brixton Prison) and his wife and Emmeline to Holloway. Keir Hardie, who had attended the trial throughout, reached out to shake Fred's hand. Outside the courthouse, supportive crowds waved handkerchiefs and called out good wishes.

Most of the press, though not wholly on the suffragettes' side, agreed the sentence was harsh, and at least one of the jury members wrote to complain to the Home Secretary claiming that the prisoners should have been given political status.

Emmeline remained incarcerated in the Second Division up until 22 June. During that time her brother Herbert, daughters Adela and Sylvia, and several friends all put in requests to visit her and were each denied. Ethel Smyth did manage to get a crate of expensive French wine to her on the grounds that she needed a half pint of Château Lafite daily for the good of her health!

In the meantime, the two new prisoners refused to be medically examined and do any work in the prison. When they threatened to go on hunger strike, the Home Office – under growing pressure from influential politicians and public figures rallying outside the prison – relented. All three WSPU leaders were moved to the First Division.

This was not enough for Emmeline. Seventy-nine other suffragettes remained in Holloway's harsher Third Division, and she demanded that they, too, be recognised as political prisoners. Meanwhile, her health continued to decline. She suffered from a persistent skin complaint, a sore throat, and significant weight loss. Concerned about the reports he was receiving, Emmeline's brother Herbert demanded that she be allowed a visit from a trusted physician, Dr Agnes Savill of Harley Street, who had been treating his sister for years. His request was ignored.

On 19 June, the suffragettes who were still in Third Division began to hunger strike. Emmeline and the Pethick-Lawrences joined them. Three days later, forcible feeding began. Emmeline, still poorly, consented to an examination by the prison medical officer, who discovered she had a very weak pulse. The doctor warned that force-feeding her could lead to serious complications, and so she was spared.[13]

Mrs Pethick-Lawrence wasn't so fortunate. Terrified, she tried to resist, but was restrained and the tube brutally forced down her throat. Emmeline, deeply distressed, heard her screams from her own cell. The shock of the event caused Mrs Pethick-Lawrence to faint almost immediately once the tube was finally removed. When she regained consciousness, the pain in her stomach was so intense that the prison doctor was called. His examination also revealed a weakened pulse and it was decided that she would not be force-fed again. In Brixton, Fred was also undergoing the same ordeal. Though equally shaken, his stronger constitution meant he was force-fed twice a day for three days. However, the strain was severe; he lost four stone and grew alarmingly weak. Eventually, on 24 June and 27 June respectively, the two women and Fred were released on medical grounds.

The day after Emmeline's release, George Lansbury strode purposefully up the floor of the House of Commons. When he reached the ministerial bench, he stopped, his hand trembling with fury as he pointed directly at Asquith, and shouted angrily: 'You will go down in history as the man who tortured innocent women.' In truth, this public accusation, which was heavily covered in the press, meant that it was Lansbury who went down in history as a defender of the people.

Emmeline spent a few days recovering at the Pethick-Lawrences' home at Clement's Inn before retreating to the countryside with Ethel for complete rest. The strain of her imprisonment had left its mark and in a letter to her closest allies in the movement, she announced that she would step back from all suffrage work and responsibilities until her health was fully restored. However, once she felt able to move around again, she quietly slipped across the Channel to see Christabel in France, using the alias 'Mrs Richards'. It would be the first of many trips she would take across the water thereafter to spend time with her daughter and Christabel recalls that these were happy days for her mother. Having the time and opportunity 'revived her schoolday memories', Christabel claims. 'It was a happy interlude for both of us in which, for a brief moment, we could prepare for the hard fight yet to come.'[14]

Deciding to take a trip to the coastal town of Boulogne, in Northern France, mother and daughter were soon joined by the Pethick-Lawrences who were themselves on their way to Switzerland for further rest and recouperation. It had been months since the four WSPU leaders had been together. Fred later recalled a walk he and Christabel took along the cliffs overlooking the sea, discussing the WSPU's increasingly militant campaign. During their holiday, news broke that Helen Craggs, Harry Pankhurst's first love, had been arrested in the early hours of the morning on the grounds of Lewis Harcourt's country home. Harcourt, a leading government opponent of women's suffrage, had unwittingly become the target of the movement's first serious act of arson.

Though another woman had been seen fleeing from the scene, Helen was not so lucky. She had been caught carrying bottles of inflammable oil, fire-lighters, matches, nine picklocks, a glass-cutter, keys, and a note declaring that after exhausting all peaceful methods of protest, she had been driven to take drastic action. Unlike Emily Davison's earlier letterbox fires, Helen's attempt carried a far greater risk of harm. Neither Emmeline nor Christabel had known about or approved it. When Helen was later sentenced to nine months' hard labour, Emmeline publicly stood by her as a fellow suffragette but made it clear that the young woman had acted 'solely on her own responsibility'.

These acts concerned Fred. Beyond their obvious danger, the ceaseless targeting of private property was alienating the public. He proposed that they focus on educating people to understand the reasons behind the WSPU's rising use of more extreme methods. His wife had already made her opinion clear that continuing to escalate militancy was now more reckless and unsustainable. But their concerns clashed with Christabel and her mother's firm convictions that attacking public and private property were a necessary strategy and required no justification. After all, these tactics were rooted in precedent, they argued. They were a deliberate echo of the tactics men had employed in their own struggles to secure the vote.

Fred had always held Christabel's political acumen in high regard. He rarely challenged her judgement and, after having her live with them for six years, thought of her almost as a daughter. He believed this bond would ensure his opinions were respected. Mrs Pethick-Lawrence, however, was less confident. In fact, she believed that Christabel was swayed fully in this matter by her mother. On stage, in front of the crowds, Emmeline captivated her audience with her poise and composure. But behind it all she was still the young girl in search of adventure. A woman, Mrs Pethick-Lawrence believed, who would always thrive best on drama and danger.

'While Christabel lived with us she agreed that we had to advance in militancy by slow degrees in order to give the average person time to understand every move and to keep pace. But since her escape to Paris, Christabel had gone completely over to her mother's standpoint,' Mrs Pethick-Lawrence later wrote.

Fred had also assumed that Christabel would soon return to London to rejoin the movement's activities, but again he was surprised to hear that this would not be the case. Christabel informed him that as the WSPU's militancy would be intensified that October, it was necessary for her to remain in Paris and outside the reach of Government – and the police – so that she could continue to 'direct it'.

Fred was disheartened. Arguments broke out, and things got heated. However, by next day, the tensions appeared to have eased, and the Pethick-Lawrences departed for their holiday in Switzerland. As hugs and smiles were exchanged, and words of well-wishing shared, it's unlikely that the couple were aware that their close ties with the Emmeline and Christabel had already started to unravel and that the time which Emmeline would later refer to as 'a four-fold partnership … in which each member played a unique and important part', was coming to an end.

Shortly after the leaders' meeting in Boulogne, another incident occurred. On 18 July, Mary Leigh and Dorothy Evans travelled to Dublin to make a protest against the proposed Home Rule Bill which made no mention of women's rights. At Dublin's Theatre Royal, during a performance attended by Prime Minister Asquith, they set fire to the curtains in his box. Later, as Asquith and the Irish leader John Redmond were being driven to the Prime Minister's hotel, Mary Leigh hurled a hatchet into their carriage. Both women were swiftly arrested and subsequently sentenced to five years in prison. However, they immediately went on hunger strike and, after weeks of forcible feeding, were released after serving just four months.

When their sentence was first announced, Emmeline briefly abandoned her plan to step back from WSPU activities. Writing in *Votes for Women*, she praised the two women 'whom we love and honour for their splendid courage', and declared that their actions now forced the Government to choose between 'sending large numbers of women to penal servitude or granting them the vote'.

In July, Adela took part in her final act as a WSPU member, campaigning alongside Helen Archdale and her sister Sylvia in the North West Manchester by-election. When the campaign ended, the youngest Pankhurst daughter stepped away from the organisation she had given much of her young life to.

In the meantime, Emmeline continued to spend her summer in France. She returned briefly to London after receiving news that the rooms in Clement's Inn that the WSPU were using had been reclaimed by the landlord. Acting swiftly, she secured new headquarters at Lincoln's Inn House. Far from being frustrated by the sudden upheaval, she welcomed it. She had never felt entirely at ease in the old Clement's Inn offices, and this move felt like a chance to start afresh. But the relocation was only the beginning of bigger changes ahead.

Christabel and Emmeline had invited Mabel Tuke and Annie Kenney to come to France for a meeting. There they discussed the next steps for the WSPU and, in particular, the Pethick-Lawrences. The concerns relating to the absent leaders wasn't just about differing opinions on strategy, though that was certainly crucial. As Annie astutely noted, once someone disagreed with Christabel on policy, 'her whole feeling towards them changed'.[15] But there was a more pressing issue involving Fred. Neither he nor Emmeline had paid the fines imposed at the conspiracy trial in May. The implications of not doing so were very different for each. Emmeline owned no assets for the government to seize, but Fred was not so fortunate. In August, while he and his wife had travelled on to Canada, bailiffs had entered their country house at Holmwood and taken all the furniture. Yet even with the contents of the house sold, Fred still owed close to £3,000.

Emmeline and Christabel saw the risk around this all too clearly. The authorities could use Fred's financial troubles to pressure the WSPU into scaling back its militancy. After all, if he had to pay the price in court every time a woman took militant action, either their campaign would have to stop, or Fred and Emmeline would face financial ruin. In addition, supporters might rally to organise fundraising efforts for the Pethick-Lawrences, diverting much-needed resources from the WSPU's war chest. To the two leaders of the WSPU, both scenarios were unthinkable. Thus, after much discussion, Emmeline, Christabel, Mabel and Annie concluded that the Pethick-Lawrences had become a liability.

Emmeline put all of this in a letter to Mrs Pethick-Lawrence, claiming that the authorities 'see in Mr Lawrence a potent weapon against the militant movement and they mean to use it. This weapon is a powerful one. By its use they can not only ruin Mr Lawrence, but they also intend, if they can, to divert our funds.'

All of this was likely true, but the situation also gave Emmeline and Christabel a convenient reason to finally sever ties with Fred. In the same letter, Emmeline suggested that the Pethick-Lawrences remove their assets to Canada and set up a branch of the WSPU there, spreading the movement to the far corners of the Commonwealth. Such a relocation was out of the question for the couple and Mrs Pethick-Lawrence didn't even refer to it in her reply. Instead she wrote, rather acidly: 'Perhaps you are not aware that the present situation does not take my husband or me by surprise,' before firmly stating they planned to continue sharing responsibility of the WSPU with Emmeline and Christabel. The threats to their fortune were also dismissed. 'The more we are menaced the harder we will fight until victory is won … We have never for a single instant allowed our individual interests to stand in the way of any necessary action on policy to be pursued by the Union, and we never shall.'[16]

The Pethick-Lawrences planned to return to England that October. Before their arrival, Emmeline herself returned in optimistic humour to oversee the move into the new WSPU headquarters. When, some weeks later, the Pethick-Lawrences arrived in Fishguard, they were met by a friend who gave them the news that they were to be ousted from the WSPU. Though they could not believe it, when they arrived at the new offices in Lincoln's Inn House, they were dismayed to discover there was no room or even a desk set aside for them to work at. In addition, they were met by awkward silences, in particular from Mabel Tuke and Annie Kenney, two women who had once been so close to Mrs Pethick-Lawrence in particular. The day after their arrival, Emmeline asked for a private meeting and informed them that their association with the WSPU was at an end. Though everything had pointed to this moment, it still shocked and hurt them. Initially they refused to accept the situation and Christabel was forced to slip into the country incognito to confirm the decision. 'The whole situation has come upon us with startling suddenness and at the time nearly stunned us,' Fred wrote to George Lansbury. 'To be asked to leave the WSPU to which we had contributed our life blood was like asking a mother to be parted from her child.' Later, he would write resignedly in his biography, 'Mrs. Pankhurst was the acknowledged autocrat of the Union. We had ourselves supported her in acquiring this position several years previously; we could not dispute it now.'[17]

A meeting with the WSPU's national committee was called to explain the changes that were occurring. Emmeline had asked Elizabeth Robins and Mary Neal, both members of the leadership committee, to attend, hoping for their support. However, when Robins and Neal tried to object to the decision to oust the Pethick-Lawrences, they were sharply silenced and dismissed as being uninformed, given their infrequent attendance at meetings. Faced with such hostility, Fred and Emmeline walked out of the meeting. In her autobiography, Mrs Pethick-Lawrence would recall:

> There was something quite ruthless about Mrs Pankhurst and Christabel where human relationship were concerned. This ruthlessness was shown not only to us but to many others – Men and women of destiny are like that … From that time forward I never saw or heard from Mrs Pankhurst again and Christabel, who had shared our family life, became a complete stranger. The Pankhursts did nothing by halves![18]

Horrified by what had transpired, Elizabeth Robins immediately handed in her resignation, followed by Mary Neal. Sylvia was also present and was torn between her conflicting loyalties. While she shared the Pethick-Lawrences' belief that escalating violence would only harden opposition to the cause, she also understood that the momentum of militant action was now unstoppable. Reflecting on the situation later, she wrote of the women suffragettes already in the field: 'I would not add one word to the chorus condemning those courageous girls who trusted implicitly in the wisdom of the Union.'

A statement as to the revised leadership of the WSPU, prepared for publication in *Votes for Women*, read:

> The first re-union of the leaders after the enforced holiday [,] Mrs Pankhurst and Miss Christabel Pankhurst outlined a new militant policy which Mr & Mrs Pethick-Lawrence found themselves altogether unable to approve.
>
> Mrs Pankhurst and Miss Christabel Pankhurst indicated that they were not prepared to modify their intentions[,] and recommended that Mr and Mrs Pethick-Lawrence should resume absolute control of the paper, Votes for Women [,] & should leave the Women's Social & Political Union. Rather than make schism in the ranks of the Union [,] Mr & Mrs Pethick Lawrence consented to take this course.

In addition, a grand event at the Albert Hall, which had been planned for the triumphant return of the WSPU's imprisoned leaders, would now serve as the moment to officially announce the departure of the Pethick-Lawrences.

On the day itself, Emmeline Pankhurst stepped out alone onto stage, Christabel having quietly returned to Paris. With her characteristic calm and elegance, the leader of the WSPU addressed the surprised crowd, explaining the recent split.

'It is better that those who cannot agree, cannot see eye to eye as to policy, should set themselves free, should part, and should be free to continue their policy as they see it in their own way,' she said graciously. She then spoke warmly of Fred and Emmeline Pethick-Lawrence, declaring:

> Although no longer working with us as colleagues, our hearts are full of gratitude to both Mr and Mrs Pethick-Lawrence for all they have done, with unsparing generosity and unfailing sacrifice of time, energy and devotion, for the Union in the past, and the memory of our association with them will always be cherished as a treasured possession.

But Emmeline's speech that day was not just an acknowledgment of the Pethick-Lawrences' contributions. It was also a rallying cry for the WSPU's next phase – a yet more defiant and unapologetic escalation of militancy. Standing before the crowd she issued a clear and bold call to action.

> Be militant each in your own way. Those of you who can express your militancy by going to the House of Commons and refusing to leave without satisfaction, as we did in the early days – do so. Those of you who can express militancy by facing party mobs at Cabinet Ministers' meetings, when you remind them of their falseness to principle – do so. Those of you who can express your militancy by joining us in our anti-Government by-election policy – do so. Those of you who can break windows – break them. Those of you who can still further attack the secret idol of property, so as to make the Government realise that property is as greatly endangered by women's suffrage as it was by the Chartists of old – do so.[19]

In *Unshackled*, Christabel's vivid imagining of her mother on that night leaves no doubt about the depth of her admiration and pride in Emmeline. Whether or not Mrs Pethick-Lawrence was correct in assuming that it was Emmeline who was urging on her daughter to announce bolder acts of militancy, it is clear that Christabel was committed to moving onward, forward, to the next defiant steps. She writes:

> I can picture Mother on the Albert Hall platform that night, slender and fragile, rather tired, yet erect, head lifted, her eyes, large under their high-arched brows, looking upon the vast audience and through and beyond that place and hour – to what was coming upon her. No alternative! That was her reason. No way but militancy, to induce a Government, founded on votes, to do justice to the voteless.[20]

In Emmeline's final, fierce message, that lack of compromise was writ large in what would become one of the WSPU's leader's most unforgettable statements: 'My last word is to the Government: I incite this meeting to rebellion.'

Drawing a parallel to the Ulster Unionists, who were continuing to resist Home Rule through threats of rebellion, she declared:

> You have not dared to arrest the leaders of Ulster for their incitement to rebellion. Take me if you dare! But I warn you, if you do, so long as those who incited armed rebellion in Ulster remain free, you will not keep me in prison. So long as men rebels – and voters – are at liberty, we will not stay imprisoned, first division or no first division.

CHAPTER

16

CAT AMONG THE MICE

Despite Christabel's advice to keep a low profile, Sylvia threw herself into the work of the WSPU with more enthusiasm than ever before. Her time in America, the inequality she had witnessed there, and the dwindling public interest in Britain's suffragettes had sparked a renewed determination to fight for the cause. For years, Sylvia had searched for her purpose, longing to play a part in righting the world's injustices. Now it seemed the answer had been in front of her all along.

Though it had not been asked of her, that spring and summer she undertook a punishing schedule of meetings across London's parks, open spaces, and street corners. She spoke until her voice was hoarse, often facing jeers and threats from men in the crowd. Much of her time was spent in the East End, where she had to dodge old fish heads, rotting vegetables, or wads of tissue soaked in urine hurled in her direction. Yet she endured it all. Like so many suffragettes, she had learnt to accept antagonism as an inevitable companion to the applause.

On 14 July, which was Bastille Day and the day her mother always claimed was her birthday, Sylvia, alongside Flora Drummond and Lady Sybil Smith, organised a huge WSPU rally in Hyde Park. They were joined by members of the ILP and the Fabians, though Millicent Fawcett's NUWSS was notably absent. While the NUWSS supported the ILP, Millicent refused to align with the WSPU's increasingly violent trajectory. The event was a marvellous success, dampened only by a telegram Sylvia claimed she had received from Christabel in Paris, urging her to burn down Nottingham Castle. 'The request came as a shock to me,' Sylvia later wrote. 'The idea of committing a stealthy act of destruction was repugnant to me.'[1]

Yet Sylvia did not condemn the 'stealthy acts of destruction' when carried out by other determined suffragettes. She had even formed a new friendship with Norah Smyth, who, it turned out, had been the 'other woman' sneaking with Helen Craggs through the grounds of MP Lewis Harcourt's home. On that occasion, Norah had managed to scale the wall and escape, while Helen had not been so lucky.

That summer, Sylvia also grew close to Zelie Emerson, the daughter of an American industrialist whom she had met in Chicago. Zelie had followed Sylvia back to Britain, exchanging her privileged life in America for a life fighting against women's inequality on the streets of Britain. Along with their determination to secure the vote for women, the trio shared a commitment to socialism, and it was this that often found them in London's East End, working alongside George Lansbury, the MP for Bromley and Bow. Lansbury welcomed the women warmly, though his wife, Bessie, initially viewed them with suspicion as nothing more than middle-class do-gooders. Over time, however, she came to recognise that they were genuinely committed to improving the lives of East End women, and, in particular, she and Sylvia developed a close friendship.

The East End had undergone notable changes in the few years since Sylvia and Annie Kenney first walked its battered streets, speaking with impoverished women about the promise of voting rights and freedom from poverty. While conditions were still deplorable, with overcrowding, poor drainage, dangerous work environments, and families living below the poverty line, new forms of transport and entertainment, such as cinemas, music halls, and pubs, had brought fresh vitality to the area.

Political activism had long gone hand in hand with East End life, though it was not always easy to sustain momentum. Many women here had supported the WSPU from its very first London meeting when Sylvia and Annie had paid train fares to bring them to Caxton Hall. In 1906, the Canning Town branch of the WSPU had been formed, though it had generally been overlooked by the organisation's leadership. Additionally, unlike their middle-class counterparts, most working women in the East End and elsewhere had other pressing demands on their time. Long hours in factories, on shop floors, or in domestic service were just the start; they also shouldered the burden of running households, and cooking and cleaning for their families. As Hannah Mitchell, who had been a former dressmaker and domestic servant, observed in her autobiography *The Hard Way Up, the Autobiography of Hannah Mitchell, Suffragette and Rebel*: 'No cause can be won between dinner and tea, and most of us who were married had to work with one hand tied behind us.'

However, Sylvia hoped to strengthen the WSPU's scant following in the East End by reigniting the socialist spirit that had originally defined the Union. There was, in many ways, a certain romanticism in Sylvia's vision, not unlike Annie's when she had first arrived in the East End as a young mill girl. But Sylvia, similar to her father, had a more instinctive understanding of the cultural as well as the environmental contexts of systemic injustice. Moreover, it was coupled with the capacity to truly imagine a future where these women –

alongside the wealthier prisoners behind the bars of Holloway – would have the right to vote.

With these ideas in mind, Sylvia, Norah and Zelie tramped the East End pathways until they found an old bakery at 198 Bow Road. It was here that they established the East London branch of the WSPU. The new premises were conveniently close to Lansbury's home, and his family enthusiastically supported the women's efforts. They brought lumber from the family's wood factory to build floorboards and shelves and helped in whatever ways they could. Lansbury himself was an outspoken advocate for women's suffrage and had been pressuring his fellow Labour MPs to support votes for women – a stance that earned him the full backing of Emmeline and Christabel. The Labour Party, however, had other priorities and would not put votes for women above Irish Home Rule and the Trade Union Bill. Party leaders demanded that Lansbury fall in line or leave. Although Emmeline urged him to stay and wield influence from within, he refused. Instead, the East End politician resigned from Labour and announced his decision to stand for re-election in the Bromley and Bow by-election as an independent socialist.[2]

Lansbury's full-hearted embrace of the movement, and the WSPU in particular, came at a critical time for Emmeline and Christabel. Despite the warm reception Emmeline had received at the Albert Hall, many in the WSPU were shaken by the recent split with the Pethick-Lawrences. Financially, the meeting brought in only £3,600 in actual funds and pledged donations – a modest amount compared to the £5,000 or more the organisation typically raised at such events in the past. The shift in leadership naturally caused anxiety among women who were literally putting their lives and reputations on the line for the organisation. There was apprehension about what a WSPU led solely by the uncompromising Pankhursts might demand of them. As Elizabeth Robins observed, the Pethick-Lawrences had provided a sense of stability to counterbalance Emmeline and Christabel's 'force and fire'. As a result, there was a lot of debate among the file and ranks as to whether this split was actually of benefit to the Union. One suffragette, Anna McLeod, went so far as to draft a petition for their reinstatement. Though she claimed the petition was not meant as an insult to Emmeline, she described the Pethick-Lawrence withdrawal as an 'irreparable loss to the Union'.

'One pair of shoulders [i.e., Emmeline's],' she wrote, 'should not and cannot bear the great weight of responsibility resting on them in this crisis of the Women's Movement.'[3]

However, the petition was completely disregarded by Emmeline, as were the conflicting feelings within the organisation itself. Annie Kenney, who had not stood up for the Pethick-Lawrences at the time, later reflected sadly that, 'The old days were over … the fight continued, but the Movement, as a Movement, was lost. The two had gone who had been the creative geniuses of the constructive side of a world-famed fight.'

That world-famed fight was now continuing in a much fiercer manner. The Young Hot Bloods (YHB) stepped up their influence, engaging in what could only be described as terrorist acts of violence. Windows were smashed, and so many fires were set in letterboxes that by early December 1912, the government claimed over 5,000 letters had been damaged. These violent activities had forced much of the WSPU activities underground, which is why Emmeline and Christabel Pankhurst were pinning so much of their hopes on George Lansbury's by-election campaign; they believed his success would demonstrate how much public support there still was for women's suffrage. It would also expose, as they saw it, the cowardice of the Labour Party in failing to fully back the cause.

So it was that the WSPU got behind a single candidate for the very first time in its history and launched an energetic campaign to help Lansbury regain his seat. However, Christabel put Grace Roe in charge, once again bypassing her sister Sylvia. It seemed a strange move considering Sylvia had gained an intimate knowledge of the East End. Yet the decision likely went beyond their ideological differences or any sibling rivalry. By this time, both Emmeline and Christabel were probably aware of Sylvia's romantic relationship with Keir Hardie and wanted to avoid any risk of the affair coming to light. Such a revelation would have been gleefully pounced upon by the press and unsupportive elements of the public and would not only have greatly embarrassed the family but also damaged Lansbury's campaign, not to mention the movement. Unfortunately, Grace proved ill-suited to the task. Likely following Christabel's instructions, she downplayed Lansbury's socialism – something that would have resonated with many of his constituents – and focused exclusively on his feminism. This alienated much of the local working-class male electorate. Meanwhile, the anti-suffrage Conservative candidate, Reginald Blair, offered a clearer, more traditional appeal, which likely struck a chord with disgruntled voters. Despite Emmeline's tireless campaigning on Lansbury's behalf, he was soundly defeated.

In the aftermath, Christabel wrote that November in the WSPU's new magazine, *The Suffragette*: 'A great mass of men are still so corrupted and led astray by party politics that to depend simply on the help of the electors to secure the enfranchisement of women is a grave and fatal mistake.'[4]

Lansbury's defeat reinforced Emmeline's belief that the path to winning the vote would not be found in legal and constitutional approaches. It also deepened her conviction that all men's political parties were fundamentally prejudiced against women's suffrage, and her mistrust of the Labour Party, in particular, grew even more.

Following the WSPU's failure to help get Lansbury re-elected, Emmeline instructed Sylvia to shut down her work in the East End. However, Sylvia was not willing to do so and managed to persuade her mother to allow her to continue her efforts for the time being. Sylvia knew support for the WSPU was dwindling, and the continuing campaign of destruction was not helping. In addition, many of the women who had poured their passion, pride, and bravery into the WSPU were leaving. Some had no choice, their health having been so badly battered by their commitment to the cause. For example, in the autumn of 1912, Mabel Tuke had suffered a nervous breakdown and left the country to recover.[5] And yet, while some distanced themselves from the escalating violence, others embraced it with a new zeal. With all of this going on, Sylvia believed that in her East End work, she had found her place, and she was resolved more than ever to build up support for votes from both the women and the men living here. She began writing for the *Daily Herald*, a newspaper set up by Lansbury and Annie Kenney's brother, Rowland. Defying a core rule of the WSPU, she also shared platforms with men in attempts to encourage votes for all, much to Christabel's chagrin. As the office was not a priority for the WSPU, funding was sparse, and Sylvia and her companions could not afford to keep on the office at 198 Bow Street. Undeterred, she, Zelie, and Norah found a new, cheaper space just a few doors away. It was a dilapidated former second-hand clothes shop infested with rats and bugs, but with help from their newfound East End friends, the three women renovated the building. Though this was ostensibly an East End premises for the WSPU, by mid-year, the building would be home to Sylvia's new, radical organisation, which, though still claiming tenuous ties with the WSPU, would also have links with the Labour movement. The new organisation would be called the East London Federation of the Suffragettes (ELFS).

However, before the new organisation came to be, Sylvia claimed she could organise a working-class deputation to meet Lloyd George and Edward Grey. A reluctant Emmeline and Christabel agreed, and on 23 January 1913, twenty East End women and 1,000 other women organised by Annie Kenney and Flora Drummond marched to the Treasury. However, as usual, the women were met with evasive, noncommittal responses when they pressed for a women's suffrage amendment to the Manhood Suffrage Bill. In fact, they got their answer clearly later that day when the Speaker of the House of Commons ruled that any amendments for women's suffrage would fundamentally alter the nature of the bill, making them inadmissible. Four days later, Prime Minister Asquith confirmed that the bill would be withdrawn for the session, though he vaguely promised support for a private member's bill in the next. In Paris, Christabel heard the news from Annie and Flora, who had travelled there almost immediately to inform her. Convinced the government had deliberately sabotaged the bill to block women's suffrage, the WSPU organising secretary initiated a full-scale arson campaign.

Back in England, Sylvia was dismayed by Christabel's violent call to action. Still, she and Flora Drummond led a deputation through torrential rain to the Commons, demanding equal suffrage. As the women marched, windows in government offices in Whitehall and in large West End shops were smashed.

The crowds that gathered around the women were also largely hostile. The *Pall Mall Gazette* later reported that many of the women had to be protected from the public by the police and claimed that this reversed relationship between police and protesters was 'a significant sign of the changed temper of the public in their attitude towards suffragette militancy'.

As tensions escalated and fights broke out, Sylvia and Flora were among forty-nine women arrested, and both women received a fourteen-day prison sentence. The following month Sylvia found herself in the dock again. At a meeting she was holding in the Bromley-by-Bow Town Hall, stones were thrown, and she was among those apprehended. She avoided prison as the WSPU paid her fine. However, a week later, in the freezing cold, she stood outside a local council school with Zelie and George Lansbury's son, Willie, delivering a passionate speech on the need for votes for women. In the heat of the moment, she hurled a stone through the window of a nearby undertaker's shop, shattering the glass. Amid cheers and chants, she, Zelie, and Willie were arrested. This time, Sylvia was sentenced to two months of hard labour, with no option of paying a fine.

Sylvia was far from alone in her arrests at this time. Across Britain, hundreds of WSPU members were being taken into custody, determined to follow Emmeline's incitement to rebellion and Christabel's call to commit arson. Women chained themselves to railings, forcing policemen to saw them free and drag them away by their hair, kicking and screaming. Stately homes were set ablaze, and golf courses and football stadiums were vandalised. Elderly women applied for gun licences, while younger women flocked to martial arts classes. As the days rolled on, the acts of defiance grew even bolder. Acid was poured onto open green spaces to burn the slogan 'Votes for Women' into the earth. The Orchid House at Kew Gardens was smashed, destroying rare plants. Priceless paintings in Manchester were ruined. On 19 February 1913, Lloyd George's unfinished and empty country home in Walton Heath, Surrey, was greatly damaged by a homemade bomb.[6]

Five days later, Emmeline was arrested at the Knightsbridge flat she had recently started to rent and was charged with procuring and inciting women to commit offences contrary to the Malicious Injuries to Property Act, of 1861. At Epsom Police Court, Emmeline was told that bail was denied and she would be committed to Holloway as a remand prisoner awaiting trial. In protest, Emmeline declared she would adopt the hunger strike. This she duly did, and after twenty-four hours, the government agreed to move her case to the Central Criminal Court at the Old Bailey so that it could be heard in the April assizes. However, for this to happen and for Emmeline to be released on bail, she had to agree not to incite agitation.

In prison, the leader of the WSPU had once again not been subjected to forced feeding. She was aware, though, that that's what was happening to her daughter, Sylvia, who had gone on hunger strike shortly after being committed to Holloway a month earlier. The authorities had denied it, insisting Sylvia was a well-behaved prisoner working out her sentence. However, Emmeline had received a letter from Sylvia that had been smuggled out of Holloway and which Sylvia requested her mother publish to counteract the authorities' claims. It read:

> I am fighting, fighting, fighting. I have four, five, and six wardresses every day, as well as the two doctors. I am fed by stomach tube twice a day. They prize open my mouth with a steel gag, pressing it in where there is a gap in my teeth. I resist all the time. … The night before last I vomited the last meal and was ill all night and was sick after both meals yesterday. I am afraid they may be saying we don't resist. Yet my shoulders are bruised with struggling … whilst they hold the tube into my throat. I used to feel I should go mad at first and be pretty near to it, as I think they feared, but I have got over that, and my digestion is the thing that is most likely to suffer now.[7]

Emmeline asked Lansbury's *Daily Herald* to publish it, and they obliged. A few days later, on Good Friday, 21 March, Sylvia was released from prison. She was immediately taken to Nurse Catherine Pine's nursing home at Pembridge Gardens to recover. At the time, Emmeline was staying at Coign, from where she had written to her long-time friend Elizabeth Robins. Despite the fallout with the Pethick-Lawrences, Emmeline had maintained a friendship with Elizabeth. 'My dear friend,' she wrote cheerfully, 'I know you will rejoice with me that Sylvia is released. The news came by telephone late last night, and in a few minutes I am leaving by car to see her.'

However, when Emmeline arrived at Pembridge Gardens, she was met by a distraught Keir Hardie, who had come to stay by Sylvia's bedside. Though Sylvia had written to her lover while incarcerated, the letter had never reached him. Seeing her now was a shock. Gaunt and pale, with both eyes horribly bloodshot from ruptured veins, she seemed a ghost of herself. Sylvia's frail appearance alarmed Emmeline too. During her five weeks of imprisonment, Sylvia had lost two stone in weight, and it would be weeks before she recovered enough to leave the nursing home.

As Emmeline stayed by Sylvia's side with Hardie, more family concerns were to trouble her. A letter arrived from Helen Archdale, mentioning that Adela was nearing the end of her horticultural course and planning a trip to Italy with her. Emmeline felt uncomfortable about this. Funds were tight, and she wasn't sure she could spare enough money for her daughter's trip. After replying to Helen, Emmeline wrote a concerned letter to Adela, sharing her worries about the trip and her daughter's next steps. 'I am really very anxious about your future and fear that if you leave the College before getting a post, it will increase the difficulty of getting one.'

Fortunately, luck was on Adela's side. Shortly after earning her diploma that Easter, she was offered a position as head gardener at Road Manor near Bath, the home of Mrs Batten Pooll, a supporter of the WSPU. For Emmeline, this was a relief. Knowing that her youngest daughter had both a roof over her head and an income was a comfort during those days when she herself was uncertain how long she would remain a free woman.

Emmeline's trial at the Old Bailey began on 2 April. The night before, she wrote to Elizabeth Robins: 'Tonight I am full of doubts and fears that I shall not be equal to the part tomorrow, but I daresay I shall be "all right on the day".' The next day, Emmeline stood before the court, pleading not guilty to charges of inciting persons unknown to place explosives in Lloyd George's unfinished house at Walton Heath. As before, she chose to conduct her own defence, though this time with support from her solicitor, Alfred Marshall. In her closing speech, she highlighted how

> over 1,000 women have gone to prison in the course of this agitation, have suffered their imprisonment, have come out of prison injured in health, weakened in body, but not in spirit. I come to stand trial from the bedside of one of the daughters who has come out of Holloway Prison, sent there on two months' hard labour for… breaking a small pane of glass … There is only one way to put a stop to this agitation. It is not by deporting us; it is not by locking us up in prison; it is by doing us justice.[8]

However, once again, while her words visibly moved those in the courtroom, the all-male jury found Emmeline guilty. As before, they recommended the judge show leniency. When asked if she had anything to say before sentencing, Emmeline calmly replied, 'I have no sense of guilt. I feel I have done my duty. I look upon myself as a prisoner of war. I am under no moral obligation to conform to, or in any way accept, the sentence imposed on me.' Justice Lush had a hard job ahead of him and claimed that the task of sentencing her was 'a very painful duty'. However, even taking on board the jury's plea for clemency, he stated that the minimum sentence he could impose on the WSPU leader was three years' penal servitude. Across the courtroom, her supporters erupted with cries of 'Shame!' and broke into verses of the 'Women's Marseillaise' as Emmeline was led out of the dock.

That evening at an organised meeting, an enraged Annie Kenney called for a fresh wave of action to show the authorities that the WSPU would continue its militancy even with its leader behind bars. Her call was eagerly met. Women around the country began smashing windows, defacing public buildings, and setting mailboxes and empty country houses alight. In Holloway, Emmeline immediately went on hunger strike. She accepted water, but her refusal to eat left many concerned, not least the Home Secretary, who feared that this small, slight woman might actually starve to death. Reginald McKenna MP, the previous First Lord of the Admiralty, had effectively switched jobs with Winston Churchill in 1911, and like his predecessor, had little sympathy for the suffragettes. Nonetheless, he did not want the suffragette leader dying on his watch. Over the next nine days, he insisted that the wardens bring her the best of meals – boiled eggs for breakfast, roast chicken and filleted plaice for dinner – but the WSPU leader would not budge. On the floor of the House of Commons, Keir Hardie regularly enquired about her health and treatment, ensuring no one forgot what was happening within the walls of Holloway.

On the 10 April, the prison doctor reported that Emmeline's pulse was racing and that the physical toll of malnutrition was becoming visible. Forcible feeding, he advised, would now be pointless as too many days had passed without food. A vigil was being held outside the prison gates, and that evening, the WSPU meeting at the Albert Hall raised an astonishing sum of £15,000 for the organisation. The following day, the Governor of Holloway entered Emmeline's cell, carrying a special licence issued under the Penal Servitude Acts. The document granted her a fifteen-day release on the condition that she desist from WSPU activities and report all her movements to the police. It was a precursor to a new Prisoners' Temporary Discharge for Ill-Health Bill, which the Home Secretary was trying to rush through its various readings in Parliament.

Emmeline took the written licence with slow, shaky hands and then proceeded to tear it into shreds. 'I have no intention of obeying this infamous law,' she told the governor. 'I shall never voluntarily return to any of your prisons.' Nevertheless, arrangements were made. A cab was summoned, and as the governor informed the Special Branch of her release, a frail and gaunt Emmeline was helped into the waiting vehicle. Her destination was 9 Pembridge Gardens, the nursing home run by Catherine Pine.

In the days that followed, Nurse Pine tended tirelessly to her friend's health. Ethel came to visit and was struck by the sight of her. 'She was heart-rending to look at,' she recalled. 'Her skin was yellow, so tightly drawn over her face … her eyes deep sunken and burning.'[9]

Emmeline was concerned about the presence of the police at the home, feeling it disturbed the peace of other patients. Detectives roamed the grounds and stood guard outside Emmeline's door. Finally, on 22 April, Dr Flora Murray called Scotland Yard to inform them that Emmeline was being moved from her current address to Hertha Ayrton's house at 41 Norfolk Square. Permission was granted, and after nightfall, an ambulance carried the frail WSPU leader to Hertha's doorstep. Hertha, who had only learnt of the plan that very day, opened the door to a woman still a shadow of her former self.

Emmeline was due to return to Holloway on the afternoon of 28 April, but her recovery had been painstakingly slow. When Dr Smalley from Holloway came to assess her, he found a thin, pale, trembling figure, far too unwell to endure the damp and punishing conditions of London's most infamous women's prison. Her return was postponed indefinitely. In the meantime, detectives swarmed Hertha's home. They were stationed by the door, in the street, and on the roof. However, this didn't stop Emmeline when, three weeks later and much improved, she slipped out of the back of the house. She clambered into a waiting motor car, which sped off to Ethel Smyth's Woking home with detectives in hot pursuit. That evening, Emmeline and Ethel enjoyed some quiet time together, amused by the detectives attempting to conceal themselves in shrubs outside the house, even as the heavy rain poured down, drenching them. The following days unfolded like a drawn-out siege, with the two women attending to their lives inside Ethel's house while detectives kept watch at every exit. Eventually, weary of it all, Emmeline declared her intention to attend the WSPU meeting at the London Pavilion on 26 May. A car from the WSPU was summoned, with Flora Drummond accompanying her. However, as Emmeline stepped forward to board the vehicle, detectives swooped in and apprehended her. Rearrested, she was hurriedly bundled into another vehicle and taken to Holloway. The drive turned into something of a spectacle, however, with four cars of her supporters trailing close behind, cheering defiantly for their captive leader as startled pedestrians stopped and stared. On arriving at the prison, her followers leapt out, rushing unsuccessfully to breach the gates, as a waving Emmeline was brought inside.

During Emmeline's weeks of recovery, the WSPU's battle with authorities had continued. The organisation's new headquarters had been raided, as had the flat the Kenney sisters shared together. Flora Drummond, Harriet Kerr, Beatrice Sanders, Rachel Barrett, Geraldine Lennox, and Agnes Lake had all been arrested at Lincoln's Inn House, while Annie herself was apprehended while returning from a clandestine meeting with Christabel in Paris. Police also swooped into Victoria House Press, the most recent printer of *The Suffragette*, and shut down production. This was particularly troublesome. With Christabel unable to conduct speeches or attend meetings on British soil, she had used *The Suffragette* as her main means of addressing the countrywide WSPU membership and directing her campaign.

However, during the raid on WSPU headquarters, a quick-thinking typist had concealed Christabel's lead article in her blouse. Surreptitiously, she had passed it onto Grace Roe who managed to escape the chaos unnoticed. Acting swiftly, Grace set about salvaging the publication. She secured a new printer and funded the critical tasks required to ensure *The Suffragette* was published on schedule. On 2 May, the paper hit the streets with a plain front page simply emblazoned with the large capitalised word: 'RAIDED!'[10]

On 6 May a private member's bill to enfranchise women of 25 years and upwards, who were householders or the wives of householders, was defeated by forty-seven votes on its second reading in the Commons. In response, the arson campaign took a more aggressive turn, with several empty churches becoming additional targets of fires and bomb attacks. Public condemnation was swift and widespread, dominating the major newspapers and escalating into panic when fears arose about a potential bomb in St Paul's Cathedral. These objections were shared with many in the WSPU, including Mary Blathwayt, who quietly resigned her WSPU membership.

The infamous Prisoners' Temporary Discharge for Ill-Health Bill had also passed into law. Nicknamed the 'Cat and Mouse Act', it allowed hunger-striking suffragettes, the 'mice', to be released from prison as soon as their health began to fail, only to be seized again without the need of warrants by the 'cat' – the government – once they had regained their strength. The recaptured 'mice' were then forced to complete their prison sentences. The Act was the government's latest attempt to manage the suffragette crisis. Forcible feeding had failed to deter the suffragettes from their guerilla warfare and, as worrying for the government, carried the grave risk of causing injury or death.

However, to the suffragettes, the Act was simply a devious attempt by the authorities to keep them indefinitely behind bars. After all, if a prisoner on a short sentence was released and rearrested multiple times, her incarceration could be extended to months and even years. Nonetheless, the women, including Emmeline, now back in Holloway, continued their hunger strikes. As before, Emmeline's health quickly deteriorated, and she was released four days later. Though she despised the thinking behind the Cat and Mouse Act, and despite how the repeated hunger strikes ravaged her health, she would continue to use the Bill to serve just six weeks in total of her three-year sentence.

CHAPTER

17

FAMILY FRACTURES

Not everything about the WSPU's campaign during this time centred on confrontation, however. In the first fortnight of June, a peaceful summer fair was planned for the Empire Rooms in Kensington. Over two weeks, the event offered stalls selling toys, books, hats, antiques, homemade food, and more. The fair opened on 3 June to great success. But the following day, a tragedy struck that completely overshadowed events.

At the Epsom Derby, as the leading horses thundered around Tattenham Corner, the 40-year-old radical suffragette, Emily Wilding Davison, stepped out onto the track. Emerging from beneath the railings, she ran directly into the path of the King's horse, Anmer. The powerful animal collided with Emily, striking her with its chest before stumbling and crashing headfirst to the ground. The jockey, Herbert Jones, was thrown from the saddle and knocked unconscious. Emily, meanwhile, was hurled violently through the air, landing lifelessly in the grass. Though she was still breathing when carried from the track, four days later she died from severe skull fractures.

Emily's death sent shockwaves through the WSPU ranks and around Britain. Mary Richardson, an active suffragette, had spotted her moments before the horrific event. Though not a personal friend of Emily's, she had waved to her as the other stood quietly by the white-painted railings watching the galloping horses speed around the bend. Emily had smiled back in return.

> She looked absorbed and yet far away from everyone else and seemed to have no interest in what was going on round her – I shall always remember how beautifully calm her face was – I was unable to keep my eyes off her as I stood holding *The Suffragette* up in my clenched hand … I watched her hand. It did not shake. Even when I heard the pounding of the horses' hooves moving closer, I saw she was still smiling.[1]

Speaking about the event many years later, Mary claimed, 'The vision I had of Emily as she darted under the rail at Tattenham Corner and then lay in the grass horribly stretched out recurred. Over and over again I saw it. And now, after nearly forty years, it remains as vivid.'

The motives behind Emily's actions remain unanswered. The police claimed that it was a suicide and nothing to do with the suffragette movement, but evidence from Emily's belongings suggested otherwise. Among the items in her purse that day were a return train ticket to Victoria Station and a helper's pass to the WSPU summer festival scheduled for that evening.

Yet with no evidence of a planned suffragette protest that day, and no banner or placard in Emily's possession, the authorities doubled down on their claim that her actions were not an act of female suffrage militancy. However, the act was caught on film, and years later, with the help of more advanced technology, the footage would show that Emily did in fact carry a scarf, which she was attempting to tie to the horse's bridle.

The police may have claimed otherwise, but the WSPU were in no doubt that Emily intended her radical action to draw attention to the cause. Following her death, an entire issue of *The Suffragette*, edged in black, was full of praise for her. 'So greatly did she care for freedom that she died for it,' wrote Christabel. 'So dearly did she love women that she offered her life as their ransom.' Her death was, as Christabel wrote, a '"martyr's death" pure and simple'.

Though the relationship between the often reckless Emily and the WSPU had not always been an easy one, Emmeline, as leader of the Union, also penned a deeply felt tribute to a woman she called 'one of our bravest soldiers', noting that 'We who remain can but honour her memory by continuing our work unceasingly.'

The WSPU took responsibility for organising and funding Emily's funeral. Christabel gave the task to Grace Roe, who had known Emily well. Grace asked another close friend, Charlotte Marsh, to serve as one of the pallbearers. The funeral procession, with 5,000 women marching in solemn solidarity, turned out to be the final, and one of the most poignant, suffragette demonstrations. Even members of other non-militant suffrage groups came out to pay their regards, though Milicent Fawcett and other leaders of the NUWSS were noticeable for their absence. When the coffin was carried into St George's Church in Bloomsbury for a brief memorial service, suffragette militants dressed in white lined the route, standing in solemn formation and offering a military salute. After the service, the coffin was taken to King's Cross station and placed on a train bound for Morpeth, Northumberland, Emily's birthplace.

Emily's death was a profound shock to the nation, but it also became a turning point in public opinion. The British public, long wearied by the grim stalemate between suffragettes and authorities and the seemingly endless cycle of arson, bombings, arrests and hunger strikes, was jolted out of its fatigue. Emily's death forced the country to confront the unsettling truth that women were willing to risk, and even lose, their lives for their beliefs, and for this reason, the struggle could not continue indefinitely.

However, change, though clearly necessary, still seemed slow in coming. Emmeline, arrested while attempting to attend Emily's funeral, was sent back to Holloway Prison and once again began a hunger strike. Within days, she collapsed and was moved to the hospital wing. Ill-natured and incoherent, she refused both food and medicine, prompting the authorities to release her on a temporary seven-day licence. The treatment of the WSPU leader, which filled the pages of newspapers, so soon after the death of Emily Wilding Davison, prompted an outcry of concern from the public and intensified criticism of the Cat and Mouse Act.

Meanwhile, Annie Kenney, another 'mouse' out on licence and as such forbidden to engage in WSPU activities, was recaptured while finishing a speech at an 'At Home' event at the London Pavilion. Sylvia had similarly returned to Holloway after organising a rally in Trafalgar Square, where she invited the Men's Federation for Women's Suffrage to join East End women in protest. The rally, however, descended into chaos as the crowd surged towards Downing Street. Two days later, Sylvia was arrested under an obscure statute from the reign of Edward III, branding her as 'a disturber of the peace of our Lord the King'.[2]

From the moment she entered prison, Sylvia refused food and water and quickly became ill. She was eventually taken by wardresses to the East End home of Mr and Mrs Payne. While detectives kept a constant watch on the Paynes' door, they did nothing to stop the steady stream of visitors, including local supporters, East End friends, prominent socialists, and even the Bishop of London, who came to check on her.

Sylvia's reputation as both a suffragette and a socialist had grown significantly since her return from America, and the East London Federation had swelled in numbers. But like Annie and countless other suffragettes, Sylvia's temporary licence would soon expire, and she would be returned to prison. This relentless cycle of arrests, releases, and hunger strikes continued to take its toll on public patience. Letters poured into newspaper editorial pages, expressing frustration and fatigue with the seemingly endless upheaval. The country was exasperated, and yet, the suffragette campaigns of militancy pressed forward, and the arrests continued.

On 14 July, Emmeline Pankhurst defied the authorities and snuck into the WSPU 'At Home' meeting at the London Pavilion that Annie would later be arrested leaving. As Annie finished her speech, Emmeline made her way onto the stage. The audience, caught by surprise, gasped. Then, as realisation dawned, they erupted into cheers, rising to their feet in a standing ovation. She stood smiling down at the enthusiastic crowds. She had missed the thrill of addressing a public gathering, and the members of the WSPU had missed her leadership.

The movement had felt adrift in her absence. With the Pethick-Lawrences gone, Christabel in Paris, and many of the WSPU's key figures either imprisoned or facing arrest, the heart of the Union had weakened. Now, Emmeline sought to strengthen that core again. She began not with grand strategies but by acknowledging the sacrifices being made, the struggles of the women before her, of those around her, and of herself, and of the commitment all had made. The audience listened, gripped. It had always been Emmeline's particular talent to weave her personal resolve into the collective spirit of the movement, and she did it now with expert grace.

'I know that women, once convinced that they are doing what is right, that their rebellion is just, will go on, no matter what the difficulties, no matter what the dangers, so long as there is a woman alive to hold up the flag of rebellion,' she said, as more cheers broke out in the hall.

> I would rather be a rebel than a slave. I would rather die than submit, and that is the spirit that animates this movement. … I mean to be a voter in the land that gave me birth, or they shall kill me, and my challenge to the government is: Kill me or give me my freedom: I shall force you to make that choice.

Over the next week, Emmeline, insistent that she would speak at the various events being held over the summer, managed to stay one step ahead of the police, attending as many WSPU meetings as possible without being caught. There were some fun and games to be had, as she and other 'mice' disguised themselves in wigs and large overcoats to slip by the police unnoticed or enlisted women of similar build to dress like them, leading detectives on a lively chase through the streets of London.

On the following Monday, as Emmeline arrived for the WSPU's At Home at the London Pavilion, however, the police were waiting. They seized her as she entered the hall. 'Women, they are arresting me!' she cried, and hundreds of militants rushed forward in a desperate attempt to protect her. They did not succeed, and Emmeline was taken back to Holloway. However, further fasting and failing health saw her released again on a seven-day licence on 24 July. By this time, the Home Office had received several individual and group petitions for a pardon for Emmeline, including two drawn up for presentation to the King by the London Graduates' Union for Women's Suffrage; the first had been signed by six prominent London men, including Sir Edward Busk, Sir Victor Horsley, Professor Karl Pearson, and Sidney Webb, and the second by 474 teachers and graduates. Even C. P. Scott, editor of the *Manchester Guardian*, wrote to Lloyd George complaining that there seemed to be 'no sense' in the way Mrs Pankhurst was being treated. 'The woman is obviously being killed by inches, and the home secretary is merely dodging death,' he penned.[3]

While out on licence, Emmeline was often too frail to walk and relied on a wheeled chair to attend events. Still, true to her word, she spoke at as many gatherings as her health allowed. However, in August 1913, when she was given permission to travel outside of Britain, she gratefully took the opportunity to go to France to relax and spend a few months with her beloved eldest daughter.

In Paris, Christabel had also been trying to maintain control of the WSPU by ensuring the weekly publication of *The Suffragette*, featuring her articles alongside updates on the movement's progress across Britain. The regularity of the publication was crucial for sustaining national morale. But in more recent issues, Christabel had begun to fill the double-sided pages of the publication with articles on male sexual violence and 'White Slavery'. This latter subject, which had been an early campaigning issue for the NUWSS, alluded to the forced prostitution of young (white) British girls and women. This narrative was deeply rooted in the racial and imperial ideologies of the time, reinforcing as it did the idea that white women were uniquely valuable (and vulnerable).[4]

But Christabel was not so much concerned with the racial implications as she was with the feminist ones. In her articles, she argued that women's enfranchisement would lead to greater protection for women against men's abuses. Her sharply feminist critique contented that prostitution was rooted in the power dynamics of a male-dominated society. Men, she claimed, deliberately kept women on low wages to ensure they were more easily driven into exploitative circumstances. This, she believed, was true regardless of a man's political ideology. 'A man-made socialism,' she wrote, 'is no less dangerous to women than a man-made capitalism. So long as men have a monopoly on political power, they will continue to ensure women's economic dependence and, in turn, their sexual subservience.'

Christabel's arguments were, as ever, thoughtful and incisive. Yet, at times, she resorted to heavy religious rhetoric to get her argument across, a step that seemed strange and would surely have disappointed her atheist father. In a 1913 article titled 'The Appeal to God', she wrote: 'Worldly justice is not yet given to women, but divine justice is theirs.'

Emmeline too began addressing issues of sexual violence and sexually transmitted diseases in her speeches, puzzling and frustrating several members of the WSPU. After all, both women were doing exactly what they had earlier forbidden other members of the Union to do, which was to shift focus from the single argument of votes for women.

Christabel believed remaining in Paris was essential for the WSPU's success. But the years she spent here also left her disconnected from the realities unfolding on the ground in Britain. In France, her life was certainly quieter. Hours stretched out before her and to keep boredom at bay, Christabel spent time studying several different topics. It was during these months that she began to show an interest in Christianity and the teachings of the Bible, which may have been the prompt to read up on the subject of sexual vice that now took up many of the column inches in *The Suffragette*.

Yet the time she spent either in study or in work for the movement was shadowed by moments of deep doubt as she felt the movement slipping out of her grasp. To provide comfort, Emmeline had brought her a little Pomeranian dog that Christabel named Fay, and which her mother hoped might offer the consistent affection and sense of daily purpose Christabel seemed now to lack. There were long, lonely days, however, when her mother's imprisonment and hunger strikes deepened Christabel's isolation and unease, and the prospects of British women's suffrage seemed painfully distant.

It's also probable that Christabel realised that her once-bright reputation as the fiery leader of the suffragette movement had begun to dim in the shadow of her mother's rising visibility. Emmeline had always been acknowledged as the leader of the movement. But in the absence of Christabel and many of the other stronger militants who had faded from the fray, her commanding presence and relentless combativeness made her the singular defining face of the struggle against the British government.

Emmeline no doubt took on this role as much as to protect her beloved daughter from the harsher realities of the campaign – arrest, imprisonment, and the life-threatening ordeal of hunger striking – as anything else. Still, for Christabel, who had once thrived on the adulation she received in London, exile in Paris was a bittersweet refuge. It's likely that this was why she felt increasingly frustrated with Sylvia's activities in the East End. Christabel would never turn on her mother whom she adored, but her sisters had always been quite another matter.

The autumn of 1913 unfolded with a steady, if thinly veiled, exchange of public criticism between Christabel and Sylvia. Emmeline had taken the opportunity to embark on another paid lecture tour of America and had left from France in mid-October. She had also been approached by William F. Bigelow, editor of the widely read American magazine *Good Housekeeping*, to pen a series of autobiographical articles. When she declined, Bigelow sent his own journalist, Rheta Child Dorr, to help her. Under Emmeline's careful direction, Rheta sifted through WSPU notes, piecing together the story of the movement and Emmeline's role within it. Rheta accompanied Emmeline back to New York, taking dictation and transforming their shared work into what would become a much-enjoyed series for the magazine and finally Emmeline's biography, *My Own Story*, which was published in 1914.

While her mother was in America, Sylvia Pankhurst had appeared on stage at a large socialist and trade union rally in the Albert Hall on 1 November. Organised by the *Daily Herald*, the event aimed to protest the mass lock-out of workers in Dublin and demand the release of Jim Larkin, one of the leading figures of the dispute.

Sylvia stood among notable figures of the labour and socialist movement, as well as previous but now alienated members of the WSPU. These included George Lansbury, James Connolly of the Irish Transport and General Workers' Union (ITGWU), Delia Larkin (Jim Larkin's sister and a key organiser in the ITGWU's women's section), Dora Montefiore, Charlotte Despard, and Fred Pethick-Lawrence. Christabel was furious, not just because her sister had appeared on a stage with men while supposedly representing the WSPU, but also because one of those men was Fred Pethick-Lawrence. The former WSPU co-leader had continued publishing the Union's old and successful newspaper, *Votes for Women*, supported by the newly formed Votes for Women Fellowship, a coalition of militant and non-militant suffrage groups. The paper sought to unify the broader movement but this, of course, was in direct opposition to Christabel's increasingly rigid vision for the WSPU.

Just days after the Albert Hall rally, the *Daily Herald* reported that Sylvia's WSPU-founded Federation was forming a 'people's army' of women and men to defend suffragettes, but also striking dockworkers, from police violence. The defence of women militants mirrored what was already happening in the WSPU; in recent years, Edith Garrud, a martial arts teacher and dedicated suffragette, had trained several women in jujitsu and self-defence. She eventually formed The Bodyguard, a group of around thirty women tasked with protecting Emmeline Pankhurst and others, especially during the current Cat and Mouse Act era when police frequently ambushed women without warning. However, the article went on to suggest this 'people's army' proved there was a growing convergence between industrial and suffrage rebels.

To Christabel, this was evidence that Sylvia was deliberately undermining her authority in the absence of Emmeline. As she saw it, by attending the rally Sylvia was attempting to pull the WSPU back towards its socialist roots and open the way for the suffragette movement to accept male membership. Fuming, she issued a statement in *The Suffragette* declaring that Sylvia had appeared at the rally in a personal capacity and that the ELFS was not formally aligned with the WSPU.

Sylvia responded with a circular clarifying that the ELFS had no affiliation with the *Daily Herald*. She also took the opportunity to critique the WSPU itself, pointing to its falling membership numbers and lamenting the noticeable decline in public meetings, an implicit jab at Christabel, who, because she had been directing the Union remotely, had not attended or spoken at a meeting since she had absconded to France almost two years previously.[5]

These sharp public exchanges between the sisters left many in the WSPU uneasy, and so it was that in January 1914, after Emmeline had returned from her American tour, and undergone two more prison stays, that Sylvia was summoned to France to discuss the future of the East London Federation of Suffragettes. Sylvia too was recovering from yet another hunger strike after her fifth arrest, and was out on licence under the Cat and Mouse Act. She slipped successfully across the Channel accompanied by Norah.

The discussion between the three Pankhurst women was never going to be easy, and, in true form, it quickly turned into a clash of ideals. Christabel took issue with Sylvia's collaboration with male suffrage support groups, reiterating that the WSPU was to remain an exclusively women-led organisation. Sylvia, in turn, passionately defended her commitment to broader labour struggles, criticising what she saw as the WSPU's social elitism.

Eventually, a resolution was reached, though it was far from amicable. According to Sylvia's account in *The Suffragette Movement*, Christabel declared that the East London Federation was to become entirely independent of the WSPU. To make the separation unmistakably clear, the split would be announced in the next issue of *The Suffragette*. 'You have your own ideas,' Christabel reportedly said. 'We do not want that. We want all our women to take their instructions and walk in step like an army!'

The decision was final. As Sylvia later recalled, they concluded the tense meeting with a drive through the Bois de Boulogne, 'Christabel with the small dog on her arm, I struggled against headache and weakness, Mrs. Pankhurst blanched and emaciated – Christabel was emphatic. "It must be a clean cut!" So it went on. "As you will then," I answered at last.'[6]

Despite pressure from Emmeline and Christabel, Sylvia refused to comply with their demand that the East London Federation of Suffragettes (ELFS) remove the word 'Suffragette' from its name. The WSPU leaders argued that the term was synonymous with their union, but Sylvia stood firm. In addition, her hurt feelings were evident in the draft announcement she prepared to formalise the split. In a kind, though in some ways manipulative letter to her daughter, Emmeline had suggested that the 'best way to make it impossible for gossipmongers & malicious journalists to foment that sort of thing is to concentrate each on our own work & make our supporters imitate our example'. She signed the letter, 'much love, mother' along with, 'Christabel joins me in love'.

When Sylvia still refused to budge, Emmeline's tone hardened, and in an angrier letter she wrote, 'You are unreasonable, always have been, and I fear always will be … You make your own difficulties by an incapacity to look at situations from other people's points of view as well as your own. Perhaps in time, you will learn the lessons that we all have to learn in life.'[7]

Sylvia did not respond. She had already stepped into her own path. Though news of the family split was widely covered in the press, even making it as far as the pages of *The New York Times*, her East End Federation soon came to be recognised as an independent organisation. Sylvia, Zelie, and Norah set up their own weekly socialist publication, called *The Woman's Dreadnought*, which, though it sold for a halfpenny, was freely distributed during processions and demonstrations. Her relationship with Emmeline faded, and the two saw little of each other in the years that followed. With Christabel, the estrangement was even sharper, marked by constant ideological clashes as their visions for female enfranchisement and their broader political beliefs continued to drift further apart.

But Sylvia was not alone in being expelled from the WSPU and, by extension, the family. During the latter months of 1913, Adela had given up her job at Road Manor, where for 35 shillings a week she had spent every weekday from 6.00am to 6.00pm toiling to the point of exhaustion. Like her brother before her, it was not a life she was cut out for. Plus, work was isolating; after years spent travelling with other WSPU women, she felt out of place among the other gardeners. Lonely and unsure of her next step, Adela knew she had to leave but had no clear idea of where to go. Certainly, she could not return to the WSPU. In any case, she found Christabel's hardline feminism and her series of increasingly strident articles about the vices of men deeply off-putting and at odds with her own beliefs. Surprisingly, Sylvia had reached out to her to suggest she come and help out at ELFS; however, taking up this offer would have meant defying her mother's strict instruction that she never speak publicly again, so she refused. Sylvia's outstretched hand to Adela of all people was likely further fuel to Christabel's determination that the WSPU sever ties with the ELFS entirely.

Eventually, Adela turned to her kind friend Helen Archdale, who insisted she come to Switzerland for the summer. Adela gladly accepted, and while there took on work as a governess for Helen's children, Alec and Betty. It gave her a sense of purpose, and for a time, she was content. Emmeline, however, was furious when she found out; she had never considered teaching of any kind a praiseworthy career and had always baulked at the idea of any of her girls becoming governesses. But Adela was delighted to be doing something useful and something she felt confident in. Her peace was short-lived, however. Annie Kenney, whom Adela had long resented for taking the affection of her mother, which Adela thought was rightfully hers, arrived in Switzerland bearing a reprimand from Christabel and Emmeline. It transpired that while in Milan, Adela had been spotted by a *Daily Mail* reporter who mistook her for Christabel. The reporter asked for an interview, which Adela obligingly gave. Christabel was furious, seeing this as confirmation of Adela's lack of trustworthiness. To Christabel's mind it also furthered the possibility that her youngest sister, always unpredictable, might join forces with Sylvia, and that was too much to bear.

Thus, just as Sylvia had been summoned to France, so too was Adela sent for at the end of that same month. She arrived to discover that the meeting was less a discussion than a decision already made. Emmeline had written to Helen Archdale ahead of time, informing her that Adela would not be returning as a governess. Instead, Emmeline had decided her daughter needed a complete fresh start – in Melbourne, Australia. The idea was not so out of the blue. The two women had corresponded that autumn with Emmeline apologising for her 'naughty child' whom she felt was giving Helen so much trouble. In that earlier letter she had mentioned that 'just before I left London [Adela] wrote about going to Canada. I replied that I would not sanction her giving up her post and could find no money this year. If next year she was still in the same mind, I would do so.' Now, with the reality of Australia, rather than Canada, on the horizon, Emmeline wrote to Helen, 'I hope A will take the right attitude about all this. We must do what we feel is best for her and all concerned.'[8]

Throughout the meeting, Adela was aware of her mother's disappointment in her, and the sense of rejection left her shattered. Lacking the strength to counter the accusations that she intended to undermine Christabel's leadership, Adela yielded to her mother's plan to send her to the other side of the world. Heartbroken, she accepted the fare to Australia, along with £20, some woollen clothes, and a letter of introduction to the Australian suffragist Vida Goldstein, whom she had met briefly in London in 1911.[9]

In Emmeline's eyes, 28-year-old Adela, like Sylvia before her, had broken the cardinal Pankhurst rule: loyalty to Christabel was absolute. With an extended prison sentence looming over her, Emmeline also truly believed she was acting in Adela's best interest. Yet, despite her determined exterior, she struggled with the decision. In a letter to Ethel who had returned to her career as a composer and was now in Egypt, she confessed, 'We are busy getting her ready for the journey … Of course, now all is settled; I have pangs of maternal weakness, but I harden my heart and have been busy with domestic cares all the time.'

Finally, the day came. On 2 February 1914, Adela boarded the *Geelong* for Australia. As the ship pulled away from London, beginning its six-week journey, the youngest Pankhurst daughter stood silently on the deck. Alone, as she had so often felt in her life, she faced a new adventure ahead. She would never again see her mother or her sisters.

CHAPTER

18

THE LAST DAYS OF MILITANCY

The year 1914 had gotten off to an unexpected start for the Pankhursts and the WSPU. Adela had left for Australia, Sylvia was building her new group in London's East End, and both had been expelled from the organisation that had dominated their adult life thus far. Christabel remained in Paris, but she would be back in England before the year was out.

In truth, she had been receiving criticisms from certain WSPU quarters for some time. That January, the Union's organising secretary received a frustrated letter from Beatrice Harraden, a writer and committed member of the WSPU Hampstead branch. Harraden chastised Christabel for allowing her mother to persist with her hunger strikes, something that she and the rest of the country believed would only end in the older woman's death. She also accused Christabel of alienating the Union's most steadfast supporters, those whose loyalty had long been the backbone of their shared struggle. Harraden claimed that without speakers to awaken and galvanise the nation, Emmeline's continual sacrifice for the cause was a 'vain and useless one'. Finally, she highlighted her heartbreak at hearing how little care was being extended to many of the 'mice'.[1] This grievance was echoed by Mary Leigh, who, despite having recently joined Sylvia's ELFS, arrived at Christabel's Parisian home with two other suffragettes to recount the desperate plight of several young, inexperienced militants. They had entered prison and endured hunger strikes out of unwavering loyalty to the Union only to find themselves 'on the run with no money, no food, no shelter'.

Christabel, however, appeared impervious to such stories. Mary later claimed that when she voiced the frustrations of those suffragettes still in the field, and in particular their resentment at taking orders from the younger, less experienced office staff, Christabel appeared visibly irked by the criticism.

February was ushered in with another unsettling letter, this time from a group announcing the formation of a new organisation, the United Suffragists (US). Comprising former members and supporters of the WSPU, this group differed from the original suffragette organisation by admitting both men and non-militant suffragists into their ranks. They had also adopted *Votes for Women*, the Pethick-Lawrences' publication, as their official publication. Its founding members read like a roll call of past allies and included Dr Louisa Garrett Anderson, Mary Neal, Emmeline and Fred Pethick-Lawrence, George Lansbury, and Hertha Ayrton, whose home had been a refuge for Emmeline during her first release as a 'mouse'.

For Christabel and Emmeline, it must have stung to see so many familiar names, companions on the long and arduous road of the suffrage struggle, now united under a banner that excluded them. Yet, for all this, the two women remained undeterred. As such, among the criticisms, the duo's singular focus on steering the WSPU through the turbulent years of 1912–1914, with an eye always on that final victory of votes for women received praise from many other suffragettes. These were those who remained steadfastly loyal to the WSPU and, as a consequence, to the constant hunger striking Emmeline undertook.

Whether the diehards truly understood Emmeline's brutal use of her own body – or why Christabel could stand back and accept it – remains unknown. Beatrice Harraden may have dismissed Emmeline's actions as 'vain and useless', but the Pankhurst women saw them differently. Christabel was far from indifferent to her mother's suffering; she worried deeply about her health. Jessie Kenney recalls a distraught Christabel weeping over the lack of news about the hunger strikers, agonising, 'not knowing whether my mother, my sister Annie … [and others] … might die in prison'.

She was not devoid of feeling, but she accepted her mother's insistence on using her own body as a site of protest. In the Victorian world that Emmeline had grown up in, the female body had been mythologised and yet stripped of all autonomy; women were deemed 'angels in the house' but had no rights in that house when it came to marriage, sex, or motherhood. This political bondage continued and with this lack of a voice, all Emmeline had left to protest with was her body. Christabel – and even Sylvia, despite her distance from both her sister and her mother – understood this in a way that many women of the era, even those fervently committed to female enfranchisement, did not.

This is not to say that Emmeline embraced hunger striking easily. She did not. She was acutely aware of how it was ravaging her health. During this period, she did everything she could to evade re-arrest and avoid serving the remainder of her three-year prison sentence. This, of course, was as much about keeping morale high among her followers through rousing speeches as it was about protecting her health. On 10 February, a notice appeared in the press announcing that she would address supporters from the balcony of the Brackenburys' London home, where she was staying at the time. Over 1,200 people crowded into the street outside the Campden Hill house, as Emmeline, from the building's first-floor balcony, alerted the crowd that she was, as always, ready to fight for the cause, and taunted the police. Whether they arrested her or not, she declared, she would never serve the full term of her sentence.

By the end of the month, she delivered another speech, this time from the private residence of Dr and Mrs Schutz. Then, in March, she travelled to Glasgow to speak at a public meeting in St Andrew's Hall. Her Bodyguard had travelled up the day beforehand and was already in the hall along with the 4,000 people who had gathered for the meeting. Earlier, knowing that many full-uniformed and plain-clothes police would also be there to try and re-arrest Emmeline, they had entwined strings of barbed wire among the flowers and garlands that adorned the front of the stage. To avoid detection, Emmeline was smuggled into the back of the hall in a laundry basket. Stepping out on the stage, she had only just begun her speech, when officers surged to the front of the hall to arrest her. As they got tangled in the barbed wire, several suffragettes ran out from the stage wings with buckets of water to drench them. Others had flag poles which were used as battering rams. Chaos erupted as more police arrived, wielding batons and brutally attacking the women. The situation escalated when Scottish suffragette Janie Allan drew a pistol from her skirt and fired blank shots into the air. In the melee, Emmeline Pankhurst was beaten, dragged from the room, and bundled into a waiting vehicle before being taken to Central Police Station.[2]

The next day, she was transported back to London by train, flanked by two metropolitan police officers, four detectives, and a matron. Despite strict measures to prevent any suffragettes from following her, at every stop several suffragettes ran along the platform, cheering and calling out, 'We are with you, Mrs Pankhurst!' As the journey continued, more suffragettes joined, speaking to Emmeline at every stop, passing flowers and notes through the small opening at her window, and climbing on board so that the train was full of suffragettes by the time it reached its final destination.

In Glasgow and across the country, there was an outcry over the brutal treatment of Emmeline. Deputations demanding an inquiry were made to magistrates in Glasgow and to Scottish MPs in London. WSPU members staged protests across Britain, interrupting church services with cries of 'God save Emmeline Pankhurst!', setting fires in deserted barns and buildings, and smashing eighteen windows at the home of Home Secretary McKenna.

On 10 March, Mary Richardson attacked the famous *Rokeby Venus* painting in the National Gallery, London, with a meat cleaver. 'I have tried to destroy the picture of the most beautiful woman in mythological history as a protest against the government for destroying Mrs Pankhurst, who is the most beautiful character in modern history,' she explained in court following her arrest.[3]

The incident sparked outrage. The *Daily Telegraph* called it 'the most wicked act of vandalism ever committed in this or any country'. Christabel Pankhurst was quick to respond, accusing the press of hypocrisy. She mocked their outrage over a damaged painting while 'beautiful womanhood is being defaced and defiled by the economic horror of sweating and by that other horror of prostitution'. She urged them to save their tears for 'the devastation their sex has wrought through political disenfranchisement, industrial robbery, and the sexual exploitation of women'.

Despite Christabel's arguments, the justice system showed no leniency. Mary was sentenced to six months in prison but was released after a month following a hunger strike. Around the same time, Kitty Marion, who had been serving a three-year sentence for setting fire to the Hurst Park Racecourse grandstand in 1913, was also released. During her imprisonment, Kitty had endured the horror of being force-fed an unimaginable 232 times.

In March, Emmeline received word from Adela, who had safely arrived in Australia and been welcomed by Vida Goldstein and Cecilia John. The youngest Pankhurst daughter initially faced intense press attention, as the Pankhurst name carried significant notoriety even in these distant corners of the Commonwealth. Declaring her visit a private one, Adela was swiftly taken to Vida's comfortable middle-class home in Melbourne.

Though Adela had been forbidden by her mother from giving public speeches, Vida, Australia's best-known feminist, did not feel this should extend to Australia and so asked Adela to join the women's movement. Australian women had achieved suffrage, but to Vida, this was only the beginning of a long battle towards true equality. Adela immediately wrote a letter to her mother seeking permission, which Emmeline graciously gave. During the next few months, Adela basked in the adulation of the crowds eager to see one of the legendary Pankhursts in person. Addressing one such gathering, she reflected on the British suffragette struggle: 'You have heard a great deal about broken windows,' she told them. 'I can tell you about the broken lives that caused the broken windows.'

Back in Britain, Sylvia was also thriving, finally free from the controlling presence of her sister and mother. She continued to be arrested and re-arrested, entering and exiting prison nine times from January to August 1914. This earned her the title, as her biographer Rachel Holmes puts it, of the nation's most 'moused' militant. Among the Pankhursts, she was the most frequently incarcerated and force-fed – a bitter irony given that she was the one who, despite her deep commitment to women's suffrage, had initially hesitated to fully embrace the militant suffragette path. Historians have puzzled over why, as this was the case, she endured such torture. Some believe it was simply in defiance of her mother. As Sylvia herself wrote, 'We were chasing each other in and out of prison, as though it had been a race between us, until she had served forty-two days in ten imprisonments, and I, in nine imprisonments, had served sixty-five days.'

Others suggest Sylvia was attempting to show her mother how far she was willing to go for the movement and thus regain her mother's trust and sympathy. Most likely it is that Sylvia had fully embraced her own vision of social feminism and was determined to prove that it could triumph. Certainly, around her imprisonments, she continued her important work with ELFS. During these months she managed to organise meetings and discussions within the East End community, growing local engagement with the Federation. The first issue of the *Women's Dreadnought* was planned for 8 March 1914. This date was significant as it was linked to the struggles of US female labourers. Six years previously, thousands of New York women textile workers had gone out on strike on this date. Two years later, at the 1910 International Socialist Women's Conference, communist and women's rights activist Clara Zetkin proposed this date as an annual Women's Day commemoration. Though it did not come into being at that time, on 8 March 1917, working-class women in Petrograd led a strike that helped spark the Russian Revolution, and after that, the date would be unofficially recognised by several communist groups as a date to celebrate womanhood. Sylvia was aware of its association with the US women's textile strike, which was why she chose 8 March not only for the inaugural edition of the *Women's Dreadnought* but also for a series of speeches and demonstrations. As such, it would be the first time 8 March would be marked as a day to celebrate women in the British Isles.

On Mothering Sunday, 14 March, Sylvia also led a procession of East End women and men from Old Ford Road to Westminster Abbey. Still recovering from her imprisonment and hunger strikes, she was too weak to walk and so was carried by stretcher. Beforehand, she had written to the Dean of Westminster, requesting that he include a reference to women's enfranchisement in his sermon. He did not, and the doors of the Abbey remained shut to Sylvia and her followers. Undeterred, the frail yet fiercely determined Sylvia delivered a speech from the steps of the Abbey, addressing the thousands who had gathered to support her.

In April, she left the country, having been invited to speak in Budapest, Hungary. Travelling through Europe was risky at this time. The Balkans were in conflict, and nationalist tensions were sweeping through Austria-Hungary and Serbia. However, Sylvia could not be dissuaded. Zelie, who had also been imprisoned and force-fed when she went on hunger strike, was also in need of recuperation, and accompanied her. While in Hungary the two women visited the women's prison of Budapest and were horrified by the misery and despair they witnessed there. Sylvia had also been invited to speak in Dresden, but a subsequent ban by the German government prevented her from entering the country.[4]

Returning to London, Sylvia and Zelie, along with Norah, turned their attention to an abandoned school building at 400 Old Ford Road, which Sylvia had discovered one misty morning during an early stroll. With financial backing from Henry Harben, a Labour Party supporter and steadfast ally of the women's movement, Sylvia secured the lease. Harben, along with his wife

Agnes, had long supported suffragette causes, even founding Victoria House Printing, which produced *The Suffragette*.

With help from the local community, the trio transformed the derelict building into a vibrant social centre, naming it the Women's Hall. It became the headquarters of the ELFS but also a place where local women could access medical aid, job training, and information, and join in the fight for female enfranchisement. The Hall offered workshops to build skills, a library, a choir, and a sense of solidarity.

Opening to the public on 5 May, the celebrations went on all afternoon, spilling out along Old Ford Road. The following day, however, was a more sombre affair. Zelie, still weak and unwell from her time in prison, departed for America on her doctor's advice to seek rest and recovery. She had fought against leaving, but Sylvia, knowing her friend was desperately ill, had finally persuaded her. It was a painful goodbye between the two women who had grown inseparably close.

As Sylvia had been building these new relationships following her return from America, her bond with Keir Hardie, once so deep, had quietly unravelled. There appeared to be no conflict or definite ending. Likely it happened for no other reason than time had passed and their lives had shifted in different directions. Sylvia's star was on the rise, while Hardie's had begun to wane. He was older now, more tired, and she no longer needed him as she once had. Reflecting on a visit he made during her recovery from forcible feeding at Catherine Pine's nursing home, Sylvia wrote: 'I saw myself now in the position toward him in which I had so often seen my mother: he trying to help her, she flouting his efforts.'[5]

Sylvia had discovered her own path – difficult though it was – and it no longer required his guidance. 'I did not want him to help me to get free or even to try,' she admitted. He had nurtured her socialism, and helped her to use it to forge the foundation of her feminist activism. Now, she was strong enough to walk forward alone, carrying the cause he had helped her make her own.

In June, Sylvia wrote to Prime Minister Asquith, requesting that he meet a deputation of six working women who had been democratically elected at the ELFS' public rallies to discuss their demand for votes for all women over the age of 21. Sylvia intended to accompany them, though she was again very frail after her latest hunger and thirst strike and would need to be carried once more on a stretcher. Asquith refused, but the march led by the deputation went ahead nonetheless. It was met with heavy resistance as policemen wielding truncheons tried to push back the crowd. The six representatives managed to gain entry to the Commons. However, they had little luck in securing their audience with Asquith so all they could do was reiterate their demands to the Liberal Chief Whip.

The Federation was not to be put off, however. They joined forces with the United Suffragists to broaden support for their campaign. In a gesture of unity, and unbeknownst to Sylvia, Norah wrote to the WSPU inviting them to collaborate. She received a curt rebuff from Emmeline who stated that ELFS methods were not aligned with WSPU policy and instead, urged Sylvia to stop endangering her health.

But Sylvia would not relent. After being briefly imprisoned, she was released on 18 June and was driven by Norah straight to the House of Commons, where she declared she would stay and starve herself unless the Prime Minister received the deputation. Caught between 'the rock' of a likely general election happening in 1915 and 'the hard place' of a possible starved suffragette on his doorstep, Asquith realised he had no choice but to meet with the women. It was Keir Hardie who knelt by Sylvia's side and broke the news to her that she had brought the Prime Minister to the table.

In truth, the tide was slowly turning for women's suffrage in the British Isles. In 1902, Australia became the first Commonwealth country to grant female British subjects the right to vote in federal elections and to stand for Parliament. Their neighbour, New Zealand, had led the way a few years earlier, enfranchising all women in 1893. In Europe, things were also changing. The Grand Duchy of Finland extended voting rights to women in 1906, followed by Denmark two years later. And across the Atlantic Ocean, individual states in America were also beginning to grant women's suffrage.

In his meeting with the East End women, Asquith gave the same vague promises he had given to the NUWSS at a meeting the previous year, but he also claimed 'that if the change has to come, we must face it boldly, and make it thoroughgoing and democratic in its basis'. Sylvia interpreted this optimistically and was convinced that the government was finally preparing to shift its stance on women's suffrage. She asked George Lansbury to organise a meeting between her, Lansbury and Lloyd George.

The breakfast meeting between the trio a short time later was encouraging, at least on the surface. According to Sylvia, Lloyd George pledged his support for a Reform Bill that would include women's enfranchisement, even claiming he would resign if it failed. However, this had to be conditional on an end to all militancy. In a critical misstep, Sylvia failed to secure his promise in writing. She also told Lloyd George that she doubted her sister Christabel would agree to a truce, to which the Chancellor of the Exchequer, unimpressed, replied curtly that he would address the matter with 'Miss Christabel' himself.[6]

Matters grew more complicated when George Lansbury, elated by the Chancellor's apparent support, relayed the news to Henry Harben, who in turn passed it on to Christabel. Sylvia had hoped to keep her negotiations quiet for the moment, giving herself time to approach other Cabinet Ministers before sharing details. She telegrammed Christabel to explain her plan, promising to visit Paris afterwards to discuss matters face to face. But to Christabel, the time for negotiations was long past. The WSPU was demanding women's right to vote, not bargaining for compromises. Additionally, Christabel was probably irked by Sylvia's growing influence among Members of Parliament. She responded to Sylvia's plans for an impending Paris visit via a telegram to Norah, tersely stating, 'Tell your friend not to come.'

Emmeline, who had been arrested protesting outside Buckingham Palace in May, released and then re-arrested on 16 July while being carried by stretcher to a WSPU meeting at Holland Park, was also adamant that there would be no negotiations. In anticipation of her detention, she had left a note to be read in her absence: 'There has been talk of negotiation and compromise. No negotiation for us. A Government measure giving equal voting rights to women with men is our demand, and we demand it NOW!'[7]

Thus, while Sylvia was attempting to thrash out new terms by which the Government could finally concede and give the vote to women, Christabel, Emmeline, and the WSPU's loyal supporters were immovable. After years of beatings, arrests, imprisonment, force-feeding, shattered health, and even deaths, they would not yield. The government, equally stubborn, refused to bend. It was a stalemate.

Then, everything changed. War broke out in Europe.

Emmeline was in France when Britain declared war on Germany on 4 August 1914. Ravaged and exhausted after being released from prison following her tenth hunger strike, she had travelled to meet Christabel and Ethel Smyth in St Malo in Brittany. Sylvia was working hard in Bow at the time. London had been brimming with speculation ever since Archduke Franz Ferdinand, heir to the Austro-Hungarian throne, was assassinated by a Serbian nationalist two months earlier. The fragile balance in Europe had begun to unravel, with nations hurriedly choosing sides. Germany aligned with Austria-Hungary, while France and Russia backed Serbia. Britain was still uncertain about its allegiances but it seemed increasingly likely the country would be drawn into the escalating conflict. On the streets, in the pubs, and in ordinary people's drawing rooms, support for the war was growing, while on the floor of the House of Commons, intense debate ensued over the possibility of Britain's participation. Keir Hardie spoke lengthily about the devastating cost war would bring to the poor and was called a coward and a traitor.

Emmeline was aware that British women's fight for suffrage was entering its final, desperate throes, yet the continued force-feeding of hunger-striking suffragettes deeply distressed her. In a letter to a WSPU benefactor in Boston, she wrote: 'Our struggle grows more and more intense as we near the inevitable end.'[8]

The toll was undeniable. More and more suffragettes were left broken and gravely ill after enduring the brutal procedure of forcible feeding multiple times. News reached Emmeline of Francis Gordon, imprisoned in Perth, Scotland, who, having been unable to be force-fed by nose or mouth, was force-fed through the rectum. When she was released nearly three weeks later, after suffering the unimaginably painful ordeal twice daily during her imprisonment for an attempted arson charge, Dr Mabel Jones, who examined her, wrote:

> Her appearance was appalling, like a famine victim – the skin brown, her face bones standing out, her eyes half shut – her voice a whisper, her hands quite cold, her pulse a thread – her wrist joints were swollen, stiff and painful – this was not from rough handling but from poisoning. The breath was most offensive unlike anything I have smelt before and the contents of the bowels over which she had no control smelt the same.[9]

In prison and now back in France, Emmeline was plagued by severe migraines and sleepless nights, consumed with worry for the women who had sacrificed their bodies, minds and everyday lives for the movement.

However, now the outbreak of war in August 1914 gave her and Christabel an unexpected opportunity to reassess their strategy. When Germany declared war on France on 2 August, followed by Britain's entry into the conflict two days later after Germany invaded neutral Belgium, the WSPU leadership saw a chance to pause their militancy and, in doing so prevent further hunger strikers from suffering the terrible pain of forcible feeding. In any case, continuing to confront the government during wartime, they realised, would almost certainly doom their cause as their actions might be seen as treasonous. After much discussion between themselves and Ethel, they issued a directive from WSPU headquarters to inform their activists that they were going to offer the government a truce. But the truce would include one essential condition – France had released its political prisoners at the start of the war, and the WSPU demanded that Britain do the same for suffragettes.

The decision wasn't just tactical, however. For both Emmeline and Christabel, the war was undoubtedly a political moment, but it was also deeply personal, stirring a profound surge of nationalist sentiment. Emmeline's love of France and lingering prejudice against Germany, rooted in her youthful days as a schoolgirl in post-Franco-Prussian War Paris, made her see Germany as a threat that needed to be defeated. As she saw it, France was the cradle of democracy, a nation that had brought the ideals of liberty, equality, and fraternity into fruition, all of which needed to be protected. It was the reason she cherished the symbolic connection between her birthday and Bastille Day, a celebration of freedom and revolutionary spirit. Christabel shared her mother's fervent affection for the country. France had been her home for the last two years. It was a country that had given her safety when her own could not. Thus when she stood in the hot, crowded streets of St Malo, listening to the mayor read Germany's declaration of war, she felt a stirring within her similar to that which her mother must have felt decades earlier as she sat listening to Lydia Becker. It was the understanding that she had a role to play. For Christabel, it was a chance to emerge again as a leader, a feminist patriot in the national struggle.

On the eve of war, the exiled WSPU organising secretary had already made her stance known in this new, urgent fight. While she travelled to meet her mother in St Malo, Jessie Kenney, her secretary, was making her way back across the Channel with a new editorial from Christabel to appear in the next issue of *The Suffragette*. The article blamed the crisis in Europe on the imbalance of power held by men and once again was peppered with religious imagery. 'This great war,' she wrote, 'is God's vengeance upon the people who held women in subjugation and, by doing so, destroyed the perfect human balance.'

Yet despite the WSPU leadership's willingness to shift focus and embrace its patriotic duty, Home Secretary McKenna was not eager to forgive and forget. Accepting the WSPU's truce, he insisted that suffragette prisoners would only be released if they promised to cease all militant actions. Amid an outcry from suffragettes and sympathetic members of the public, Emmeline reached out to her well-connected contacts who persuaded the Archbishop of Canterbury to act as an intermediary in this instance. Archbishop Randall Davidson approached McKenna, advocating for unconditional releases. Three days later, on 10 August and after intense negotiations, the Home Secretary finally rolled back his response and announced that all suffragette prisoners would be released unconditionally. Emmeline immediately issued a notice to WSPU members to cease militant activities for the duration of the war and with that, the WSPU's years of rebellion came to a halt.

CHAPTER

19

PATRIOTIC FEMINISM

In France, Christabel was confident that neither she nor her mother would face arrest if they returned to England and so once negotiations with Home Secretary McKenna had been agreed upon, they announced plans to return in the autumn. The WSPU's mission, as they now saw it, was to throw their full support behind Britain's war effort. As Christabel wrote later in her memoir:

> War was the only course for our country to take. This was national militancy. As suffragettes, we could not be pacifists at any price. Mother and I declared support of our country … We offered our service to the country and called upon all members to do likewise … As Mother said, 'What would be the good of a vote without a country to vote in!'[1]

Where once the WSPU had organised massive public gatherings inciting their audiences to fight in whatever way they could against Britain's government, they now planned events encouraging young men to enlist in the British Army. *The Suffragette* ceased publication, and when it did resurface nine months later in the spring of 1915, its pages were full of articles about France, Russia and Britain's efforts on the Front. Even Christabel's highly anticipated return speech at the London Opera House centred entirely on the war. She made a passionate case for women to support Britain's fight, but, to the surprise and disappointment of many in the audience, barely mentioned votes for women at all.

Sylvia was horrified at the position her mother and sister took, feeling they had betrayed the pacifist ideals their father, Richard Pankhurst, 'his unswerving, life-long advocacy of Peace and internationalism, in which for nineteen years [Emmeline] had supported him', and which he had instilled so passionately in all his children. While the country was swept up in war fever, the working classes, as Hardie had so rightly pointed out, bore the brunt of the hardships that followed. In the East End, factories shuttered, work at the docks dried up, and luxury goods from silk to sugar that once flowed into the port simply stopped arriving. Many East End households lost their incomes overnight. Determined to act, Sylvia began writing hundreds of letters and articles highlighting the East End people's plight, something she would continue to do throughout the four years of war. She also organised a deputation to the Board of Trade, presenting ministers with stark evidence of the financial struggles faced by these families.

At the same time, she used her newspaper, *The Women's Dreadnought*, to publicly track rising rent and food costs, exacerbated by panic buying after the war's outbreak. Britain imported two-thirds of its food, including 80 per cent of its wheat used in the bread that formed the staple of most working-class diets. When prices shot up, many families found themselves unable to afford even this basic necessity. The government's strict food laws, like banning bread for livestock or rice at weddings, compounded the crisis. Bakers were required to produce 'regulation bread' using alternative grains, while posters urged the public to win the war by 'eating less bread'.[2]

As the war dragged on, more East End men were conscripted, leaving women to manage families alone. Separation allowances and pensions for soldiers' families were introduced but often delayed due to bureaucratic inefficiency. Women had to submit marriage and birth certificates, but lost documents and slow processing left many waiting weeks or months for payments. For struggling families, these delays meant hunger and mounting debts, with little relief in sight.

Sylvia and her team at ELFS' Women's Hall launched a series of fundraisers to address the pressing needs of the community. They began with a milk distribution drive, providing milk, eggs, and barley to struggling households. As donations came in, ELFS was able to open a clinic dedicated to treating malnourished children and those suffering from related illnesses. This clinic, located in a former pub in Bow, was aptly renamed The Mother's Arms, and during its first year of opening treated no fewer than 1,000 mothers and babies.[3] In addition, thanks to contributions of food, crockery and cutlery, ELFS established a series of soup kitchens, offering daily meals at cost price. According to Nellie Cressall, an East End suffragette and ELFS member, each meal cost just one penny. 'It did not pay, of course,' she later remarked, 'but I think many a life was saved by the sacrifice and service of the people who carried on all through the war and after.'[4]

Sylvia's most innovative initiative was the East London Toy Factory. Before the war, Germany had been Europe's leading toy manufacturer. Now Sylvia decided to open her own small factory in October 1914 to combat unemployment and meet wartime demand for toys. The East London Toy Factory, based at 45 Norman Road, provided women with training, a new trade, and at five pence an hour, or £1 a week – the same as the men's minimum wage at the time – gave women a fair wage. Despite anti-German sentiment, Sylvia employed H. Niederhofer, a local German toymaker, to train workers.

The factory produced a variety of toys, including stuffed animals and wax-headed baby dolls. In a remarkable act of inclusivity for the time, the toy makers produced dolls with different skin tones, including Asian and Black dolls. Financially, the factory thrived. Its toys were sold at fairs across London and, thanks to Sylvia's persuasiveness, even made it onto the shelves of upper-class store, Selfridges.[5]

Still, not all historians agree on the effectiveness of Sylvia and the ELFS' efforts. Based in London's East End, they served but a small strata of British society at the time, and one deeply entrenched in poverty and unemployment, challenges that could hardly be solved through the donations of one small organisation. Yet to criticise Sylvia for not addressing every issue is to overlook the impact she did have. For the families who benefited from the ELFS' soup kitchens and workshops, their struggles would undoubtedly have been even harder without her efforts. George Lansbury commented on how 'Sylvia Pankhurst worked day and night, rushing from town to town, from one Government office to another … It is certain, that many thousands of women and children owe her, and the rest of the committee, thanks for securing something approaching decent treatment…'

Meanwhile, on the other side of the world, Adela was also making her voice heard protesting Britain's involvement in the war. Socialism thrived in Australia, and Adela quickly found a home among Melbourne's radical socialist circles. These groups reminded the young émigré of the lively gatherings in her childhood homes and her mother's political salons. Renowned for her powerful oratory skills, Adela drew large crowds. She spoke passionately against the conditions in British women's prisons and the exploitation of female labour. At a meeting in July 1914, she even made an emotional plea for her mother's release from prison, moving half the audience to tears.

However, as war fever gripped Australia, 28-year-old Adela's determined pacifist stance became increasingly controversial. Initially welcomed in her socialist circles, her outspoken opposition to Britain's entry into the war began to clash with public sentiment. Her speeches were not only rooted in the pacifism her father had instilled in her but also in her own memories of the Boer War and her deep disdain for British jingoism. As sensational propaganda stories circulated about German atrocities against Belgian women and children, Adela rejected the narrative, arguing that Germany was the underdog, oppressed by Britain and France. All her years of standing in front of hostile crowds, ignoring the missiles of rotten vegetables thrown in her direction, using her voice to rise above their jeers, had brought her to this moment, and so she saw herself as a lone rebel, an independent voice unafraid to speak truths that others would not.

Sylvia, who had been at Christabel's address at the Royal Opera House, wept at what she had heard, and afterwards, immediately wrote a letter to her mother decrying their war stance. Emmeline replied with her own curt condemnation, claiming 'I am ashamed to know where you and Adela stand.'[6] Later, Sylvia would write to her younger sister in Australia complaining that their mother 'takes the opposite view in everything. The most extreme jingoism is scarcely enough for her and I can only look in wonder and ask "Can those two really be sane?"'

However, in Britain, many people believed Emmeline to be at her most sane in years. She seemed a world apart from the woman who, only a few years earlier, had urged supporters to smash windows and set fires to force the nation to listen. Now, she, Christabel, Annie Kenney, Flora Drummond and Grace Roe among many others, returned to their spotlights on the stage but this time urging men to sign up to fight on the Front, while on the streets they handed out white feathers to those 'cowards' who refused to do so. Also campaigning for women to be allowed to contribute more in the way of work to the war effort, their 'patriotic feminism' was embraced by many of the same women who had once been willing to follow them to prison.

Trade unions were less enthusiastic about Emmeline's campaign for women to join the workforce, fearing it would undercut labour standards and wages. But in WSPU's 'At Homes' and at events up and down the country, Emmeline argued that enlisting women, especially in munitions factories, was essential. The war effort was in desperate need of an unprecedented output of guns, bullets, and aircraft parts. Lloyd George, who had been appointed Minister of Munitions, had recently introduced the Munitions Bill in Parliament and called for more men to enrol for this work. However, Emmeline argued that by taking over men's jobs, women could free up more men to fight at the Front without slowing production.

Some critics suggest that Emmeline's support for the war marked a betrayal of feminism in favour of militarism and imperialism. However, this view oversimplifies her position during these years. Far from abandoning her feminist principles, Emmeline interwove them with the war effort, framing women's contributions to wartime labour as both a patriotic duty and a pathway to political enfranchisement. She continued to challenge traditional notions of femininity but did so in a way that aligned with the nation's urgent needs, making her efforts more socially acceptable in the process.

In her speeches and interviews, Emmeline was candid about her pacifist past but explained that while she still believed the Boer War was unjust, she had come to see this war as both righteous and necessary. Again, it is crucial not to oversimplify this stance or judge it by contemporary standards. The First World War was an unprecedented conflict, and many in Britain believed their national identity was under existential threat. For Emmeline and Christabel, this fear extended to the identity of British women. Emmeline often highlighted the plight of German women, whom she described as enduring the lowest status in Europe, confined by the rigid traditions of the so-called 'four Ks' –

Kinder (children), *Kirche* (church), *Küche* (kitchen), and *Kleider* (clothes). Both she and her eldest daughter were convinced that a German victory would unravel everything British women had fought for over the past decade. Indeed, in Christabel's speech at the Opera House, she claimed, 'We women are determined that the British citizenship for which we have fought in the past … shall be preserved from destruction at the hand of Germany.'

In late June 1915, Lloyd George received a letter from the secretary of King George V. The King, after reading an article in *The Observer* on the urgent need for women workers in munitions – written by none other than Christabel Pankhurst – was moved to act. He inquired whether it might be 'possible or advisable' for Lloyd George to enlist the help of the Pankhursts so as to allow women into the war workforce finally. The Minister of Munitions must surely have baulked at the idea of working with Emmeline Pankhurst, the woman who had so long been a thorn in his side and whose very health he'd had a hand in ruining. Still, his King had made a request and it was his duty to comply. He asked Emmeline to meet with him to discuss her potential contribution. The request shocked Emmeline, but, still, she agreed to meet her once-adversary, bringing Annie Kenney with her.

At the meeting, Lloyd George laid bare the dire situation on the front lines. The war had drained the nation's male workforce, and, just as she had been suggesting all along, it was now imperative to mobilise women for the war effort. He proposed that they finally set aside their grievances so that Emmeline could organise a public demonstration to show whether women were truly ready to step into working roles that had long been dominated by men. Emmeline, though it must have taken a deep inner courage to disregard all that had passed between them and accept Lloyd George's white flag, agreed. This event was to take place in a fortnight's time and received £3,500 from the ministry's propaganda fund to help fund it. Grace Roe was put in charge of organising it and over the next two weeks, she and other WSPU women worked tirelessly day and night to plan what would be a massive women's march. They took out a full-page advertisement in the *Daily Mail*, boldly announcing 'The Great Women's Procession'. They used the tactics that had worked so well in the past to mobilise women against the government in ensuring that, this time, those women would march in solidarity with their national leaders.

On 17 July 1915, over 50,000 women wove through the heart of London, marching from the Victoria Embankment past the Houses of Parliament, Pall Mall, Piccadilly, Park Lane, and Trafalgar Square, all sites of past violent suffragette protests. Women carried banners with slogans such as 'Mobilise the Brains and Energy of Women' and 'The Situation is Serious, Women Must Help to Save It'. Bands played patriotic tunes and the crowds, shouting and cheering made their voices and their willingness to serve unmistakably heard.

The event culminated with a rally at the Ministry of Munitions. In a moment almost unthinkable a few years earlier, Emmeline stood on a platform, speaking alongside Lloyd George. Newspapers seized on the image, running headlines the following day like 'Once They Were Enemies, the War Made Them Friends'.

However, the results of this unlikely alliance had the effect that Emmeline had been lobbying for since the beginning of the conflict. Women and girls poured into munitions factories. By mid-1918, approximately one million women were working in these industries. It should be noted, however, that many of these 'munitionettes', as they were nicknamed, endured gruelling conditions and handled toxic substances like TNT. Their efforts, however, were transformative, not just for the war but, finally, for Britain's perceptions of its women's capabilities.

Less than a year after the march, Lloyd George stood before the House of Commons and with praise levied at women that would have been unimaginable before the war, stated:

> It is not too much to say that our armies have been saved and victory assured by the women in the munition factories, where they helped to produce aeroplanes, howitzer bombs, shrapnel bullets, shells, machine tools, mines, and even took part in shipbuilding.[7]

War work for women wasn't the only issue that concerned the former WSPU leader. Her years as a Poor Law Guardian had left her deeply concerned by the plight of so-called 'war babies' born to single mothers, and she felt moved to do something to help.

Emmeline set about establishing an adoption home at Campden Hill, despite criticism for aiding unwed parents. Unfortunately, the home quickly ran out of funds and was forced to close. Nonetheless, Emmeline adopted four war babies herself, renaming them Kathleen King, Flora Mary Gordon (later Mary Hodgson), Joan Pembridge, and Elizabeth Tudor. She and her new family moved into a house in Holland Park, her first permanent address in years, and remained there throughout the war years. Later, she was asked how, with such little means, she could afford to adopt the four children and her answer was simply, 'I wonder I didn't take forty.'

As the war progressed, the rift between the Pankhurst women deepened, each championing causes the others found insupportable. While Sylvia and Adela both held pacifist beliefs, Adela's rhetoric veered sharply into anti-British and pro-German territory. Her speeches, delivered from the platforms of the Women's Political Association (WPA), where she became secretary in January 1915, and her articles for *The Woman Voter* and *The Socialist* wove together a perplexing blend of grievances. She railed against the armaments of monarchs, and the Allies' use of colonial troops, and repeatedly cast Germany as a beleaguered scapegoat. She also, quite bizarrely, warned that an Allied victory would force women into prostitution, leaving them victim to venereal disease.

Still, she was a passionate speaker and had thousands of followers. When she condemned rising food prices, the Australian Parliament threatened to defund the WPA, branding her dangerous. In defiance, she led a dramatic torchlight march through Melbourne, by all accounts, the first large-scale women's political demonstration in the city.

However, her radical rhetoric began alienating Australia's moderates. The popular morning newspaper, *The Argus*, denounced her as treasonous, and readers offered to fund her passage to Germany. Adela eventually resigned from the WPA but found a new purpose in January 1917, when she became an organiser for the Victorian Socialist Party. Leaving the security of Vida Goldstein's home, she moved in with socialist allies Robert and Ethel Ross, embarking on yet another bold chapter of her tumultuous life.

Emmeline and Christabel were horrified by Adela's public stance against Britain's war effort. They denounced both her and her sister, Sylvia, in the pages of their publication which they newly titled *Britannica* on 15 October 1915. Later, Emmeline would go so far as to send a telegram to Australian war-time Prime Minister Billy Hughes with the claim: 'I am ashamed of Adela and repudiate her.'[8]

However, while both women had immediately involved themselves in rallying support for the war among suffragettes, Christabel found herself struggling to find her footing upon her return to Britain. She confessed to feeling uneasy about the prison sentence that loomed over her now that she was back on British soil. More deeply, the country she returned to after two years abroad, and now several months into a war, had shifted in ways that left her unmoored. Shortly after delivering a speech at the Royal Opera House, she decided to leave again, this time for America, ostensibly to rally support for Britain's cause.

Travelling incognito on the Red Star Liner *Finland* under the name Miss Margaret MacDonald, she was accompanied by Olive Bartels, who adopted the alias Miss Mabel Barton. The three weeks of rest aboard the ship may have done Christabel some good, as once in New York, she seemed to rediscover her confidence. Speaking to audiences in cities like Chicago, Minneapolis, Washington, and New York itself, it was clear that her years in Paris had done little to dull her formidable powers as an orator.

Her message, however, was not universally embraced. The United States, not yet embroiled in the war, leaned towards pacifism, and many suffragists found her overtly patriotic stance distasteful and at odds with the fight she had been undertaking for years with the same government she now praised. Christabel, however, remained resolute. To her, the war was more than justified. In a characteristic blend of anti-male feminism and strategic conviction, she argued that allowing a 'male nation' like Germany to spread its ideals unchecked would be catastrophic for humanity.

As a skilled debater she was also able to overcome the scepticism of the pacifists in her audience. When they questioned her stance, she deftly pointed out that America's own War of Independence had been fought for principles of freedom and self-governance, which, she highlighted, were ideals no less just than those underpinning the current fight against Germany and its allies. The sharp wit and humour that had been so beloved by her WSPU audiences were also on full display during this tour. At the end of her six-month journey, she addressed a packed room at Carnegie Hall, where, as on other occasions, a heckler interrupted her. Without missing a beat, she turned to him and quipped, 'If you were a suffragette, you would have been thrown out – and after you'd been thrown out, I'd have said I didn't believe in your violent methods!' The audience chuckled warmly. With a sly smile, she continued, 'But you men are always so indulged. You are the privileged sex, the sheltered ones. We haven't the heart to treat you as cruelly and as roughly as you treat us.' At that, the hall erupted in laughter and applause.

In January 1916, Emmeline travelled to North America with Čedomilj Mijatović, Serbia's former Secretary of State, to rally support for the Allies. Touring the US and Canada, she appealed to suffragettes, including Alice Paul, who had once been a member of the WSPU and had been imprisoned with her British suffragette compatriots, urging them to channel their militancy into supporting the war effort.

On her tour, Emmeline also highlighted her worry about a communist insurgency in Russia. Russia's army was dealing with major defeats on the German Front, and the collapse in morale made the threat of large-scale mutiny alarmingly real. Under advice from his officials, Tsar Nicholas II abdicated the throne on 15 March 1917, believing the unrest that had risen across Russia would subside. Instead, his abdication served to embolden the Bolsheviks, an uncompromising Marxist group who had opposed the war from the beginning and now, calling for an immediate end to the war, sought to seize power.

While Russia grappled with its internal turmoil, Britain faced its own political upheaval. The catastrophic losses at the Battle of the Somme had intensified discontent with Prime Minister Asquith's leadership. His government, already strained by divisions, struggled to manage the mounting challenges of the war. As his inability to unite factions or inspire confidence became clear, his position crumbled. In December 1916, Asquith resigned, making way for Lloyd George, whose reputation as an energetic war minister had already won public favour.

After returning from America, Emmeline saw an opportunity to bolster the war effort by urging Russian peace terms. Though she opposed Czarist Russia, she feared a 'premature peace' would doom the Allies. Emmeline approached Britain's new Prime Minister with her proposal, who surprisingly agreed to sponsor a trip for her and other WSPU colleagues to Russia.

Her trip, however, was not welcomed by all women across the country. Glasgow-born Helen Crawfurd, a former WSPU member who had been part of Emmeline's Bodyguard and helped smuggle her into St Andrew's Hall in March 1914, had since broken ties with the organisation over its pro-war stance. Crawfurd co-founded the Women's Peace Crusade and publicly opposed Emmeline's Russian mission. In an impassioned letter to the publication *Forward*, Crawfurd wrote: 'Does Mrs Pankhurst speak for us? Has her voice ever been raised since this war started on behalf of the workers of this country against the profiteers or exploiters? SHALL WE NOT SPEAK FOR OURSELVES?'[9]

Despite criticism, Emmeline's June 1917 visit resonated with some Russian feminists and militarists, including Maria Bochkareva, leader of an all-female military unit. However, Russia's political chaos after the February Revolution overshadowed the former suffragette leader's agenda. Food shortages and Emmeline's own declining health further hampered her efforts. For a finish, her message urging Russia to continue fighting for 'civilisation and freedom' received mixed reactions from the people and the right-wing and left-leaning press.

Towards the end of her three-month tour, Emmeline met Alexander Kerensky, the revolutionary who had become Prime Minister of the fledgling Russian Republic. However, the meeting proved futile, and returning to Britain, exhausted and ill, her three-month tour was not considered a success. That autumn, the Bolsheviks stormed the Winter Palace in St Petersburg. Emmeline reacted with alarm, writing for *Britannica* that Russia was now under siege by a minority she claimed was inspired and directed by German agents.

Yet, returning from the chaos abroad, Emmeline found that the war was profoundly changing Britain. Society's attitudes toward women were shifting in astonishing ways. Women had stepped into roles previously deemed unsuitable for them, not only in munitions factories but across virtually every sector of the workforce.

The introduction of male conscription in 1916 – a policy Emmeline and Christabel had actively supported – had further expanded opportunities for women. With men called to the front, women took on non-combatant and administrative roles in the army, freeing even more men for active duty. This shift culminated in the formation of the Women's Army Auxiliary Corps (WAAC) in 1917, under the leadership of Dr Mona Chalmers Watson. A pioneering Scottish physician and suffragette, Dr Watson had been instrumental in advancing women's rights in medicine and, along with Dr Mabel Jones, had previously treated suffragettes released from hunger strikes in Perth Gaol.

The WAAC was structured into four divisions – cookery, mechanical, clerical, and miscellaneous – and became the first female military unit of its kind in the Western world. While most of the 57,000 women in the WAAC served on the Home Front, approximately 9,000 were deployed to France, marking a historic step in women's participation in military operations.

That autumn also brought changes of a more personal kind. Emmeline heard that on 30 September 1917 Adela had married Irish-born radical trade unionist Tom Walsh. Fourteen years her senior, Walsh was an ex-Catholic divorced father of three teenage daughters. Emmeline was aghast at the idea that this rough-cut Irishman, who had grown up as a poor orphan with little formal education before becoming a seaman, was now her son-in-law.

However, Walsh's passionate advocacy for workers' rights resonated deeply with Adela. Known for his commitment to 'the workers first, second, and always', Walsh earned the respect of several Australian suffragettes who had crossed paths with Emmeline's family. Nellie Martel described him as well-read and cultured, while Dora Montefiore called his company 'delightful'.[10]

Adela herself appeared content with her choice. In response to a congratulatory letter from Sylvia, she wrote enthusiastically, 'This is the life, isn't it, and I am happy – more than happy – to carry on Father's work.'

'Their father's work' is something that both Sylvia and Adela believe Christabel and their mother had abandoned when they stepped out as patriotic feminists. However, the truth is more complex than that. Though Emmeline opposed both Czarist autocracy and German imperialism equally, she viewed the Bolsheviks with particular suspicion. The Bolshevik Revolution inspired workers around the world who saw it as a successful uprising against capitalist oppression. Yet like many others, Emmeline feared that this revolutionary influence would dismantle the existing political framework, which, though she knew it to be deeply flawed, was still the one through which she advocated for votes for women. Plus, what good would the rise of the labour movement do for women's equality? She had long lost faith in the Labour Party as a reliable ally for the women's cause and saw their pacifist socialist stance during wartime as a betrayal of national interests. Additionally, her own experience of the socialist trade unionism movement had been that it systematically sidelined women's issues, prioritising male workers' interests instead. This bias became even more apparent during the war, as the influx of women into the workforce prompted many men to go out on strike. To Emmeline, this proved that the labour movement failed to grasp a fundamental truth: as she and Christabel saw it, only a society that achieved equality for women could deliver lasting prosperity to the working classes.

Sylvia, on the other hand, approached these issues through the lens of class struggle. Through her staunch opposition to the war, she championed a revolutionary form of socialism that prioritised the working class and rejected imperialism. Her belief was essentially the inverse of her mother's: if the working class could achieve prosperity, then women's equality would naturally follow. In truth, the Pankhurst split was reflective of a wider tension that was growing within the feminist movement in Britain. And yet, despite these divisions, the reality of votes for women was steadily approaching.

In 1917, the House of Commons passed a clause granting the parliamentary vote to certain categories of women aged 30 and over who were either householders or the wives of householders. This historic step awaited final approval from the House of Lords and was set for early 1918. As anticipation grew, debates about the future of women's political involvement intensified. At a meeting of the Standing Joint Committee of Industrial Women's Organisations – formed in 1915 to advocate for women workers during the First World War – Millicent Fawcett and socialist feminist Marion Phillips championed a collaborative approach. They argued that men and women should work together to achieve equality after women won the vote.

Emmeline and Christabel Pankhurst strongly disagreed. They believed that women, with their distinct perspectives and experiences, could best serve the nation by operating independently from traditional male-dominated political structures. Their vision culminated on 7 November 1917, when the Women's Social and Political Union was officially dissolved. That same day, they launched the Women's Party, shifting their focus from winning the vote to preparing women for their new role as citizens. The Party's slogan – 'Victory, National Security, and Progress' – emphasised their commitment to recognising women's contributions to society and ensuring their active role in shaping the nation's future.

Sylvia, however, was not happy with the proposed Franchise Bill. While the inclusion of women in the electorate was a significant victory, she felt the bill fell far short of true equality. In a letter to the socialist newspaper *The Call*, she questioned why women, legally considered adults at 21, could only vote at 30. Of course, she knew the answer. With millions of young men lying dead on the battlefields of Europe, allowing younger women to vote would create a female majority in post-war Britain, something the government refused to allow.

She also criticised several discriminatory provisions of the Bill such as the fact that if women or their husbands received Poor Law Relief, then the women in question would lose their parliamentary and local government votes, while their husbands would lose only their local vote. In addition, a woman separated from her husband, even due to his desertion, would forfeit her local government vote, yet her husband would retain his. Finally, Sylvia condemned the disenfranchisement of conscientious objectors to military service, seeing it as another unjust exclusion.

However, she and other critics could not stop the turning tide. The war was coming to an inevitable close, and the significant contributions women made to the war effort left the government with no choice but to extend voting rights to a portion of them. On 6 February 1918, the Representation of the People Act became law, allowing 8.5 million British women to finally cast their votes. Around the islands women came together to hug, cheer and weep for a day many thought they wouldn't live to see happen. Receptions were held by suffrage groups and reform clubs in cities such as Manchester and Glasgow where some of the most active suffrage campaigning had taken place. The vote was finally in their hands, or, at least, the hands of a vast majority. It was a long-overdue if bittersweet victory, shaped both by the sacrifices of the war and by the sacrifices of the thousands of women who had, over years and centuries, fought passionately for this moment.

CHAPTER

20

BEYOND SUFFRAGE

The war had irrevocably transformed Britain and the wider world – and with it, Emmeline and her daughters. Emmeline, once a stalwart upholder of the class-conscious values that had brought her and her husband, the 'Red Doctor', together, now turned her back completely on socialism in favour of a fervent patriotism. She saw clearly now how socialism had betrayed women's interests, and she viewed the class-based politics of groups like the Labour Party as being the true threat to democracy.

In June 1918, Emmeline returned to the US and Canada for another short tour. According to *Britannica*, her mission was to rally American support for Japanese intervention in Siberia, effectively endorsing military aid to anti-Bolshevik forces. Back in Britain, opposition MPs in the House of Commons expressed outrage, questioning whether Emmeline was acting as a representative of the government and, if so, in what capacity. The government, keen to avoid the fallout from admitting to such interference in the affairs of another nation, offered only evasive responses.

Emmeline, however, was not deterred. Ever in search of drama and excitement, she had a new mission. The passage of the 1918 Representation of the People Act had been a watershed moment, and laid the groundwork for women's participation in Parliament. Soon after the armistice was declared on 11 November 1918, the Qualification of Women Act followed, allowing women to stand for election to Parliament. Seizing the moment, Emmeline swiftly decided that Christabel would run as a candidate for the Women's Party.

Around this time, Emmeline received word that Adela had given birth to a son, whom she had named Richard, after his grandfather. Whatever Emmeline felt about the arrival of a grandson into the world, she did not spend time dwelling on the details, or her youngest daughter's new role as a mother. Christabel's ambitions remained her primary focus, consuming her attention as they always had.

However, the war had also profoundly changed Christabel. She had spent fifteen years of her life devoted to the struggle for women's suffrage, and now that it was here, she couldn't help but question how these hard-won votes would shape a world so scarred by the recent and devastating war. With these thoughts crowding her mind, she had stumbled upon the writings of Dr Henry Grattan Guinness, an Irish Nonconformist Protestant preacher and evangelist, and the author of several books on eschatology and biblical prophecy. His words spoke to her in a clear and compelling way, and led her towards what would eventually become the next major phase of her life – the Second Adventist Movement. This newfound faith provided her with a moral framework in a fallen world. It helped her shape her future political strategies and goals by offering her an intersection of the spiritual beliefs she had recently begun to nurture and the feminist convictions that had formed the core of her being since early adulthood.

Initially, Christabel kept her conversion to herself, though she did finally tell her mother in October 1918. Emmeline, who knew her daughter deeply, was neither surprised nor against it. She herself had drifted from the fierce agnosticism her late husband had once championed, finding her own anti-religious beliefs softening over the years, particularly during the horrors of the war. She welcomed Christabel's spiritual awakening, though the two chose to keep her daughter's new faith discreet as they worked together to secure a parliamentary seat for Christabel in the working-class constituency of Smethwick.

The Pankhursts wrote to Prime Minister Lloyd George to inform him of Christabel's candidacy under the Women's Party banner. He welcomed the news, recognising the party's staunch opposition to pacifism and Bolshevism as a valuable parliamentary asset. While her campaign was funded in part by the Women's Party, Christabel also received a £1,000 contribution from the British Commonwealth Union.[1]

Meanwhile, Sylvia had been invited – but refused – to stand as a Labour candidate for Sheffield Hallam. Increasingly drawn to radical left-wing ideals, she rejected the parliamentary process, believing it incapable of fully supporting workers' interests. Just as Emmeline had dismissed the Labour Party as betraying women's causes, Sylvia now viewed it as inadequate for the revolutionary change she envisioned.

Emmeline threw herself into her daughter's campaign, helped by stalwart allies from the WSPU – now the Women's Party – such as Jessie Kenney, Flora Drummond, and the disabled Rosa May Billinghurst. Christabel had planned to contest the Westbury constituency in Wiltshire. However, at the last moment, she shifted to the more industrial, working-class constituency of Smethwick, where she ran against Labour candidate and trade union leader John Davison.

Christabel's campaign focused on powerful themes that resonated with many in a post-war Britain. These included calls for the Germans to bear the full cost of the war and the slogan 'Britain for the British'. She capitalised on the prevailing fear of Bolshevism, framing the post-war struggle as a battle between 'the Red Flag and the Union Jack'. As always, Christabel's wit was sharp. When, during a public speech, a working-class heckler challenged her by asking if she had ever worked in a factory, she retorted, 'No, I have not. Neither have your friends Ramsay MacDonald and Philip Snowden.'[2]

Despite her skill and energy, Christabel's campaign ultimately fell short. The ballot results were delayed to allow votes from soldiers still stationed in Flanders and France, but when they were finally tallied, Davison narrowly claimed victory by 775 votes. Emmeline was devastated by the loss, perhaps more so than Christabel herself.

There was some solace to be found by both women when they heard that of the seventeen women that had stood in the 1918 December elections, one had been elected. This was Countess Constance Markievicz, the Irish nationalist and suffragist who stood as a member of the Sinn Féin party in Dublin's St Patrick's constituency. However, because she represented the nationalist movement in Ireland and therefore refused to swear the mandatory oath of allegiance to the King, Markievicz did not take her seat in Westminster.

More women, however, would follow. On 1 December 1919, Conservative candidate Nancy Astor who had defeated Liberal Isaac Foot, became the first woman to take her seat in the House of Commons. Astor was not a suffragette but over the next few years, many who were such as Dorothy Jewson, Susan Lawrence, Mabel Philipson and Vera Terrington would gain their place in Parliament and history.

❁ ❁ ❁

The suffragette story of Emmeline Pankhurst and her three daughters more or less ends here. Although each Pankhurst remained active in public life, continuing to fight the causes that had become crucial to them, their paths rarely crossed again.

Christabel finally left England in 1921 and moved to the United States. There, she embarked openly on a spiritual journey, becoming an evangelist affiliated with the Plymouth Brethren, a non-conformist group that had originated in early nineteenth-century Dublin. She would go on to become a prominent member of the Second Adventist movement, writing several books on the topic and being, as always, a highly in-demand speaker.

She returned to Britain in the late 1920s and was appointed a Dame Commander of the Order of the British Empire for 'public and social services'. She stayed in Britain for a short period, returning to California following the onset of the Second World War. Christabel adopted a daughter, Betty, and spent her remaining years on the West Coast of America, continuing to inspire those around her with the same fervour and conviction that had defined her earlier suffrage work.

Sylvia's path after the First World War led her inevitably towards Communism and, as it turned out, further imprisonment for these beliefs. In her publication, now called the *Workers' Dreadnought*, she had published articles encouraging Royal Navy sailors to mutiny. Though the incendiary pieces were actually written by the publication's first black correspondent, Jamaican author Claude McKay, Sylvia refused to name him. Instead, she took responsibility for their publication and, in 1921, was sent to prison for the last time for sedition.

In 1915, while the war still raged, Keir Hardie had passed away. He had been unwell for some time and, recognising that his health would not improve, announced his retirement from Parliament in May of that year. Sylvia was the first person he confided in about his decision. She had immediately gone to see him at Nevill's Court, a place steeped in memories of countless evenings spent sharing a warm cup of tea among the piles of books and papers, and discussing their dreams of a better world.

When she arrived, he was packing, preparing to return to Scotland and the comfort of his home with Lillie. Sylvia knew instinctively that this would be their final meeting and struggled to hold back her tears. Hardie, ever stoic, seemed unable to summon the words for a proper farewell. Instead, he simply said, 'You have been very brave.'[3] Months later, while weaving through a demonstration in London, Sylvia spotted a newsboy holding a placard. Three stark words were written across it: *Keir Hardie Dead*. The man she had first met as a teenager in her parents' parlour, a figure who had profoundly shaped her life and ideals, was gone. Hardie had succumbed to pneumonia following a series of strokes on 26 September 1915, at the age of 59.

Though her romance with Keir Hardie had long since ended, such had been Hardie's impact that Sylvia doubted she would ever find another man to journey alongside her in life. She was wrong. Toward the end of the First World War, she met Silvio Corio, an Italian anarchist, trained as a printer and typographer, whose passion for politics matched her own. The couple moved in together, and in 1927, they welcomed a son. Following her younger sister Adela's example, Sylvia named her infant Richard, in honour of the father she had so adored. Her son's middle names, however, were Keir Pethick, a salute to two other people who had had a profound effect on her life. Sylvia's decision to remain an unmarried mother caused a public outcry, particularly given her visibility as a writer and advocate for human rights. Yet, characteristically defiant, Sylvia refused to yield to pressure to tie the knot with her lover, asserting that 'marriage without legal union' was a more fitting arrangement for liberated women.

For the next several decades, Sylvia's unrelenting fight against oppression saw her championing causes as diverse as Irish independence, Indian Home Rule, and, from 1935 onwards, a battle against the rise of fascism. She also continued to use her pen to make these causes known, writing prolifically, including a biography of her mother in 1935. That same year, her focus shifted sharply toward Ethiopia after Mussolini's invasion. Sylvia threw herself into the Ethiopian cause, decrying both fascism and Western colonial ambitions. Following the Allied liberation of Ethiopia in 1944, she visited the country, but was openly critical of British aspirations in the region.

She returned to Ethiopia in 1950 and 1951, this time visiting Eritrea, then under British military administration, and voiced support for Eritrea, Djibouti, and Somaliland joining Ethiopia. Finally, in 1956, at the invitation of Emperor Haile Selassie, Sylvia moved to Ethiopia. There, she dedicated her remaining years to improving maternal and infant healthcare, spearheading efforts to establish a specialist women's hospital. Her profound commitment to Ethiopia was honoured at her death in 1960 when she became the only foreigner to receive a state funeral and was buried among Ethiopia's national heroes.

Though Sylvia and Christabel never reunited in person, they began a poignant correspondence during Sylvia's final years. The exchange, later made public by Sylvia's son, Richard, was initiated by Christabel, who wrote to her sister on Sylvia's 71st birthday in 1953. Hearing that Sylvia had suffered a serious heart attack and was recuperating at home, Christabel reached out with a letter that bridged the long years of estrangement:

'Your mind often goes back, I know, as mine does,' Christabel wrote, 'to those good years of our childhood, when we still had Father and Mother & the home they made for us.'[4]

Sylvia immediately responded, and over the next few years, they corresponded regularly, revisiting shared memories from their childhood and the suffragette movement they had brought into being, along with the wider political concerns of the day.

In one of her final letters before her death on 13 February 1958, Christabel reflected on the enduring legacy of the suffragette struggle that had so shaped their lives, and its fading prominence in history:

> This is a very different world and much less tranquil than it was in the days of our movement when, thanks to that relative tranquillity, we were able to make the stri[de] needful for a British victory and to prepare other countries, even the most unlikely ones, to give the vote to their own women. We seized the ideal moment for our suffragette campaign. Now there is inflation, there is nuclear warfare, East – West tension and many another problem[s], even that of increasing crime, even among juveniles, and so on and so forth. Do you think that the women who have the vote are much more interested in how it was won for them than are men voters in how their vote was won for them?[5]

Adela, like Sylvia, had been drawn to Communism during the First World War. By 1920, she and her husband, Tom, became founding members of the Communist Party of Australia. Imaginative and idealistic as ever, the youngest Pankhurst daughter dreamed of a new social order grounded in cooperation and mutual support. However, eventually disillusioned with the movement's rigidity, both she and Tom withdrew from the party and were eventually expelled.

During this time, Adela focused on her growing family, giving birth to four more children after her first son, Richard. Significantly, her next two children were named Sylvia (born in 1920) and Christian (born in 1921), echoing the names of her sisters and subtly binding herself to her family's legacy. Ursula was born in 1923, followed by a daughter, Faith, in 1926, who tragically died in infancy.

As Emmeline before her, Adela did not give up her political work as a result of motherhood. In 1928, she founded the anti-communist Australian Women's Guild of Empire, a group dedicated to relieving the suffering of working-class women and children. Ironically, her eloquence and organisational skill attracted a predominantly middle-class following, marking a shift in the Guild's influence.

Adela and Tom's interest in internationalism eventually led them to sympathise with Japan's industrialisation and trade ambitions, viewing Japan as a more favourable trade partner for Australia than the United States. As tensions in Europe grew, the couple advocated for a trade agreement with Japan. In late 1939 and early 1940, they travelled to Japan as guests of the Japanese government – their only holiday together – and returned to assure Australians of Japan's peaceful intentions.

However, Adela's support for Japan alienated her followers. After the bombing of Pearl Harbor in 1941, she was interned in March 1942 as a potential security risk. Tom, now in his early 70s, had fallen gravely ill and Adela, desperate to be free so that she could care for him, used a suffragette tactic of old – she began a hunger strike. It was effective. She was released in October, just days before her husband's death in 1943.[6]

Tom's passing marked the end of Adela's political life. In 1960, she converted to Roman Catholicism, having never forgotten the fondness for the stories she had once secretly listened to, enthralled, at the back of the classroom in the first school she had ever attended. A year later, on 23 May 1961, she passed away and received a Catholic burial.

As her daughters forged their own paths across the world, Emmeline Pankhurst attempted to retreat from public life by moving to Canada. In 1922, she rented a house in Toronto, bringing with her her four adopted children. Yet true to form, Emmeline could not remain idle. She became involved with the Canadian National Council for Combating Venereal Diseases (CNCCVD), delivering lectures across Ontario. During a tour of Bathurst, when the mayor proudly introduced her to a new facility for 'Fallen Women', Emmeline retorted pointedly, 'Ah! Where is your Home for Fallen Men?'

Despite her activism, Emmeline struggled financially, having never earned a stable income. The harsh Canadian winters, coupled with her declining health, made life increasingly difficult. Her old friend and literal saviour of so many battered suffragettes, Nurse Catherine Pine, travelled to see her and took care of her for a short while.[7] However, finally, it was too much for Emmeline and in 1925 she returned to England, leaving behind the icy landscapes of her brief Canadian chapter.

When Emmeline returned to England, she moved in with her sister, Ada Goulden Bach, in Kensington. News of her return quickly reached Sylvia, who decided to visit her mother after years of estrangement. At the time, Sylvia was living in her unconventional relationship with Silvio, an arrangement that Emmeline found deeply objectionable, even though, ironically, she had once suggested a similar lifestyle for herself and Richard Pankhurst in their early years together. The mother and daughter's reunion was fraught with tension. Sylvia later recalled that their meeting was initially emotional as 'The old affection overwhelmed us. Then as the first rush of joy and sadness passed, a gulf remained.'[8]

Emmeline's adopted daughter, Mary, claims there was little in the way of joy, however. According to her, Emmeline simply set down her teacup and walked out of the room in silence, when Sylvia appeared, leaving her daughter to dissolve into tears. The ideological divide between them would prove insurmountable. When Sylvia attempted to visit her mother again on several occasions, her requests were consistently refused.

In contrast, Emmeline was heartened to receive a letter from Adela, who wrote to say that she and her husband, Tom, had abandoned their socialist ideals. Adela now recognised, she claimed, the destructive nature of class conflict and embraced views closer to Emmeline's. Emmeline responded with warmth, admitting she was 'full of regret for their long rift'.

If those who loved her had thought that Emmeline's frailty would slow her down, they had greatly underestimated her. In truth, Emmeline was keen to become active in politics once more. In 1926, she startled many by joining the Conservative Party, and stood as a parliamentary candidate for Whitechapel and St George's, though she was ultimately unsuccessful. Her transformation from the militant suffragette who led a campaign of civil disobedience that landed her behind bars on several occasions, courting near-death for her cause, to a Conservative candidate was bewildering to many of her contemporaries. When questioned about her change in allegiance, Emmeline simply claimed, 'My war experience and my experience on the other side of the Atlantic have changed my views considerably.' However, historians suggest the actual truth was that Emmeline believed the Conservative Party offered the most viable path to achieving the suffragettes' ultimate goal: votes for all women on the same basis as men. It was a belief that Christabel had also harboured during her time at the WSPU helm.

Finally, Emmeline could not ignore her failing health. Christabel, who had returned from America to care for her mother, and Ada, were compelled to move her into a nursing home at 43 Wimpole Street in Hampstead. Here, she reminisced with her beloved daughter about bygone days. 'She spoke much of her husband Richard and beloved son, Harry, her "greatest griefs". According to Christabel, she claimed 'she had never recovered from them. She had always been silent about things too deep for words, but she spoke more of them now than she had ever done.'[9]

Frail and in constant pain, Emmeline insisted on being treated by the same doctor who had restored her to some semblance of health after her thirteenth hunger strike fourteen years earlier. Unfortunately, even he could do nothing for her now. The years of torture her body had endured had caught up to her and she would not recover. Her condition worsened rapidly, and on 14 June 1928, just one month shy of her 70th birthday, Emmeline passed away peacefully in her bed.

Christabel, who was at her side during her final moments, later wrote to Emmeline's lifelong friend, Esther: 'My greatest comfort is the look of joy on her face that I saw ... it seemed to fade afterwards, and just peace and contentment and beauty were left – as I have never seen them on any other.'[10]

News of Emmeline's death echoed across the globe, with newspapers heralding the loss of a pioneer who had reshaped the political landscape. In Britain, thousands of mourners – women and men alike – paid their respects as her body lay in state in the chapelle ardente at Cambridge Place.[11] Four days later, a grand funeral was held at St John's Church, Smith Square, Westminster. The church was packed with women of all ages and backgrounds, many adorned in the suffragette colours of purple, white, and green. Among them were those wearing the silver brooches that signified time served in prison, or the tri-colour ribbons bearing bars that marked the harrowing experience of hunger striking.

The air was thick with the scent of flowers and wreathes that had been laid in tribute. Among the floral offerings was a wreath from Herbert Jones, the jockey who had ridden Anmer on the fateful day that Emily Davison sacrificed her life for the cause. His simple yet poignant message read, 'To do honour to the memory of Mrs Pankhurst and Miss Emily Davison.'[12]

The service included Emmeline's favourite hymn, 'Sun of My Soul, Thou Saviour Dear', followed by prayers and an address delivered by Reverend William Frederick Geikie-Cobb. Speaking of Emmeline as a woman who had fought heroically and purposefully both for suffrage and the war cause, he said:

> We wondered in those days what was to come, and then there came bursting upon us a war mightier than this civil war. Emmeline

> Pankhurst realised that the issues in both were identical, and she threw her energies into the new fight for freedom. We salute her as an heroic leader, we acclaim her as a friend, and we respect her as a wise counsellor. We owe her a deep debt of gratitude which we can best discharge by carrying on still farther the cause to which she gave her life.

After the service, the coffin was carried to the church door by the pallbearers, all of whom were former WSPU members and included Marion Wallace Dunlop, Barbara Wylie, and Kitty Marshall. From there, a solemn cortege of more than a thousand women marched eight abreast, just as they had done on so many past suffragette marches. Once more under the command of Flora 'The General' Drummond, and passing crowds of silent onlookers who lined the streets to bid goodbye to this extraordinary woman, they accompanied the coffin to Brompton Cemetery.

Among the chief mourners were Emmeline's surviving siblings, Ada and Robert Goulden, and her daughters Christabel and Sylvia, the latter of whom had arrived with the son Emmeline had never met. Annie Kenney and Flora, Emmeline's supporters to the last, were also present. Meanwhile, across the ocean in Australia, Adela privately mourned her mother, a woman she had loved as fiercely as she had feared, much like many of the others who had known her during her remarkable life.

Less than three weeks later on 2 July 1928, the Equal Franchise Act was passed, granting equal voting rights to all women and men over the age of 21. With this historic milestone, women became a majority of the British electorate, comprising 52.7 per cent of all eligible voters.

NOTES

Chapter 1

1. E. Pankhurst, *My Own Story*. 1914. London, Hesperus Press, 2015, p. 17
2. University of Manchester LUNA Catalogue, Peterloo Collection, English MS 1197/22, To the Inhabitants of Manchester and Neighbourhood at www.digitalcollections.manchester.ac.uk/view/MS-ENGLISH-01197-00022/1 Accessed 13 March 2024
3. M. L. Bush, *The Casualties of Peterloo*, Lancaster, UK, Carnegie Publishing, 2007, p. 33
4. Powered By Reason – poweredbyreason.co.uk. 'The Women of Peterloo – People's History Museum', *People's History Museum*, 30 March 2023, phm.org.uk/blogposts/the-women-of-peterloo. Accessed 13 March 2024
5. E. Pankhurst, *My Own Story*. 1914. London, Hesperus Press, 2015, p. 11
6. E. Pankhurst, *My Own Story*. 1914. London, Hesperus Press, 2015, p. 18
7. E. Pankhurst, *My Own Story*. 1914. London, Hesperus Press, 2015, p. 15
8. E. Pankhurst, *My Own Story*. 1914. London, Hesperus Press, 2015, p. 14
9. Poetry Foundation, 'The French Revolution as It Appeared to Enthusiasts at Its Commencement by William Wordsworth', *Poetry Foundation*, 6 September 2022, www.poetryfoundation.org/poems/45518/the-french-revolution-as-it-appeared-to-enthusiasts-at-its-commencement
10. R. West, 'Mrs. Pankhurst', *The Post Victorians*. London, Ivor Nicholson, 1933, pp. 479–500
11. C. Pankhurst, *Unshackled: The Story of How We Won the Vote*. London, Hutchinson & Co., 1959, p. 18
12. C. Pankhurst, *Unshackled: The Story of How We Won the Vote*, London, Hutchinson & Co., 1959, p. 8.
13. E. Pankhurst, *My Own Story*. 1914. London, Hesperus Press, 2015, p. 41

Chapter 2

1. C. Pankhurst, *Unshackled: The Story of How We Won the Vote*, London, Hutchinson & Co., 1959, p. 22
2. E. Pankhurst, *My Own Story*. 1914. London, Hesperus Press, 2015, p. 21
3. C. Tuttle, *Hard at Work in Factories and Mines*, 7 October 2021, https://doi.org/10.4324/9780429036989. Accessed 1 March 2024
4. 'Chetham's Library – Karl Marx's Desk', *Chetham's Library*, library.chethams.com/collections/101-treasures-of-chethams/karl-marxs-desk
5. V. Coleman, *Adela Pankhurst: The Wayward Suffragette 1885–1961*, ebook ed. Melbourne University Press, 1996, Chapter 1
6. E. Pankhurst, *My Own Story*. 1914. London, Hesperus Press, 2015, p. 25
7. S. Harrison, *Sylvia Pankhurst: Rebellious Suffragette*, ebook ed. Sapere Books, 2018, Chapter 2
8. C. Pankhurst, *Unshackled: Story of How We Won the Vote*, London, Hutchinson, 1959, p. 27
9. R. West, *The Young Rebecca: A Reed of Steel*, p. 249
10. S. E. Pankhurst, *The Suffragette: The History of the Women's Militant Suffrage Movement 1905–1910*. 1911. Rimbault Press, 2009, p. 103

Chapter 3

1. V. Coleman, *Adela Pankhurst: The Wayward Suffragette 1885–1961*, ebook ed. Melbourne University Press, 1996, Chapter 3
2. J. Purvis, *Emmeline Pankhurst: A Biography*, Oxfordshire, Routledge, 2002, p. 39
3. V. Coleman, *Adela Pankhurst: The Wayward Suffragette 1885–1961*, ebook ed. Melbourne University Press, 1996, Chapter 3
4. E. Pankhurst, *My Own Story*. 1914. London, Hesperus Press, 2015, p. 32
5. E. Pankhurst, *My Own Story*. 1914. London, Hesperus Press, 2015, p. 33
6. R. Holmes, *Sylvia Pankhurst: Natural Born Rebel*. London, Bloomsbury, 2021, p. 34

Chapter 4

1. C. Pankhurst, *Unshackled: The Story of How We Won the Vote*, London, Hutchinson & Co., 1959, p. 35
2. E. Pankhurst, *My Own Story*. 1914. London, Hesperus Press, 2015, p. 37
3. C. Pankhurst, *Unshackled: The Story of How We Won the Vote*, London, Hutchinson & Co., 1959, p. 35

4. C. Pankhurst, *Unshackled: The Story of How We Won the Vote*, London, Hutchinson & Co. 1959, p. 35
5. V. Coleman, *Adela Pankhurst: The Wayward Suffragette 1885–1961*, ebook ed. Melbourne University Press, 1996, Chapter 3
6. NUWSS typescript, n.d., Manchester Central Library, M50/2/10/20, accessed 22 April 2024
7. E. Pankhurst, *My Own Story*. 1914. London, Hesperus Press, 2015, p. 41

Chapter 5

1. S. Harrison, *Sylvia Pankhurst: Rebellious Suffragette*, ebook ed. Sapere Books, 2018, Chapter 6
2. J. Purvis, *Emmeline Pankhurst: A Biography*, Oxfordshire, Routledge, 2002, p. 71
3. 'Women's Enfranchisement Bill', WOMEN'S ENFRANCHISEMENT BILL. (Hansard, 12 May 1905), api.parliament.uk/historic-hansard/commons/1905/may/12/womens-enfranchisement-bill-1. Accessed 30 April 2024
4. C. Pankhurst, *Unshackled: The Story of How We Won the Vote*, London, Hutchinson & Co., 1959, p. 46
5. C. Pankhurst, *Unshackled: The Story of How We Won the Vote*, London, Hutchinson & Co., 1959, p. 48
6. *Nottingham Evening Post*, 10 September 1906

Chapter 6

1. C. Pankhurst, *Unshackled: Story of How We Won the Vote*, London, Hutchinson, 1959, p. 57
2. D. Morgan, *Suffragists and Liberals: The Politics of Woman Suffrage in England*, Totowa, Rowman and Littlefield, 1975, p. 38
3. L. Jenkins, 'Annie Kenney and the Politics of Class in the Women's Social and Political Union', *Twentieth Century British History*, Volume 30, Issue 4, December 2019, pp. 477–503
4. E. Pankhurst, *My Own Story*. 1914. London, Hesperus Press, 2015, p. 48
5. E. Pankhurst, *My Own Story*. 1914. London, Hesperus Press, 2015, p. 51
6. *Manchester Evening News*, 16 October 1905
7. 'Missive from a Militant: Testimony from the First British Suffragette Revealed – University of Oxford', www.ox.ac.uk/news/arts-blog/missive-militant-testimony-first-british-suffragette-revealed
8. S. Harrison, *Sylvia Pankhurst: Rebellious Suffragette*, ebook ed. Sapere Books, 2018, Chapter 6
9. C. Pankhurst, *Unshackled: The Story of How We Won the Vote*, London, Hutchinson, 1959, p. 54
10. C. Pankhurst, *Unshackled: The Story of How We Won the Vote*, London, Hutchinson, 1959, p. 52

11. M. Pugh, *The Pankhursts: The History of One Radical Family*, ebook ed. Vintage, London, 2008, Chapter 7
12. S. Harrison, *Sylvia Pankhurst: Rebellious Suffragette*, ebook ed. Sapere Books, 2018, Chapter 5
13. L. Broad, *Winston Churchill 1874–1945*, London, Hutchinson & Co., 1945, p. 53
14. C. Pankhurst, *Unshackled: The Story of How We Won the Vote*, London, Hutchinson, 1959, p. 62
15. C. Pankhurst, *Unshackled: The Story of How We Won the Vote*, London, Hutchinson, 1959, p. 62
16. J. Purvis, *Emmeline Pankhurst: A Biography*, Oxfordshire, Routledge, 2002, p. 78
17. A. Kenney, *Memories of a Militant*. 1924. London, Edward Arnold, 2015, p. 68
18. A. Rosen, *Rise Up Women! The Militant Campaign of the Women's Social and Political Union 1903–1914*, Oxfordshire, Routledge, 1974, p. 60

Chapter 7

1. S. Harrison, *Sylvia Pankhurst: Rebellious Suffragette*, Sapere Books, 2018, Chapter 6
2. J. Purvis, *Christabel Pankhurst: A Biography*, Oxfordshire, Routledge, 2018, p. 105
3. M. Pugh, *The Pankhursts: The History of One Radical Family*, ebook ed. Vintage, London, 2008, Chapter 7
4. E. S. Pankhurst, *The Life of Emmeline Pankhurst*, 1936, Kessinger Publication, 2007, p. 60
5. A. Pankhurst Walsh, *My Mother: A Vindication and an Explanation*, Australian National Library, Canberra, 1933

Chapter 8

1. K. Atherton, *Suffragette Planners and Plotters: The Pankhurst/Pethick-Lawrence Story*, Pen and Sword, 2019, p. 47
2. E. Pankhurst, *My Own Story*. 1914. London, Hesperus Press, 2015, p. 74
3. E. S. Pankhurst, *The Suffragette: The History of the Women's Militant Suffrage Movement 1905–1910*. 1911. Rimbault Press, 2009, p. 120
4. E. Pankhurst, *My Own Story*. 1914. London, Hesperus Press, 2015, p. 83

Chapter 9

1. J. Purvis, *Emmeline Pankhurst: A Biography*, Oxfordshire, Routledge, 2002, p. 90
2. E. S. Pankhurst, *The Suffragette Movement: An Intimate Account of Persons and Ideals*, Longmans, 1931, pp. 261–262

3. M. Pugh, *The Pankhursts: The History of One Radical Family*, ebook ed. Vintage, London, 2008, Chapter 8
4. E. S. Pankhurst, *The Suffragette Movement: An Intimate Account of Persons and Ideals*, Longmans, 1931, pp. 269
5. E. S. Pankhurst, *The Suffragette Movement: An Intimate Account of Persons and Ideals*, Longmans, 1931, pp. 263
6. J. Purvis, *Emmeline Pankhurst: A Biography*, Oxfordshire, Routledge, 2002, p. 93
7. E. Pankhurst, *My Own Story*. 1914. London, Hesperus Press, 2015, p. 263
8. E. Pankhurst, *My Own Story*. 1914. London, Hesperus Press, 2015, p. 61
9. E. Pankhurst, *My Own Story*. 1914. London, Hesperus Press, 2015, p. 91.
10. J. Marlow (Ed.), 'From Life's Fitful Fever "Go it, old gal!"' Margaret Wynne Nevinson, *Suffragettes: The Fight For Votes for Women*, ebook edition, Virago, 2015

Chapter 10

1. E. S. Pankhurst, *The Suffragette Movement: An Intimate Account of Persons and Ideals*, Longmans, 1931, pp. 266–267
2. E. Pankhurst, *My Own Story*. 1914. London, Hesperus Press, 2015, p. 63
3. E. S. Pankhurst, *The Suffragette Movement: An Intimate Account of Persons and Ideals*, Longmans, 1931
4. C. Pankhurst, *Unshackled: Story of How We Won the Vote*, London, Hutchinson, 1959, p. 83
5. M. Pugh, *The Pankhursts: The History of One Radical Family*, ebook ed. Vintage, London, 2008, Chapter 8
6. E. Pankhurst, *My Own Story.* 1914. London, Hesperus Press, 2015, p. 99
7. E. S. Pankhurst, *The Suffragette Movement: An Intimate Account of Persons and Ideals*, Longmans, 1931, p. 278
8. E. Pankhurst, *My Own Story*. 1914. London, Hesperus Press, 2015, p. 101
9. E. Pankhurst, *My Own Story.* 1914. London, Hesperus Press, 2015, p. 101
10. E. Pankhurst, *My Own Story.* 1914. London, Hesperus Press, 2015, p. 108

Chapter 11

1. C. Pankhurst, *Unshackled: The Story of How We Won the Vote*, London, Hutchinson, 1959, p. 97
2. E. Pankhurst, *My Own Story*. 1914. London, Hesperus Press, 2015, p. 114
3. K. McInerney, 'Reclaiming space: enacting citizenship through embodied protest during the British suffragette movement', 2023, *Gender, Place & Culture*, pp. 1–22. https://doi.org/10.1080/0966369X.2023.2249260. Accessed 20 August 2024

4. C. Pankhurst, *Unshackled: The Story of How We Won the Vote*, London, Hutchinson, 1959, p. 99
5. J. Purvis, *Emmeline Pankhurst: A Biography*, Oxfordshire, Routledge, 2002, p. 110
6. C. Pankhurst, *Unshackled: Story of How We Won the Vote*, London, Hutchinson, 1959, p. 105
7. S. Harrison, *Sylvia Pankhurst: Rebellious Suffragette*, Sapere Books, 2018, Chapter 10
8. J. Purvis, *Emmeline Pankhurst: A Biography*, Oxfordshire, Routledge, 2002, p. 116
9. E. Pankhurst, *My Own Story.* 1914. London, Hesperus Press, 2015, p. 122
10. J. Marlow (Ed.), 'Portia breaks Down', *The Evening News*, October 1908. *Suffragettes: The Fight For Votes for Women*, ebook edition, Virago, 2015

Chapter 12

1. E. Pankhurst, *My Own Story.* 1914. London, Hesperus Press, 2015, p. 124
2. S. Harrison, *Sylvia Pankhurst: Rebellious Suffragette*, Sapere Books, 2018, Chapter 10
3. E. Pankhurst, *My Own Story.* 1914. London, Hesperus Press, 2015, p. 125
4. C. Pankhurst, *Unshackled: The Story of How We Won the Vote*, London, Hutchinson, 1959, p. 118
5. M. Pugh, *The Pankhursts: The History of One Radical Family*, ebook ed. Vintage, London, 2008, Chapter 9
6. H. Moyes, *A Woman in a Man's World*, Alpha Books, 1971, p. 30
7. S. Harrison, *Sylvia Pankhurst: Rebellious Suffragette*, Sapere Books, 2018, Chapter 10
8. E. Pankhurst, *My Own Story*, 1914. London, Hesperus Press, 2015, p. 147
9. J. Purvis, *Emmeline Pankhurst: A Biography*, Oxfordshire, Routledge, 2002, p. 135

Chapter 13

1. E. S. Pankhurst, *The Suffragette Movement: An Intimate Account of Persons and Ideals*, Longmans, 1931, p. 320
2. S. E. Pankhurst, *Life of Emmeline Pankhurst: The Suffrage Struggle For Women's Citizenship*, T. Werner Laurie Ltd, 1935, pp. 93–94
3. E. Pankhurst, *My Own Story.* 1914. London, Hesperus Press, 2015, p. 150
4. S. E. Pankhurst, *Life of Emmeline Pankhurst: The Suffrage Struggle For Women's Citizenship*, T. Werner Laurie Ltd, 1935, p. 94
5. *New York Times*, 21 October 1909
6. F. L. Bullard, 'Mrs. Pankhurst at close range – a talk with a remarkable personality', *Sunday Herald Boston*, 31 October 1909

7. S. E. Pankhurst, *The Suffragette Movement: An Intimate Account of Persons and Ideals*, Longmans, 1931, p. 326
8. C. Pankhurst, *Unshackled: Story of How We Won the Vote*, London, Hutchinson, 1959, p. 147
9. S. Harrison, *Sylvia Pankhurst: Rebellious Suffragette*, Sapere Books, 2018, Chapter 11
10. J. Purvis. *Emmeline Pankhurst: A Biography,* Oxfordshire, Routledge, 2002, p.143
11. S. E. Pankhurst, *The Suffragette Movement: An Intimate Account of Persons and Ideals*, Longmans, 1931, pp. 439–442
12. C. Pankhurst, *Unshackled: Story of How We Won the Vote*, London, Hutchinson, 1959, p. 146
13. M. Pugh, *The Pankhursts: The History of One Radical Family*, ebook ed. Vintage, London, 2008, Chapter 9
14. 'Two of a Kind: Youth and Age – Votes for Women', *BBC Archive*, www.bbc.co.uk/archive/two-of-a-kind-youth-and-age--votes-for-women/zmb9f4j
15. C. Pankhurst, *Unshackled: Story of How We Won the Vote*, London, Hutchinson, 1959, p. 153
16. E. Smyth, *Female Pipings in Eden*, London, P. Davies Ltd, London, 1933, p. 192
17. M. Pugh, *The Pankhursts: The History of One Radical Family*, ebook ed. Vintage, London, 2008, Chapter 9
18. V. Iglikowski-Broad, 'Suffragettes and the Black Friday Protests: 18 November 1910 – the National Archives Blog', *The National Archives Blog*, 19 November 2019, blog.nationalarchives.gov.uk/suffragettes-and-the-black-friday-protests-18-november-1910. Accessed 9 September 2024

Chapter 14

1. S. Harrison, *Sylvia Pankhurst: Rebellious Suffragette*, Sapere Books, 2018, Chapter 12
2. E.S. Pankhurst, 'A Red Indian College'. In K. Connelly (Ed.), *A Suffragette in America: Reflections on Prisoners, Pickets and Political Change*. Pluto Press, 2019, pp. 137–143
3. J. Purvis, *Emmeline Pankhurst: A Biography*, Oxfordshire, Routledge, 2002, p. 161
4. J. Purvis, *Emmeline Pankhurst: A Biography*, Oxfordshire, Routledge, 2002, p. 161
5. J. Purvis, *Emmeline Pankhurst: A Biography*, Oxfordshire, Routledge, 2002, p. 156
6. E. S. Pankhurst, *The Suffragette Movement: An Intimate Account of Persons and Ideals*, Longmans, 1931, p. 367
7. V. Coleman, *Adela Pankhurst: The Wayward Suffragette 1885–1961*, ebook ed. Melbourne University Press, 1996, Chapter 7

8. A. Raeburn, *The Militant Suffragettes*, New English Library, 1974, p. 163
9. A. Raeburn, *The Militant Suffragettes*, New English Library, 1974, p. 163
10. 'No Vote, No Census – 1911 Census Protests', *Historic UK*, www.historic-uk.com/HistoryUK/HistoryofBritain/No-Vote-No-Census-1911-Census-Protests
11. E. Smyth, *Female Pipings in Eden*, London, P. Davies Ltd, London, 1933, p. 194.
12. 'Plaque to Emily Wilding Davison – UK Parliament', *UK Parliament*, 1991, www.parliament.uk/about/living-heritage/transformingsociety/electionsvoting/womenvote/case-studies-women-parliament/ewd/tony-benn-plaque
13. J. Purvis, *Emmeline Pankhurst: A Biography*, Oxfordshire, Routledge, 2002, p. 171
14. C. Pankhurst, *Unshackled: Story of How We Won the Vote*, London, Hutchinson, 1959, 192
15. E. Pankhurst, *My Own Story.* 1914. London, Hesperus Press, 2015, p. 193

Chapter 15

1. E. Pankhurst, *My Own Story.* 1914. London, Hesperus Press, 2015, p. 196
2. E. Pankhurst, *My Own Story.* 1914. London, Hesperus Press, 2015, p. 196
3. J. Purvis, *Emmeline Pankhurst: A Biography*, Oxfordshire, Routledge, 2002, p. 179
4. J. Purvis, *Emmeline Pankhurst: A Biography*, Oxfordshire, Routledge, 2002, p. 180
5. C. Pankhurst, *Unshackled: The Story of How We Won the Vote*, London, Hutchinson, 1959, p. 203
6. E. Pankhurst, *My Own Story.* 1914. London, Hesperus Press, 2015, p. 206
7. 'The Proceedings of the Old Bailey', oldbaileyonline.org, 2025, www.oldbaileyonline.org/record/t19120514-54. Accessed 25 January 2025
8. J. Purvis, *Emmeline Pankhurst: A Biography*, Oxfordshire, Routledge, 2002, p. 182
9. 'Sir Almroth Wright's Letter to the Times on the Suffrage', 6 April 1912, *The Spectator Archive*, 2025, archive.spectator.co.uk/article/6th-april-1912/3/sir-almroth-wrights-letter-to-the-times-on-the-suf. Accessed 9 September 2024
10. E. Pankhurst, *My Own Story.* 1914. London, Hesperus Press, 2015, p. 216
11. E. S. Pankhurst, *The Suffragette Movement: An Intimate Account of Persons and Ideals*, Longmans, 1931, p. 384
12. E. Pankhurst, *My Own Story*. 1914. London, Hesperus Press, 2015, p. 216
13. J. Purvis, *Emmeline Pankhurst: A Biography*, Oxfordshire, Routledge, 2002, p. 189
14. C. Pankhurst, *Unshackled: Story of How We Won the Vote,* London, Hutchinson, 1959, p. 203
15. A. Kenney, *Memories of a Militant*. 1924. London, Edward Arnold, 2015, p. 192

16. K. Atherton, *Suffragette Planners and Plotters: The Pankhurst/Pethick-Lawrence Story*, Barnsley, Pen & Sword, 2019, p. 97
17. F. W. Pethick-Lawrence, *Fate Has Been Kind*, Hutchinson & Co, publishers, 1943, p.100
18. E. Pethick-Lawrence, *My Part in a Changing World*, London, Hyperion Press, 1938, p. 285
19. E. Pankhurst, *My Own Story*, 1914. London, Hesperus Press, 2015, p. 243
20. C. Pankhurst, *Unshackled: The Story of How We Won the Vote*, London, Hutchinson, 1959, p. 229

Chapter 16

1. E. S. Pankhurst, *The Suffragette Movement: An Intimate Account of Persons and Ideals*, Longmans, 1931, p. 398
2. J. Purvis, *Emmeline Pankhurst: A Biography*, Oxfordshire, Routledge, 2002, p. 204
3. A. McLeod, 'Petition for the Pethick-Lawrences', *The Fight for Votes for Women*, ebook edition, Virago, 2015
4. *The Suffragette*, 29 November 1912
5. M. Pugh, *The Pankhursts: The History of One Radical Family*, ebook ed. Vintage, London, 2008, Chapter 11
6. C. Pankhurst, *Unshackled: The Story of How We Won the Vote*, London, Hutchinson, 1959, p. 240
7. Letter to Emmeline Pankhurst from Sylvia Pankhurst, 18 March 1913, WSPU Collection, Museum of London
8. E. Pankhurst, *My Own Story*, 1914. London, Hesperus Press, 2015, pp. 266–269
9. E. Smyth, *Female Pipings in Eden*, London, P. Davies Ltd, London, 1933, pp. 213–214
10. E. Pankhurst, *My Own Story*, 1914. London, Hesperus Press, 2015, p. 283

Chapter 17

1. M. Richardson, 'Laugh A Defiance'. *Suffragettes: The Fight for Votes for Women*, edited by J. Marlow, London, Virago, London, 2015
2. S. Harrison, *Sylvia Pankhurst: Rebellious Suffragette*, Sapere Books, 2018, Chapter 15
3. J. Purvis, *Emmeline Pankhurst: A Biography*, Oxfordshire, Routledge, 2002, p. 229
4. C. Devereux, '"The Maiden Tribute" and the Rise of the White Slave in the Nineteenth Century: The Making of an Imperial Construct', *Victorian Review*, vol. 26, no. 2, 2000, pp. 1–23. *JSTOR*, www.jstor.org/stable/27793436. Accessed 31 October 2024

5. S. Harrison, *Sylvia Pankhurst: Rebellious Suffragette*, Sapere Books, 2018, Chapter 15
6. E. S. Pankhurst, *The Suffragette Movement: An Intimate Account of Persons and Ideals*, Longmans, 1931, pp. 517–518
7. J. Purvis, *Emmeline Pankhurst: A Biography*, Oxfordshire, Routledge, 2002, p. 248
8. J. Purvis, *Emmeline Pankhurst: A Biography*, Oxfordshire, Routledge, 2002, p. 233
9. V. Coleman, *Adela Pankhurst: The Wayward Suffragette 1885–1961*, ebook ed. Melbourne University Press, 1996, Chapter 8

Chapter 18

1. M. Pugh, *The Pankhursts: The History of One Radical Family*, ebook ed. Vintage, London, 2008, Chapter 12
2. E. Pankhurst, *My Own Story*, 1914. London, Hesperus Press, 2015, p. 311
3. 'Mary Richardson, who slashed the "Rokeby Venus" by Valesquez, leaving for police court, 10 March, 1914', *London Museum*, www.londonmuseum.org.uk/collections/v/object-294074/mary-richardson-who-slashed-the-rokeby-venus-by-valesquez-leaving-for-police-court-10-march-1914
4. M. Pugh, *The Pankhursts: The History of One Radical Family*, ebook ed. Vintage, London, 2008, Chapter 12
5. S. Harrison, *Sylvia Pankhurst: Rebellious Suffragette*, Sapere Books, 2018, Chapter 15
6. E. S. Pankhurst, *The Suffragette Movement: An Intimate Account of Persons and Ideals*, Longmans, 1931, pp. 582–583
7. J. Purvis, *Emmeline Pankhurst: A Biography*, Oxfordshire, Routledge, 2002, p. 266
8. J. Purvis, *Emmeline Pankhurst: A Biography*, Oxfordshire, Routledge, 2002, p. 264
9. S. Pedersen, *The Scottish Suffragettes and the Press*, Springer, 2017, p. 152

Chapter 19

1. C. Pankhurst, *Unshackled: The Story of How We Won the Vote*, London, Hutchinson, 1959, p. 288
2. 'Eat Less Bread', *Imperial War Museums*, www.iwm.org.uk/collections/item/object/31473. Accessed 22 October 2024
3. Londonist (2021), 'The East London pub taken over by Suffragettes', *Londonist*. Available at: https://londonist.com/london/drink/the-mothers-arms-pub-suffragette-pankhurst. Accessed: 22 October 2024
4. S. Harrison, *Sylvia Pankhurst: Rebellious Suffragette*, Sapere Books, 2018, Chapter 17

5. 'Suffragette Teddy Bears: WWI and Women's Rights', *London Museum*, www.londonmuseum.org.uk/blog/suffragette-teddy-bears-wwi-and-womens-rights
6. E. S. Pankhurst, *The Life of Emmeline Pankhurst*, 1936, Kessinger Publication, 2007, p. 153
7. 'Civil Services and Revenue Departments Estimates, 1916 – Hansard – UK Parliament', 2025, hansard.parliament.uk/commons/1916-08-15/debates/248167b9-c188-4e20-a0a0-b2643fe6c2d8/CivilServicesAndRevenueDepartmentsEstimates1916%E2%80%9317. Accessed 22 October 2024
8. Archivist, Katie Wood, University of Melbourne, 'Why Emmeline Pankhurst Criticised Her Daughter', *Pursuit*, 19 January 2016, pursuit.unimelb.edu.au/articles/why-emmeline-pankhurst-criticised-her-daughter
9. Lesley Orr, '"Shall we not speak for ourselves?" Helen Crawfurd, war resistance and the women's peace crusade 1916–18', Academia.edu, 20 May 2017, www.academia.edu/33114337/SHALL_WE_NOT_SPEAK_FOR_OURSELVES_HELEN_CRAWFURD_WAR_RESISTANCE_AND_THE_WOMENS_PEACE_CRUSADE_1916_18?auto=download. Accessed 26 October 2024
10. V. Coleman, *Adela Pankhurst: The Wayward Suffragette 1885–1961*, ebook ed. Melbourne University Press, 1996, Chapter 11

Chapter 20

1. J. Purvis, *Emmeline Pankhurst: A Biography*, Oxfordshire, Routledge, 2002, p. 312
2. M. Pugh, *The Pankhursts: The History of One Radical Family*, ebook ed. Vintage, London, 2008, Chapter 14
3. S. Harrison, *Sylvia Pankhurst: Rebellious Suffragette*, Sapere Books, 2018, Chapter 18
4. R. Pankhurst, 'Suffragette Sisters in Old Age: Unpublished Correspondence between Christabel and Sylvia Pankhurst, 1953–57', *Women's History Review*, vol. 10, no. 3, 1 September 2001, pp. 483–537, https://doi.org/10.1080/09612020100200295. Accessed 10 November 2024
5. R. Pankhurst, 'Suffragette Sisters in Old Age: Unpublished Correspondence between Christabel and Sylvia Pankhurst, 1953–57', *Women's History Review*, vol. 10, no. 3, 1 September 2001, pp. 483–537, https://doi.org/10.1080/09612020100200295. Accessed 9 February 2020
6. V. Coleman, *Adela Pankhurst: The Wayward Suffragette 1885–1961*, ebook ed. Melbourne University Press, 1996, Chapter 21
7. C. Pankhurst, *Unshackled: The Story of How We Won the Vote*, London, Hutchinson, 1959, p. 296
8. E. S. Pankhurst, *The Life of Emmeline Pankhurst*, 1936, Kessinger Publication, 2007, p. 172

9. C. Pankhurst, *Unshackled: The Story of How We Won the Vote*, London, Hutchinson, 1959, p. 298
10. J. Purvis, *Emmeline Pankhurst: A Biography*, Oxfordshire, Routledge, 2002, p. 352
11. J. Purvis, *Emmeline Pankhurst: A Biography*, Oxfordshire, Routledge, 2002, p. 352
12. V. Thorpe, 'Truth behind the Death of Suffragette Emily Davison Is Finally Revealed', *The Guardian*, 19 December 2017, www.theguardian.com/society/2013/may/26/emily-davison-suffragette-death-derby-1913

BIBLIOGRAPHY

Atherton, K, *Suffragette Planners and Plotters: The Pankhurst-Pethick-Lawrence Story*, Barnsley, Pen & Sword, 2019

Atkinson, D., *Rise Up Women! The Remarkable Lives of the Suffragettes*, London, Bloomsbury, 2018

Broad, L., *Winston Churchill 1874–1945*, London, Hutchinson & Co., 1945

Burkhardt, F. et al. (Ed), *Correspondence*: *The Correspondence of Charles Darwin*. Vol. 14, Cambridge University Press, 1985

Bush, M. L., 'The Women at Peterloo: The Impact of Female Reform on the Manchester Meeting of 16 August 1819', *History*, Vol. 89, 2004

Coleman, V., *Adela Pankhurst: The Wayward Suffragette 1885–1861*, Melbourne, Melbourne University Press, 1996

Engels, F., *The Condition of the Working Class in England*, 1845, Panther Edition, 1969

Frances, H., '"Dare to be free!": the Women's Freedom League and its legacy', in *Votes for Women*, eds J. Purvis and S. Stanley Holton, Oxfordshire, Routledge, 2000

Harrison, S., *Sylvia Pankhurst: Rebellious Suffragette*, Ilkley, Sapere Books, 2018

Holmes, R., *Sylvia Pankhurst: Natural Born Rebel*, London, Bloomsbury, 2021

Howarth. J., *Fawcett, Dame Millicent Garrett*, Oxford Dictionary of National Biography, 4 October 2007

Jenkins, L., 'Annie Kenney and the Politics of Class in the Women's Social and Political Union', *Twentieth Century British History*, Vol. 30, Issue 4, December 2019, pp. 477–503

Joannou, M. & Purvis, J. (Eds), *The Women's Suffrage Movement: New Feminist Perspectives*, New York, Manchester University Press, 1998

Kenney, A., *Memories of a Militant*, London, Edward Arnold, 1924

McInerney, K., 'Reclaiming space: enacting citizenship through embodied protest during the British suffragette movement', *Gender, Place & Culture*, 2023

Marlow, J., *Suffragettes: The Fight for Votes for Women*, London, Virago, 2015

Mitchell, D. J., *Queen Christabel: A Biography of Christabel Pankhurst*, London, Macdonald and Jane's, 1977

Morgan, D., *Suffragists and Liberals: The Politics of Woman Suffrage in England*, Totowa, Rowman and Littlefield, 1975

Pankhurst, C., *Unshackled: The Story of How We Won the Vote*, London, Hutchinson, 1959

Pankhurst, E., *My Own Story*, 1914, London, Hesperus Press, 2015

Pankhurst, E. S., *The Life of Emmeline Pankhurst*, 1936, Kessinger Publication, 2007

Pankhurst, E. S., *The Suffragette: The History of the Women's Militant Suffrage Movement 1905–1910*, Rimbault Press, 2009

Pankhurst, E. S., *The Suffragette Movement: An Intimate Account of Persons and Ideals,* Longmans, 1931

Pankhurst, R., 'Suffragette sisters in old age: unpublished correspondence between Christabel and Sylvia Pankhurst, 1953–57', *Women's History Review*, Vol. 10, Issue 3, 2001

Pethick-Lawrence, E., *My Part in a Changing World*, London, Hyperion Press, 1938

Pethick-Lawrence, F. W., *Fate Has Been Kind*, Hutchinson & Co, publishers, 1943

Pugh, M., *The Pankhursts: The History of One Radical Family*, Vintage, London, 2008

Purvis, J., *Christabel Pankhurst: A Biography*, Oxfordshire, Routledge, 2018

Purvis, J., *Emmeline Pankhurst: A Biography*, Oxfordshire, Routledge, 2002

Purvis, J., 'Emmeline Pankhurst: suffragette leader and single parent in Edwardian England', *Women's History Review*, Vol. 20, Issue 1, pp. 73–91, 2011

Purvis, J., & Hannam, J., *The British Women's Suffrage Campaign*, Oxfordshire, Routledge, 2020

Rollyson, C., 'A Conservative Revolutionary: Emmeline Pankhurst (1857–1928)', *The Virginia Quarterly Review*, 2003

Rosen, A., *Rise Up Women! The Militant Campaign of the Women's Social and Political Union 1903–1914*, Oxfordshire, Routledge, 1974

Smyth, E., *Female Pipings in Eden*, London, P. Davies Ltd., 1933

Tickner, L., *The Spectacle of Women: Imagery of the Suffrage Campaign 1907–14*, Chicago, University of Chicago Press, 1988

Tuttle, C., *Hard at Work in Factories and Mines: The Economics of Child Labor During the British Industrial Revolution*, Oxford, Westview Press, 1999

West, R., *The Young Rebecca: Writings of Rebecca West, 1911–17*, New York, Viking Press, 1982

Journals, Newspapers and News Websites

Aberdeen People's Journal
Argus
BBC Education
Britannia
Daily Express
Daily Herald
Daily Mail
Daily News
Daily Sketch
Daily Telegraph
Dundee Evening Telegraph
Evening Standard
Fife Free Press
Historic UK
Leicester Daily Post
Manchester Evening News
Manchester Guardian
New York Evening Sun
Nottingham Evening Post
Pall Mall Gazette
The Edinburgh Evening News
The Freewoman
The Guardian
The New York Times
The Suffragette
The Times
The Woman's Dreadnought
Votes for Women
Women's History Network

Paper Collections

A. Pankhurst Walsh, *My Mother: A Vindication and an Explanation* (Australian National Library, Canberra, 1933)

Richard Pankhurst (2001), 'Suffragette sisters in old age: unpublished correspondence between Christabel and Sylvia Pankhurst, 1953–57', *Women's History Review*, Vol. 10, Issue 3, 483–537, DOI: 10.1080/09612020100200295

E. Sylvia Pankhurst to Adela Pankhurst, 11 July 1918, Pankhurst-Walsh Papers, 20/61

HC Deb Civil Services and Revenue Departments Estimates, 1916–17

HC Deb 12 Women's Enfranchisement Bill, May 1905 Vol. 146 cc217-36